another way to play

another
way to play

POEMS 1960-2017

michael lally

introduction by eileen myles

seven stories press

new york · oakland · london

Seven Stories Press
140 Watts Street
New York, NY 10013
sevenstories.com

Library of Congress Cataloging-in-Publication Data

Names: Lally, Michael, 1942- author. | Myles, Eileen, writer of introduction.
Title: Another way to play : poems 1960-2017 / Michael Lally ; introduction by Eileen Myles.
Description: A Seven Stories Press first edition. | New York : Seven Stories Press, [2018]
Identifiers: LCCN 2017056451 | ISBN 9781609808303 (paperback)
Subjects: | BISAC: POETRY / American / General.
Classification: LCC PS3562.A414 A6 2018 | DDC 811/.54--dc23
LC record available at https://lccn.loc.gov/2017056451

Printed in the United States of America

9 8 7 6 5 4 3 2 1 .

Thanks to all the editors and publishers of the books, anthologies, and magazines these poems appeared in and to those who helped or inspired me with some of these poems, especially: Hey Lady and Morgan Press, Some Of Us Press, The Stone Wall Press, Blue Wind Press, Wyrd Press, Salt Lick Press, Vehicle Editions, Jordan Davies, Hanging Loose Press, Little Caesar, Coffee House Press, Quiet Lion Press, Black Sparrow Press, Libellum and Charta Presses, Word Palace Press; and Morgan Gibson, Peter Schjeldahl, Robert Slater, Lee Lally, Ed Cox, Tina Darragh, Ed Zahniser, Kim Merker, George and Lucy Mattingly, Janey Tannenbaum, Jim Haining, Annabel Lee, Bob Hershon, Ron Schreiber, Dick Lourie, Emmet Jarrett, Mark Pawlak, Susan Campbell, Alex Katz, Dennis Cooper, Lynn Goldsmith, Edie Baskin, Allan Kornblum, Brian Christopher, John Martin, Vincent Katz, Paul Portuges, Ray DiPalma, Aram Saroyan, Eve Brandstein, Eileen Myles, Ted Berrigan, Karen Allen, Jamie Rose, Hubert Selby Jr., Gus Van Sant, Paul Abruzzo, Dan Simon, Rachel E. Dicken, and to all I am forgetting, and last but not least my lifelong "irreplaceable" friend and consultant on all things poetic, Terence Winch, and my children Caitlin, Miles, and Flynn.

contents

ROCKY DIES YELLOW

MY LIFE

CHARISMA

CATCH MY BREATH

JUST LET ME DO IT

WHITE LIFE

ATTITUDE

HOLLYWOOD MAGIC

CANT BE WRONG

OF

IT'S NOT NOSTALGIA

IT TAKES ONE TO KNOW ONE

MARCH 18, 2003

SWING THEORY

THE VILLAGE SONNETS

NEW POEMS

Actual Lally

This is an awesome book and you should read every word of it. You won't do it in a day or in many days but during the passage of reading *Another Way To Play* you will learn something about time. *Another Way To Play* seems to offer advice – and it's advice from self *to* self, which might be the only way to enact advice truly. Plus who is that "another"? Somebody else?

As I'm climbing over the rocks, the poems of Michael Lally, this incomplete utopia, a rugged landscape of a book, it occurs to me that what Michael takes on is nothing less than the feat of being alive and the exploding and strewn nature of that exactly on its own terms (living in a body) while this writer keeps trotting out his own arrogance like a family joke and deep humility is in there too, humility is the gas station of so much of what Michael Lally does and is, poet and man. Lally is mostly a straight guy but you may viscerally experience the embrace of another man in "Watching You Walk Away" which was dedicated to Gregory Millard, one man who died collectively—of AIDS, so there's an imputation here—of being a survivor of love, even being a man of a certain age or moment who knows that being a loving man AND loving men now has both its glory and its price:

> The world is all around us, even at night, in bed
> in each others arms
> distilled & injected into the odor we leave on each others
> backs & thighs, between the knots & shields of all we lay
> down in the dark to pick up in the morning
> I like your brown eyes when you talk

This collected poems or collected poem is constructed of similar yet all different mostly brave moments. It's a compendium of what one is possibly brave enough to do—to labor, to fail, to lounge, to love. Lally's not fessing up, but he's proud. This is undoubtedly the book of a proud man. Proud to a fault, and he's the first to tell you that as well. I mentioned family before. Yet what one more likely feels throughout the four hundred-odd pages of *Another Way to Play* is that you're kind of in a relationship with this guy. Whether you're male or female. Which is kind of octopussy, but stylistically Lally is a dancer, habitually reeling from form to form. It's a broken book in the best sense. There's no whole here, the self is never resolved, but what's delivered, weltered in poem form, is a novelistic series of impressions. It's a real thing and a changing thing. An aesthetic and a biographical one. Years ago I read in James Schuyler's "Morning of the Poem" that Schuyler approved of Michael Lally because he looked you straight in the eye. Here we've got an extended Lally poem ("The Jimmy Schuyler Sonnets"), which tells us much the same thing—that "Jimmy knew what mattered." The men's mutual admiration, their like for one another has a special feeling, a leveling affect. They invite us into their intimacy. Their public "like." Which makes me want to step out too and acknowledge that I'm discovering that I'm extremely influenced by Michael Lally and I hadn't thought so much about that until I was dwelling here in this book. Because his affect occurs through so many different gestures. In the most existential way, his poem is an act.

He starts one like this:

SUPERREALISM

First of all I'm naked
while I'm typing this,

I mean I know *I* tried it. Was it after him. Perhaps. I think I tried fucking myself while writing. Inserting a dildo and then writing an art review. I've read in Chris Kraus's biography of her that Kathy Acker sometimes wrote naked. And I kind of remember Peter Schjeldahl telling me a long time ago that he wrote naked too. And Peter *wrote* long naked poems. So naked that he stopped writing poetry entirely. The trick is to manage to stay in. And this, Lally's, was a way. Michael *began* his poem like that. Naked. Yet it wasn't about it at all. It was another way to begin again. Which Lally is always doing. Here nakedness kind of invented the studio of the poem. Just matter of fact. Which is the constant position in the work. He's a working class man so it's a chore. To be real. And to make *that* new.

Open my brain, poems fly out.

And it pretty much looked that way when I first met, or really laid eyes on Michael Lally in about 1975.

Two poets I knew, Harry and Larry, invited me to go up with them to the Gotham Book Mart to hear some famous poet from DC. Or maybe the poet had just moved to New York. Harry and Larry explained that Michael was more than a bit of a showman, a sham perhaps but winning finally, definitely worth going to see. I was a new kid in town and female so these guys, all men, were responsible for my education. Harry and Larry admired Michael Lally they blushingly admitted. They had a boy crush on him. They also loved Janey Tannenbaum of the Gotham book mart and she had made a little chapbook of Michael's *My Life* through her own Wyrd Press. That publication was the reason for the event. The room was packed. This good looking dark haired Irish guy—someone who had run for office in that counter culture way (and lost!) who slept with men and women and the breadth of Michael's living absolutely impressed the two guys who invited me. It's true, they gasped, exasperated, delighted and there he was seated at a table in a clean blue (I think) shirt presenting his poem in a low key almost cowboy way. Like you all know *this*. I am a ritual. He calmly looked up. Lally looked like someone I might have grown up with, very Irish, cute, but carrying himself like a man, not a pretty boy yet someone firmly planted in his own affect. The Gotham being at its zenith at that time only hosted stars. Ntozake Shange gave a solo reading as well around then and saintly Patti Smith had read to this glamorous room a few years earlier. Mid seventies was a moment of poetry stars, these people were not soo apart from the wider culture yet they were *ours*, each an example, pamphleteers in a way, speaking for the vitality of small culture then. They were not larger culture's absence but its depth. And each of these cults opened onto other cults of sex, politics, and race, music and painting. It was acidy. It was a wide counter culture then, and poetry was the mouthpiece of it and Michael was that day's star. He refers to "My Life" in other poems in this book as his famous poem and it is and was plaintively that. The poem revels in its own facets. Contradictions. Though the poet's not too hard on himself. The poem's sort of funkily buffed like *Just Kids*. I like "My Life" as an example of how a poet can occupy space and stand as pure legend yet it's by far not his most interesting work. You can see the echoes building up to it within this book and poems later on audition a similar stance in short and long versions for the rest of his writing life. What I love about Michael's writing is that he really isn't trying to do it again. His most famous poem is his emptiest poem. He knows that. That's its joke. His last poems in this volume are his best poems and so are his earliest ones. He's so big as a flawed human, as the apologist of Michael Lally, as the St. Augustine of Michael Lally, so endlessly expansive in his context yet still not ever breaking into prose. He's holding the line, so that finally if you just wanna talk about Lally as a poet, he's a sonneteer. A guy with a lute. A maker of that precise little form that spawns so many multiples of itself, "The South Orange Sonnets," "The Village Sonnets" reveal the classiness of a poet. He's the novelist who just wouldn't *bother* he is so busy living and dreaming. He is real *because* he's courting the myth. "My Life" is such an arrival, here's the boat, that he exhausted the approach in a one off, sort of ended his life early on so he could keep going cause so what. Why be a star really? Isn't that missing the point. This is a wise book. And a book of life has to be a book of wisdom. It's really so much more moving to read a love poem to a woman or man – or talking to his children. Or going to Ireland to find a few Lallys and not be corny about it and it's not. Or to read the much older Michael's sonnets about the village when he was a kid. This is a poet who is probably more shaped by his love for black girls than being Irish. Or is it both. Part of the wonder of Lally's work is that he is the performance of how race and class dovetail. One punk kid who makes poetry all his life about a black girl who he loved all his life and she him is the living coalition. What I mostly finally love about Lally is that like Gertrude Stein he insists we all stand *with him* while he's living and writing. Which is easy to play. Cause it's your book too.

No, all I want to do
is sound like what I am always becoming,

—Eileen Myles
NYC, June 2017

POEMS

whatever it is I want to do it
like I want to sit down for awhile
by myself this week, get a personal
letter from William Saroyan as though
he'd been reading my books since childhood,
stand up at the reunion of everyone
who ever did me a favor & those I lied to
& abused or made an ass of myself trying to
impress and say, very softly, in a voice
like the works of an Indian we all expected
to be a poet but instead was warrior:

                              "everything is a fiction"

sounding more like a Spanish philosopher
afraid to kick Franco in the ass and
spit on the church
                    No, all I want to do
is sound like what I am always becoming,
you know, what I am, and I want to call it
"poems"
            & I want the poems to fit
in your pocket and as easily lost
to turn up on washday with the half used
books of matches and lint
to be left in the bathroom to be read
by visitors taking a shit or trying to

I want these poems to be written now
while you're listening, later, when
we're both doing something else
maybe we'll remember, maybe we won't
and no one will ever test either of us on it

I

and our children will be spared
embarrassing questions about their parents

I want these poems to fly south
when they have to
to cover the ground when it is time
to be used to wrap sandwiches in
for the kids to take to school
I want a concert to be given with my poems
as the audience
I want them to die on their feet or
going down on a lover
                              I don't want anyone
to take my poems to bed with them
I want everyone to take my poems to work
to read instead of working
I want my poems to meet themselves
on their way from me to you & be surprised

I never want my poems to be mistaken
for something to be judged or eaten
fucked or framed   anthologized or
criticized, I just want them to be
taken for what they are, simply,
almost embarrassingly: possible

(broadside c. 1970)

STUPID RABBITS

(Morgan Press 1971)

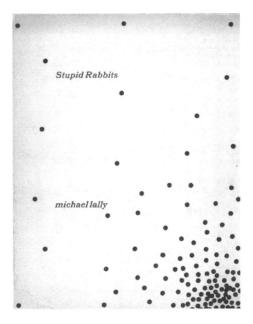

So, the novels I forgot to write were really
frightened into the road like stupid rabbits
& this is their blood & bits of fur

HITCHHIKING TO ATLANTIC CITY

to marry my first black bride I was
taken for a ride in North Carolina
by 2 teenybop divorcees & their angel
a drunken truck driver
                                    I lied
about my future while they fed me
full of J. W. Dant and bad jokes
about my future family, or theirs,
and opened up their narrow unlit
alley lives for me to smell & touch
& share
            They laughed when I cried
& blamed it on an old street wound &
pretty soon we were all skunky drunk
laughing crying parking somewhere
dark to make our own bad jokes on
come stained upholstery so colorless
it was impossible to say whose bride
black why was sharing what with someone

LETTER TO JOHN COLTRANE

I believe in you
When you died Pharoah Sanders said: John Coltrane was a man of God
I thought yes, this is all true
like the first time I saw you there was nothing to say except:

John Coltrane is a big man I mean, a big man
I remember thinking: he's too big god, he stands out
You walked among us as though you already weren't there
J. C. is a serious man people said, your drinking days forgotten
He's   clean   was the rumor
He's   thoroughbred   was the word
He's   Trane   was the fact
You said Giant Steps and they were taken
You said Blue Train and it was on
You said Ascension and there we were   watching
Talk about a big man

November 1967

HARD RAIN

Met Bob Dylan
in The Fat Black Pussycat
same way my father met my mom:
workin.
We was always workin.
If we woke up sick an complained
fathered say: Eat some breakfast
then get a little exercise
workin.
If one of us met a girl n started stutterin . . .

sure.

Comin out a the Pacific
met Buddy Holly
soakin wet.
Ya look like me with yer glasses on he said.
I don't wear no glasses I said

my father wouldn't like it.
Try to see me he said . . .

sure.

Workin comes close to prayin where I come from.
My father usta say three things: Work, work,
work.
Some people are like that.
I told my mom, god rest her soul
There's a Rangoon in Illinois you aint heard of
place to go for tattoos so peoplell know who ya are.
Met Alan Ladd there
told me to go home.
Go home boy he said
getcherself a job.
Getcherself a father I said.
Where am I I said.
Rest yer soul I said.
Work I said, work, work . . .

Sure.

IN THE DISTANCE

In the distance called My Father
I rode my innocence down, rode it
down on its hands and knees like
the people whose dance created the world

What do we know about the world
or the distance we create for our personal atmosphere

What we know is the way we fall

when we fall off the little we ride
when we ride away from the things we're given
to make us forget the things we gave up

How far is it to where my son
will break my bones and dance on them

May 1970

THE SOUTH
ORANGE SONNETS

(Some of Us Press 1972)

from THE SOUTH ORANGE SONNETS

I

In books it was the Lackawana Valley.
The Lackawana railroad ran through it
separating those on the hill from us.
Lackawana Place was the toughest block
in the neighborhood until 1952 when
the temptations and reputation moved
to Church Street where *THE PINK DEVILS*
had roses tattooed between their thumbs
and forefingers, wore delicate gold
crucifixes on chains around their
brown Italian necks, and carried porno
playing cards from Newark, the city
where parades got lost and statues
died. Newark, where we all had lived.

2

My brother brought the moon back from
Okinawa. I mean, there they learned of
the surrender three days late and then
they danced all night. My brother played
the saxophone. Junkman Willy did a one
step that most girls didn't want to do.
They called him that for all the old cars
he worked on til he was old enough to
drive. He was a paddy cat like me and we
lived on Cabbage Hill til we were old
enough to live anywhere. We believed
Italians and Jews ran *THE SYNDICATE*
maybe the world. In West Orange a man
hung himself higher than he could reach.

3.

The girls liked to dance with Eddie
we believed. He came back from jail
with big muscles and, it was rumored
bleached blonde hair. He had a tattoo
with the name crossed out and dimples.
One girl's father sent Eddie to school
in Las Vegas to learn to be a shill.
The girl's father was a big man in Las
Vegas it was rumored. Eddie was a big
man in South Orange. While he was gone
I met an Italian girl with hair on her
chest and poured beer out my side of
Junkman's truck when nobody was looking.
After only two weeks Eddie came home.

4.

In East Orange Carol Robinson decided I
was her boyfriend. Her father found out
before I did. Told his friends and neigh-
bors how he didn't want no white boy hang-
ing around his little girl. One asked me
not to pass the time at his house anymore
listening to his son's Clifford Browns or
talking to his twin daughters. Walking
home that night three teenagers sitting
on a stoop on Halstead Street yelled: Hey
white boy, whatchu doin aroun here? You
know where you are? Where you from? When
I answered South Orange this fat girl said
Shoot, that muss be Carol Robs turkey.

5

Little Robert called himself a sporting man
at fourteen. Came by Charlie's house talking
about being a gambling fool and losing a
hundred dollars a minute and who has got
the playing cards. A friend of Charlie's wife
laughed and said Ain't you too old for card
games now? Charlie's wife made most men turn
around. When I was fourteen I watched her
walk by the store where I swept the floor.
Seven years later Charlie's cousin told me I
danced too close to Charlie's wife. My father
figured Charlie, Kenny, Bobby and the other
friends I loved were lazy cause they didn't
have good jobs. Kenny didn't even have a job.

6

In 1959 I thought of myself as *NEVER
FEAR* and liked to talk about a door
that when you walked through it you were
dancing. My father thought we had to be
up to no good out til two o'clock in the
morning. We rode around in Charlie's car
and talked. We decided one difference
between white girls and black girls was
the way you danced with them. White girls
you held around the waist with your right
arm. You put the same arm over a black
girl's shoulder. That was in 1959. Did you
ever have a woman's cunt wrapped around
your head asked Eddie. That was in 1956.

7

One year our people refused to buy Christmas
cards that said *SEASONS GREETINGS* A year
later we christened the new homes on the hill
JEWSTEAD. Three years later we sang Guns for
the Arabs, bicycles and sneakers for the Jews.
Then a year came when the Jewish girls turned
soft and ripe and full of round things we
longed to hold. That was the year we all wanted
to be Jewish. We wanted to kiss the thing
they hung on their doors. We wanted to dip
our fingers into whatever holy water was theirs.
But most of all we didn't want to wait to be
the forbidden goyim they would sneak down
from their hill three years later to sample.

9

When my mother died two Irish great aunts
came over from New York. The brassy one
wore her hat tilted and always sat with
her legs wide apart. At the wake she told
me loud You look like your grandfather
the cop if you ever get like him shoot
yourself. The other one waited til after
the funeral to pull my ear down to her
level and whisper You're a good looking
young man but if you don't shave off them
side boards people will mistake you for
a Puerto Rican. We had so many cousins
in our neighborhood everybody called my
mother Aunt Irene. Even the Italians.

10

My uncle shot himself before I was born.
My grandfather who carried an old petri-
fied potato in his pocket for his arthi-
ritis got up and walked out of the funeral.
His sons slipped out of their pews as
piously as they knew how and went to find
him. He was buttoning up his fly as they
came through the big oak doors of the
church and caught the reflection of the
sunlight on his piss. He used to open the
door of a fast moving vehicle which the
driver would hysterically beg to a stop
squeezing everything. He'd say It's time
to shake a little water off the potatoes.

12

The Lackawana Railroad was an electric commuter
special that cut off the head of a ten year old
Boy Scout one summer. He was listening to the
tracks to hear if the train was coming. His
cousin saw it happen and was sick for a week.
He was seven. In bed when I was a kid listening
to the sound of the Lackawana rolling by I'd
dream of the places it would take me someday.
And it did. It took me to all the places it goes
to like Orange East Orange Maplewood Movies
Brick Church Newark and Hoboken. Sometimes
we jumped off halfway home to avoid paying.
One year somebody got a plate in his head from
jumping off onto something hard like my cousins.

14

The tree between the sidewalk and the curb
attracted me. The leaves turning up in the
breeze before a summer storm revealed a side
that glowed, flashed like the palms of a
dark woman shaping castles in the air. My
father didn't like it. He'd ask why a boy sat
on the stoop staring at trees when he could
be watching TV learning the things a boy
should know to be well liked by the men who
could help him. Golfing terms, starting line
ups, some news. Too much thinking can ruin
you, he'd say. When we were alone my mother
would ask Don't you think there might be
something wrong with having no white friends.

15

My cousin was an artist but no one knew.
They thought he was only a work of art
like a pinball machine made of marble.
When someone deliberately broke the first
two letters of the ESSEX HOUSE sign, my
cousin did the same with a new kids head.
He grew bigger than any cousin and more
gentle. Eddie no, I said, I never did
have a lady's cunt wrapped around my head.
I knew Eddie was an artist when he ate
the aspirin. Girls from *THE KRAZY KITTENS*
played EDDIE MY LOVE eighteen times in a
row that night. Eddie looked at me and
said Whadja do, come out of a horses ass?

16

They say prospectors saved their scalps
by acting crazy. I acted as crazy as I
could when white guys asked me what it
was like with a, didn't want to say it
but afraid to look like they didn't want
to say it, said it: *nigger.* I hit them.
Or I told them Fine as 400 wine. Like
laying under that tree before a storm
watching the leaves turn over and shine.
Like getting it steady and nice. Like
the first time twice. Like standing in
the rain laughing. Like sitting at Broad
and Market, spitting at the moon and
hitting it. The word I wanted to marry.

17

There is some music you have to listen to.
In South Orange there were rich Catholics
rich Protestants and rich Jews. My cousin
became a cop. His brother was stabbed by
an Italian called Lemon Drop. Across the
street lived two brothers called Loaf and
Half a Loaf. My brother became a cop. On
St. Patrick's Day 1958 I came home drunk. My
mother said He's only fifteen. My father:
It had to happen once. My grandfather was
a cop. One cousin won a beauty contest at
thirteen. My sister married a cop. By 1959
I knew I was going to be a jazz musician.
My father joined AA before I was even born.

18

At first the world's great heroes were FDR
Churchill and Uncle Joe Stalin. The block
hero was FLYING ACE who shot down Krauts
on a seven inch screen. One brother served
with the Navy Band, one with the US Army
Air Corps. Before TV we sat through Sunday
matinees with newsreel footage of Nazi war
crimes. The boarder in our house had been
a dough boy in World War I. We called him
uncle. My third brother worked on tanks in
Germany during the Korean thing. I joined
the Air Force on February eighth 1962. I
went AWOL July fourth 1962. For a long time
no one we knew ever went away a civilian.

19

There were people who didn't need nick-
names. Love I'd say to myself walking
those streets under the old gas lights.
The woman on Valley Street who waited
after her friend went home. The eyes of
pretty Italian girls as their boyfriends
pulled up to the curb. The voice on the
phone from West Orange saying love the
first time saying What saying Wait saying
Say it again. Or like getting on the bus
to Newark six thirty in the morning
with a beautiful black girl in a party
dress and all the people going to work.
In 1960 you could star in South Orange.

My father lost the store, we all went to
work when I was ten. Then he became a
ward heeler. My grandfather was dead before
I knew he spoke Gaelic. My father could
remember when they had mules instead of
automobiles and you had to remove your cap
and step to the curb to let the rich walk
by. My grandfather was glad to die in the
USA. He'd say if you can't find a job within
thirty miles of New York City there aren't
any jobs to be found. My father would say
You can write all the poetry you want to
when you're a millionaire. Eddie would say
You got to try a shoe on before you buy it.

1960-69

DUES

(The Stone Wall Press 1975)

AMERICAN RENAISSANCE

For Emily Dickinson

She always reported to herself
first, then the world, then
nature or what the *mythic poem*
might someday become. The idea.

And it cost her: the butter-
flies she mistook for mari-
golds, the blank blackboards.
As Thoreau said to a friend,
'One world at a time.' Only
faster, she might have added.

And in the end, for radio, for
television, if it wasn't, she
could not become 'the purest
of poets,' or even assume the
role. Genuine culture was an
unreasonable aspiration & poetry.

She left behind even the *frissons*.

RE

We are reminded of a new
gas station inserting the
million gallon storage tank
beneath its inviting apron

The sun continues to set and
the sounds of traffic
you call the auto harp

                    Why is it
we can get nothing on the radio
today but Johnny Ace singing of
his suicide and that tinselly
background piano

TWO POEMS WHILE SOMETHING CRUMBLED 1967

1
There's no voice to my wife
the FBI took it away with them on the phone today
all she could get from them
                              was fear

our kid sits in her belly
waiting to grow fingernails to bite
hair to pull out
in the face of such subtle suppression

                                   no goddamit
   he waits to get even
                     which is worse

2
There is always the sound
                     of women
crying

(in the hallways of my head)

                         do I know them?
                         are they 'mine'?
when the door is closed
                    I must feel my stomach for wounds

& continue to suck at dry eggs

>   why?
>   do they know me?

so I destroy the calendar (paint it blue)
take down Marlon Brando for Che Guevera
pretend it is the wind

>   and you?

ONCE

>   when I lived in a cemetery on a hill
played with a birch tree
>   called the wind lover
read sermons to Five Mile Valley
& taught lessons to the snow like:
>   The wooden clock was
>   invented by an American
>   Negro
there was a trenchcoated redhead.
So I wore brand new shirts & drank beer
leaving the headstones to weather
>   still
one day I came across some black sedan against my birch
from the back seat she smiled over his shoulder
>   snow
>   fell
my face went through the shattering glass laughing
my hair turned red, my eyes, my words, I said:
>   The traffic light was
>   invented by an American
>   Negro.
This had been my home.

AINT NO

for Boles

Never been sick
never been sick a day in my life
until today

Until this machine moved over me
until I couldn't move no more
couldn't move over, couldn't make room

Make room, they said
make time while the match still glows
make yourself presentable

I didn't move, I couldn't
move, I wouldn't move if I could've
I didn't even scream

or stroke your leg and purr
like they taught us to do in school
No legs, no sound, no way out

until they moved
until I could see the glow from the flames
until I could feel the fire

This machine felt like what is left
what couldn't be moved
but burned

WATCHING YOU WALK AWAY

For Greg Millard

Today
your back, cocked hat, thick clothes for cold
the way you turned around to look again for
what? It wasn't there last night
We were there, 'it' wasnt, why,   why not

The world is all around us, even at night, in bed
in each others arms
distilled & injected into the odor we leave on each others
backs & thighs, between the knots & shields of all we lay
down in the dark to pick up in the morning
I like your brown eyes when you talk
you know who you are, I like your knowing this
maybe that's not enough

Let's talk, go to plays, see each other sometimes just to
see each other
If we lie down in each others bodies again
let it be for the music we hold
not the music we might make

REVOLUTION

When the back of my swan
divides your body with feathers
it doesn't matter that they are
                              white or black
              only that they are soft

COUNTERREVOLUTION

Sometimes early, the children
or maybe one child begins
to coo to herself or maybe
someone we cannot see
inventing sounds we
only remember while we hear them
like knowing the sea intimately

Like women children
sometimes see us saying: love
not saying anything
but moving the floor in time to
their vibrations from everything
and us. The incredible smallness
of their heads.

           Living with us
they are constant reminders of
what we had hoped to be by now.

WEATHERMAN BLUES

I have a brother made of cockroaches.
Every morning I wake him and the bugs rustle
make noises like breakfast cereal until
he gets out of bed and starts shaving.
Then they're all quiet watching him scrape off
the unlucky eggs of his chin roaches.

I have to help him start moving and
help him sit down and so on because
the roaches in his joints die from the heat

of his energy at the end of the day
but his heart roaches and lung roaches never die
and the roaches of his eyes and mouth are
always fucking so that everyday he sees
new things and tells me words
I never heard before
and never remember.

Someday the roaches in his throat will
choke him or the ones in his stomach will have
cancerous babies that will kill him as though
he'd starved but until then all I can do
is help him around the house
keep him covered when we go out
find women who don't care who they embrace or
what enters them . . .

Why couldn't I have had a brother
made of butterflies
like other people.

ROCKY DIES YELLOW

(Blue Wind Press 1975)

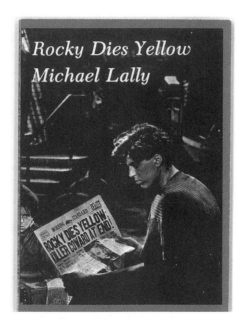

"NOW I'M ONLY THIRTY-TWO"

from 5 to 30 it was
only women, then
for almost one year
it was only men
now it's like the first
5 years and back
to everyone again

YOU REMEMBER BELMAR NJ 1956

ethnic beaches, ethnic streets,
ethnic hangouts, jetties, kids

got sand & their first glimpse
of hair where it never was

you piled into nosed & decked Chevies & Mercs
carried baseball bats to Bradley Beach to
beat up on Jews—You knew, they had all the
money & no restrictions on their sex like
Christians
        who said Hitler's only mistake was
        being born German but
        your own Jews rode with you:
        class warfare after all

Crazy Mixed Up kids with names like
Sleepy, Face, Skippy, Skootch, Me Too Morrisey
& Nutsy McConnell imitated themselves & Marlon
Brando, danced to *Frankie Lyman & The Teenagers*
or *Little Richard* & sometimes
holding their fathers' guns

made women girls light their cigarettes trembling
letting them see just enough of it beneath their
pink or charcoal grey to make them happy or sick
always glad god made man out of dirt & not sand

you got drunk in your clubhouse or rented rooms
pretended you were really recording *In The Still of The*
Night or your own secret sleeper under
some name like *The Shrapnels* or *The Inserts* not
Spartans AC (Athletic Club) or *The Archangels SC*
(social . . .

the way we're still lining up

SONG

Where we bend
the world bends
Where we join
the air joins
Where we lie
the land lies
Where we move
the sea moves
Where we break
where we break
the air breaks
the land breaks
the sea divides
Where we break
the world bends

KENT STATE MAY 4, 1970

I
This is the night they turn out the trees,
the rope we skipped, the sound of
asphalt cooling. This is the night they
left us. You used to say: This is
the night they are always leaving us.

2
In the puzzle there are four pieces:
the soap, the boat, the fish and the—
It's green, we remember that much, very
far away and steep and has a place
for each of four parts which are the
boat with the sail and the bar of soap
and the fish from the bottom of this
puzzle, but what have you done with

3
Don't even try to turn around

4

NEWARK POEM

I never made it to Morocco, Paris, Tangiers,
Tokyo, Madrid. I just live here, in Newark
& wait, for Morocco, Paris, Tangiers, Tokyo,
& Madrid to make it to me, here in Newark.

DREAMING OF THE POTATO

your grandfather being
alone lived in it loved
it & gave birth to another
felt his arms noticed the potato skin
he was hard & white & something to chew
inside

He had a dream called him-in-America
where potatoes were roses

He carried one gnarled & petrified
to keep away arthritis

Where he lived if you dug too deep
the earth was white wet & hard

"With people there has been trouble
With the potato we have been happy"

"WE WERE ALWAYS AFRAID OF"

the quiet ones

It was a myth we believed
we invented but

now we know while we were busy
watching the quiet ones

the others led us into the sea

* * * MARILYN MONROE * * *

Everybody

                    wanted her

                                        to do

a trick

for them

                      but

                she had a trick of her own

that she wanted to do for   herself

                    only

                  she hated

                  tricks

POEM TO 1956

Can you hear the adolescent
laughter in the Jersey pines?
That sound of a gas station turning
over in its long nights sleep?
What is the meaning of summer
if the menthol of your fingernails

doesn't touch me from the grave?
Anemone bones we whispered of
between trips to the car trunk
and quick changes behind towels
or the rest rooms of gasoline
stations whose owners were called:
Ma.
      Can you hear that rustling
on the highway where the tires
trailed our innocence behind
like the intestines of the desire
we kept hanging on the rear view?
Ma, we said, where in those pine
woods, under the tender feet of
tourists, where in all that fur
is there a place to tie ones skates
and hang a key around your lovers neck?

POETRY 1969

The guy down the street just
"blew his brains out" They

carried him out on a stretcher
all bloody faced and torn and

the kid next door ran home
told his ma who told us, said

"Some guy down the street just
got stabbed in the nose & died"

but we found out, we found out
different "blew his brains out"

"Just back from Vietnam" the
kid said later "like my dad"

*

Last week across the street
some lady was raped by a tight

rope walker, now this is true
he lost his job in the circus

when he fell off and hurt his
neck so it would swing all day

like this, while he worked here
as a janitor and handy man and

told all the housewives tales
about the circus and his neck

until the other night he tapped
softly on this foreign womans

door and said "It's the main-
tenance man, your power's off"

She tried the lights and said
"What do I do?" "Let me in"

he said "and I'll check your
fuse box" here the story gets

confused but it's clear he had
a knife and somehow got naked

and raped the woman before she
got the knife away and screamed

My wife rolled over and said
"Did you hear that, sounded like

five quick shots" but I wasnt
saying a thing They caught him

The bullets were fired by the guy
across the hall from the woman

He said he just fired to make the
rapist halt, said he saw this man

running out of the building, naked
in the moonlight, but it turns out

this guy with the revolver had
been the best of buddies with the

tight rope walker who happened to
have already served time for rape

Now they got a new janitor who has
a neck like everybody else here

*

Today the guy next door told me
if it comes down to it and we all

find ourselves on the barricades
we'd probably be on opposite sides

but he promised me this "I'll
only shoot at your legs, cause

youre my friend" which is better
than my brother-in-law the cop who

said "I'd shoot my own father if he
was breakin the law and tryin to

get away" he shook his head then said
softer "Ya gotta respect the law"

WEATHERMAN GOES OUT 1969

I strap on my holster
the one with the pine cone design
shove my automatic into it
slip a small book of famous quotations into
my pocket to offset the weight of the gun
take an ice pop out of the freezer
the paper sticks to the popsicle
sticks to my fingers sticks to my coat
I put the popsicle down on the sink
wash my hands and wipe off my coat
when I pick it up again it's melting
I try to suck the moisture from it
I try to avoid dripping some on my coat
or pants or shirt or holster
with the pine cone design on it
or the automatic with the gas station design
on the handle
I fail and now the automatic is sticky
I try to take off my coat
without getting it sticky too
I fail to keep the coat clean
but succeed in removing it
I wash my hands while whats left of the
popsicle melts on the kitchen sink
I roll up my sleeves
I remove the sticky automatic from
the holster with the pine cone design

I wash the automatic handle with the
gas station design I'm looking
at the popsicle and trying to hurry
so I can get whats left of it before it all
melts away when the automatic goes off
the bullet enters my forehead with
the boulevard design and I forget
about the popsicle I forget
about the bullet
I go out

CONVERSATION WITH MYSELF

"un   natural"

(un   natural?

                to love yourself
                those like you?

"It's only   natural   with   a woman"

(think   of   sucking   a cock   )

"UGH!!!   THAT DIRTY SMELLY   UGLY   SWEATY
        THING!!!"

(think of   a woman   sucking
                    your
                    cock
        not so ugh?

then   what must you think of her   "them"

any woman is a fag   & vice versa?

meaning you don't like men   &
you don't like women
or think much of them
if you can

        see
        enjoy
        desire   to have them do
              things you despise doing

&
you don't like yourself

                  after all
     it could be your cock   )

I WISH I COULD TELL YOU ABOUT IT,
HOW IT REMINDS ME OF YOU

There's a window in our house looks out on 1956
every time I draw the blinds a thirteen-year-old kid
       cries himself to sleep
and in a ladies room on the boardwalk somewhere
a nineteen-year-old woman with a moustache doesn't
       even wonder why she did it
can't remember his name
sits on a wood slat chair and dreams, no, tries to remember
doesn't know he cried in the sand under the boardwalk she
       works on
doesn't know he was thirteen
doesn't give a shit
doesn't, isn't, sure of anything but boardwalks, sitting down,
       how people act
in bathrooms
in her

Not even thirteen, eleven, twelve, just barely a bird

with feathers

Usually we just leave the blinds down, turn over the record,
go back to sleep til the kids come
then its time to do: what it was like before good old
        rock'n'roll

I wish I could tell you about it.

MY LIFE

(Wyrd Press 1975)

MY LIFE

I ate everything they put in front of me
read everything they put before my eyes
shook my ass, cried over movie musicals
was a sissy and a thug, a punk and an
intellectual, a cocksucker and a mother
fucker, helped create two new people,
paid taxes, voted and served four years
and a few weeks in the United States Air
Force, was court martialed and tried
civilly, in jail and in college, kicked
out of college, boy scouts, altar boys
and one of the two gangs I belonged to,
I was suspended from grammar and high
schools, arrested at eleven the year I
had my first "real sex" with a woman
and with a boy, I waited nineteen years
to try it again with a male and was sorry
I waited so long, I waited two weeks to
try it again with a woman and was sorry
I waited so long, wrote, poetry and
fiction, political essays, leaflets and
reviews, I was a "jazz musician" and a
dope dealer, taught junior high for two
weeks, high school Upward Bound for two
years, college for four years, I got up
at 5 AM to unload trucks at Proctor and
Gamble to put myself through classes
at the University of Iowa, I washed
dishes and bussed tables, swept floors
and cleaned leaders and gutters, washed
windows and panhandled, handled a forty
foot ladder alone at thirteen, wrote
several novels not very good and none
published, published poems and stories

and articles and books of poems, was
reviewed, called "major," compared to
"The Teen Queens," mistaken for black,
for gay, for straight, for older, for
younger for bigger for better for richer
for poorer for stupider for smarter for
somebody else, fell in love with a black
woman at 18, kicked out of the family
for wanting to marry her at 20, I sucked
cock and got fucked and fucked and got
sucked, I was known for being a big
jerk off, a wise ass, for always getting
my ass kicked so bad neighborhood kids
would ask to see the marks, for running
for sheriff of Johnson County Iowa in '68
on the "Peace and Freedom" ticket and
pulling in several thousand votes, for
winning people to the cause with emotional
spontaneous speeches at rallies and on TV,
for being a regular guy, a romantic
idealist, a suicidal weatherman, a bomb
throwing anarchist, an SDS leader, a
communist, a class chauvinist, an
asexual politico, a boring socialist,
the proletarian man, a horny androgyne,
a junkie, a boozer, a loser, a nigger
lover, a black woman's white man, a
race traitor, a greaser, a fast man
with my hands, a hood, a chickenshit,
a crazy head, an unmarked thoroughbred,
a courageous human being, a Catholic,
a fallen away Catholic, An Irish American
Democrat, a working class Irish American
writer from a family of cops, a skinny
jive time street philosopher, a power
head, an underground movie star, a

quiet shy guy, a genius, an innovator,
a duplicator, a faker, a good friend,
a fickle lover, an ass lover, a muff
diver, another pretty face, a lousy
athlete, a generous cat, an ambitious
young man, a very tough paddy, a macho
hippie, a faggot gangster, a faggot,
a big crazy queen, a straight man, a
strong man, a sissy, a shithead, a
home wrecker, a reckless experimenter
with other peoples lives, a demagogue,
a fanatic, a cheap propagandizer, a
fantastic organizer, a natural born
leader, a naive upstart, an arrogant
jitterbug, a white nigger, an easy lay,
a pushover, a hard working husband,
a henpecked husband, the black sheep,
a crazy mixed up kid, a juvenile delinquent,
a misfit, a surrealist, an actualist,
an Iowa poet, a political poet, an open
field poet, a street poet, a bad poet,
a big mouth, a voice of the sixties,
a pretty poet, a gay poet, a clit kissing
tit sucking ass licking body objectifying
poet, a gigolo, a jerk, a poor boy, an
old man, an assman, unsteady, immature,
charismatic, over confident, over 30,
impetuous, a rock, a pawn, a tool, a
potato lover, a great teacher, loyal
friend, concerned citizen, a humanist,
the bosses son, Bambi's old man, Lee's
husband, Matthew's ex-lover, Terry's
partner, Slater's main man, the bishop's
favorite altar boy, the landlady's pet,
the class clown, the baby of the family,
the neighborhood stranger, the hardest

working kid, with the rosiest cheeks, who
was an instigator, a trouble maker,
too smart for my own good, too soft,
too distant, too honest, too cold, too
tactless, uncommunicative, anal retentive,
self-sufficient, shameless, unsophisticated,
too butch, too skinny, too white, too
defensive, too hungry, apologetic, in-
decisive, unpredictable, I never hit a
woman or woke up gloomy, I'm a light
sleeper, an affectionate father, a bad
drinker, a city boy, paranoid, compulsive,
and a terrific body surfer, I love the
hipness in me I thought was black back
in the '50s, the vulnerability I took for
feminine in the '70s, I hate the poor kid
act I've pulled on strangers and friends
to start them out owing me, I learned to
cook and to sew, stopped chewing gum and
biting my nails, I was a weather observer,
a map maker, a printer's devil, a
carpenter's helper, a glazier, a locksmith,
editor, publisher, promoter and critic,
I stopped dancing at 15 and started again
at 30, math was my best subject, languages
my worst, I've been knocked out several
times but only one black eye and one
fractured thumb, I've totaled several
cars but I'm an ace driver especially
in cities, I haven't had an accident since
I stopped drinking, knock on wood, I'm
extremely superstitious, don't speak too
soon, I gave up cigarettes and coffee and
using the words chick, spade and asshole,
I've read Confucius, Buddha, Lao Tzu,
The Upanishads, The Bhagavad Gita, The

Koran, The Bible, The Prophet, Thus Spake
Zarathustra, Marx, Trotsky, Stalin, Lenin,
Mao, Che, Hesse, Proust, Firestone, Fanon,
Castenada and Davis, I read all of Joyce
and all of Dostoevsky in translation
at least two times through on night shifts
in weather towers through 1961 and 62,
I love all of William Saroyan, Van
Morrison, Jane Bowles, Samuel Beckett,
Joe Brainard, and Bertold Brecht, I'm
finally getting to know and like some
"classical music," I went to my first
ballet, opera, and concert this year and
loved all of it, took my first trip out
of the country and was glad to get back
although it was great, I love the USA and
many of the people in it, I'm afraid of
my own anger, and any kind of violence,
I've been the same weight since 1957 though
I have an enormous appetite, my hair's
turning gray, I've had it cut three times
since 1966, I spit a lot and pick my nose
too much, I could buy new shoes, eat ice
cream, chicken or chocolate pudding anytime,
I'm afraid of dogs and hate zoos, I'm
known for my second winds especially
when dancing or eating, I used to think
of myself as a dreamer, I had a vision
at 9 that I'd die between 42 and 46,
the image was me doubling over clutching
my stomach, whenever I'm embarrassed I
see that in my head, some of my nicknames
have been Faggy, Rocky, Spider, Brutus,
Paddy Cat, Newark, Irish, and The Lal,
I'm a father, son, brother, cousin,
brother-in-law, uncle, record breaker,

war child, veteran, and nut about Lauren
Bacall, James Cagney, Robert Mitchum,
Bogie and Brando, *Last Tango* and *The
Conformist* are the favorite movies of
my adult life, I've fallen in love with
eyes, asses, thighs, wrists, lips, skin,
color, hair, style, movement, bodies,
auras, potential, accents, atmospheres,
clothes, imaginations, sophistication,
histories, families, couples, friends,
rooms full of people, parks, cities,
entire states, talked to trees since
1956 and the wind since '52, between '56
and '59 I had few friends and a "bad
reputation" which made it difficult
to get dates with "nice girls," in 1960
and '61 I had more friends and several
lovers, I was at the SDS split in Chicago
in 1969 and didn't like either side's
position or tactics, I almost cried
when I heard John Coltrane had died,
and Ho Chi Minh, Babe Ruth, Jack
Kerouac, Eric Dolphy, Roberto Clemente,
Moose Conlon, Frankie Lyman, Fred
Hampton, Allende, Clifford Brown,
Richie Valens and Buddy Holly in that
plane crash, the four little girls
in that Alabama church, the students
at Orangeburg, the "weather people"
in the town house explosion which I
always figured was a set up, my uncle
Frank and my uncle John, my grandparents,
lots of people, I did cry when I thought
about the deaths of the Kent State and
Jackson State students, when I heard
Ralph Dickey had "taken his life" or

the first time I heard Jackson Browne
do his "Song for Adam" or when Marlon
Brando as Terry finds his brother Charley
(Rod Steiger) hanging dead on the fence
in *On the Waterfront* and before going
to get the murderers says something to
Eva Marie Saint like "And for god's sake
don't leave him here alone" or when he
talks to his dead wife in *Last Tango*
or finds Red Buttons and his wife
have committed suicide in *Sayonara*
I've cried a lot over movies especially
old ones on TV, I've never cried at a
play but I still haven't seen many, the
only Broadway plays I've seen were *My
Fair Lady* and *Bye Bye Birdie*, I
watched my mother die, I've paid my dues,
been through the mill, come up from the
streets, done it my way, had that once
in a lifetime thing, had trouble with
my bowels ever since I can remember
then in '72 my body became more relaxed,
I've had the clap, crabs, scabies,
syphilis, venereal warts, and unidentified
infections in my cock, my ass, my throat,
all over my body, I've been terribly
sunburned and covered with scabs from
fights and accidents, I only had stitches
once at 4 when I had my appendix out,
I've been earning money since I was 10,
supporting myself since 13, others since
22, I got "unemployment" once, been
fired several times, never paid to
get laid, I lost money gambling but
quit after I had to give up my high
school ring in a poker game at the Dixie

Hotel in Greenville South Carolina in
1962 waiting for my friend Willy Dorton
to come out from the room where he was
proposing marriage to his favorite
whore who always turned him down after
they fucked and she got most of his
paycheck from him, some of my best
friends were hookers and strippers,
postal clerks and shills, supermarket
managers and factory workers, heavy
revvies and punks, actresses and junkies,
who were and are the most difficult
of friends, art dealers and artists,
musicians and hustlers, dykes and critics,
shit workers and liberals, gringos and fags,
and honkies and bastards, queer and old
and divorced and straight and Italian
and big deals and dipshits, I know at least
six people who think they turned me on
to dope for the first time in 1960 in
New York City, in 1962 in Rantoul Illinois,
in 1964 in Spokane Washington, in 1966 and
67 in Iowa City, in 1969 in Washington
DC, I once was high on opium and didn't
want to come back, I was a recreational
therapist at Overbrook Hospital in Essex
County New Jersey in 1966 where James Moody
wrote "Last Train From Overbrook" before
he was discharged, in 1960 I had a tremendous
crush on Nina Simone, I always wanted to
name a child Thelonious, I was sure
I was an orphan at 10, I wished I was
an orphan at 18, my father's alive so
I'm still not an orphan at 32, I know
a lot of orphans, I once had an
orphan for a lover, I suppose my kids

could be orphans some day, I was never
good at planning the future for more
than a couple of days, friends have
told me I always do things the hard way,
my family's response to tough times or
catastrophes was usually humor, I'm
grateful to them for giving me that,
I find cynics boring although there's
a lot of the cynic in me, I find
depression dull, mine or anyone else's,
I'm no good at small talk, I feel
an undercurrent of violent tension
in most "straight" bars and on late
night city streets that intimidates
me, I find jealousy useless and
depressing, I know people who find
jealousy exciting and even rewarding,
something to live for, I'd love to
make love all the ways I haven't yet
or haven't thought of yet, with all
the people I haven't yet or haven't met
yet, although sometimes I could care
less about sex, I write everyday
and listen to music everyday and cant
imagine living without either,
libraries and hospitals intimidate me,
being around people who seem to feel
comfortable anywhere used to make me
feel insecure, I'm getting over that,
I used to feel obliged to apologize
for or defend people whose goals I
shared even though I might not like
them or their tactics, I'm getting
over that too, I've learned to love
or at least appreciate a lot of things
I used to despise or ignore, I've had

trouble getting it up and trouble
keeping it down, I'm tired of a lot
of things but curious about more, I'm
tired of this but that's history now.

March 1974
Washington DC

CHARISMA

(O Press 1976)

LISTEN
for Caitlin Lally

pianos in the clouds

showering us with music

of a kind

not often appreciated

and us here under the covers

MORE THAN

                                    for Joan Manson

it was more than "the fifties"
you were more than "fabulous"
I was more than a "punk"
we had more than "young love"
that was more than "right"
and I remember more than
they said I would

SONNET FOR MY 33rd

Bridget Bardot
Abbott & Costello
Hound Dog
The Dickey Bird Song
The Girl Can't Help It

T.S. Eliot
Cassius Clay
JFK
Thelonious Sphere Monk
On The Waterfront
Bird
Pope John XXIII
Ezra Pound
Clifford Brown

TESTIMONY

for Robert Slater

when he was young
they called him the carpetbagger
because whenever he went south
he fucked them up

now he can fuck them up
without even moving

ABOUT THE AUTHOR

I cant sing too good
but I can write good
I cant play too good either
but I can write good
I cant last at anything too long
even writing
but when I do it
it's something
and writing something

is always adding something
and that's supposed to be good
I can make love okay
but I cant do it forever
or too long with the same person
unless I really convince myself it's love
and then it's good
but not always good even then
but when I write about it it's great
and the writing is good
I'm not too good with languages
though I'm finally learning some Spanish
and I studied German, French, and Latin
but still, even English gives me trouble
I just go on speaking and writing
my brand of American
and the writing is good
sometimes it's very good
I was never very good at sports
even indoor sports
not enough patience for pool or shuffleboard
but I can always write
and I write good
I've never been able to make much money
I haven't tried too hard but
I've thought about it very hard
and tried some
but I've always been able to write
and write good
sometimes I wish I was a wealthy man
or a famous musician
or a great painter or something like that
but I never wished I was a writer
I just knew one day I was
and that I was good
and so I wrote

and keep writing
and keep reading what I write
and even when it's terrible
I know it's good

CATCH MY BREATH

(Salt Lick Press 1978)

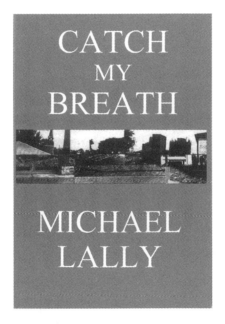

NEED

I used to argue with my father
None could be more sincere than mine
want to do something different
no place
Viet Nam
that was later with my wife
Max Ernst   David Smith etc.   *then*
Father Knows Best had me scared
where was the USA big rocks & cars
long white highways & afternoon dark bars
& my neighborhood
nobody knew anything
especially if anyone else asked
my father never asked so why should I
I don't know
I just did
& that would start the arguments until
somebody died of cancer or suicide
I got a job playing piano
washing dishes or recreational therapist
James Moody wrote Last Train From Overbrook
my father opened my mail when I was 21
and hadn't lived at home for over three years
still muttering about the rubber in my wallet
when I was 15
or the address of the sweet black girl
when I was 15
or the way the priests wanted me out of school
when I was 15
or the noise I made re entering their atmosphere
when I was 15
or the guilt I felt among the civilized
when I was 15
or the nightly rituals of Bridget Bardot fantasies
when I was 15

my father was born in the last century
and if I'm allowed I'll live into the next
that's enough to forgive anyone for

from RUNNING AWAY

            you all anxiously
tore the bouquets from your
wrists and tight little tits

In the morning the telephone wires
resembled hot nerves in a dying
Indian's spine as he watches a
white man cut off his nuts for
an unusual tobacco pouch. This
[. . .]
seeing more ways in more ways
of seeing
and getting jacked up for it

EMPTY CLOSETS

I.

When it comes time.

Take it away, demand that could make a marshmallow loud.
Everywhere, children who didn't want to go anywhere.

"I usta just wail on that mutha fucka.
Now that mutha fucka just wails on me."

"IN THE BEGINNING WAS THE ROOT OF ALL EVIL"

carrying a silo full of animals around in his arms.

"I don't know *what* I want to be."

The fallen parallel lines of white.
You break down in a grin. Leather,
the spider behind. Either. Yet and still.

"I was a fool who thought woman had to be in love with
somebody else to be worth anything to me. In fact
blew me away."

It was a case of love at first sight
and the case was closed. And the pale old men say,
"loosen."

Okay, touching and then opening the wounds
for the salt you always carry. This many times
I've been awake all night and we continue to act
as though we were sleeping. My heritage is
the way you look tonight.

Covering that black was. I got a job. Something forced home
and beat my head on the wall, a fragile, gnawed, paganism in
the back:
          Mecca.

"Of course we are all one. Rocknroll music any KARATE! hah,
rubbers, the parking lot's legs as miles on the kids. Be big,
be busy, be the walls."

Your eyes and eyes. Outside the elevator one night.
Ready this time for liberation you know what that means.
Your name has come up again and again. This is

the Bob Dylan one this is the Janis Joplin one this is
the John Coltrane one this is the Charlie:
YOU CAN'T EVEN SPELL LEROI JONES NEW NAME???

Goodly inclinations. Stop it. Knowing what you care about.
D) Your kit.

Resting night loons behind your cock.
Try to do anything to us.
There's something beautiful Mao.
For all?
The little good in everything.
White sisters are coming home with or without Ted Joans.
The fat black sparrow with way to marry a beautiful and
black woman on orders of the commander who wanted me.

On a lonely airstrip in the great NorthWest the dig it I
can kick your ass and commies all wear grey brain change
until you a white dog bite yourself there, up there.
Listening to Marion Brown shit I don't know. He said son
I love to touch inside my cells.

"White and short and stocky ones."

Round shoulders a new guy came. I walked up to the big
country boy. I never saw Nutsy, Andre, or Dolores again.
It was the year they discovered Jim Carroll.

"Everything is quiet. My hand feels pretty bad."

Getting them together
because I love. And now it's me.

2.

July 2nd and suddenly ungrateful! Old one

we demand the sun on my ass. It comes out at night.
Half shit the rest sugar.

"I jus tellsem I don know what it mean
but I sure know what it do."

     "WORLD'S LARGEST PRAIRIE DOG 8,000 POUNDS"

Ted's case.
He waspingly gruff embraces steel snow. Common stew whore.
One is enough.

No more annexing the gris-gris. Me they generally call
THE SHELF. They call him DRY the way your balls feel
when you been put away AGAIN. She forgives the future
when we take out each others' eyes
to fill in the blanks. Blue gorges.

"Way uptown on a hundred, hanging from my action back, you're
supposed to watch tv."

Once a year the sharks would come to
singular execution of snow fields,
o, in piles behind the early fifties.
On top of that we move around,
gored silver following ourselves. Getting fucked.

JUST LET ME DO IT

(Vehicle Editions 1978)

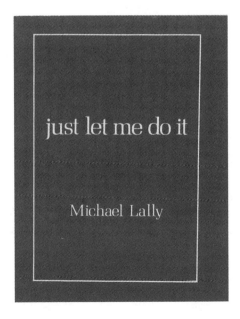

just let me do it

Michael Lally

VIOLETS

That Spring there were no violets . . .
only in the shops,
where, captive, they wilted too soon
and were too dear.

The Woolworth stores sold plastic ones:
everlasting,

not too expensive. I bought some;
you seemed delighted.
They're here, still, beside your picture.

2: TALKING

Lee, it's more than the organ music that
defines the organs inside my body / it's
as though you were walking around the in
side of my eyes until you found yourself

IN HARLEM IN 1961

for Bambi

I didn't think about it
I was in harlem with you
it was 1961 and we were
alone, in love, uptown
way uptown on a hundred
and thirty something street
heading downtown where
people didn't stare, that's

all the way down although
even there, on weekends
if you went out they
might look a little bit
longer than they would
not midtown times square
where out of state sailors
on leave left their spit
hanging from my action back
skinny shoulders three
button high front french
sport coat from klines on
the square in newark back
in jersey where the rest
of the squares didn't want
me back no more, or you
saying white and black
don't mix like sheep and
horses like cement and
fertilizer like your face
and their stomachs like
the way we walked down
that dark street after mid
night with our hands in
each other's feeling fine
and these little kids not
more than twelve years out
on the street not more
than twenty strong stopped
us and asked me what the
fuck I was doin up there
out there walkin around
with you like there was
nothing to it but to do it
and I said what I'm doing
is walking on the street

with the woman I love and
I sounded a little afraid
not enough to look like I
wouldn't be ready to go down
if I had to but enough to
let everybody know I wasn't
any hero including myself
and you looked mad afraid
and smiling at the same time
and some one of the others
not the leader said, shit,
let the dude and his woman
alone man and they did

THEIR IMAGINATION SAFE

you, wing like across the bright animals

       I taste the metal of my death, your tongue

(remember Sonny Rollins blowing with Thelonious Monk at the Five Spot)

   one foot stiffens with muscle cramp

          on your tongue
          that dark inside
          we love to fill
          but pray each day
          will open up to someone new
          & beautiful & loose like dreams

   my mouth opens like a floor, walk around in it

flash cards flash: Open / Relax / Lie back / Wider /Relax / Be filled

we are fine together, one safe smell
in it the metal of what dies in us each day
the rinse of knowing who we are
what honor we can give
they are afraid to know

brother, stretch across my map your face & ass & toes
insert your A's & B's into my Y's and Z's
lie back again with me before we go
& go with me to where they can't imagine
taste death & know what they cannot know
we are each other's children
alchemists

midwives
peasants

in each others crevices creating seed from shit & loving it

(there are those who have never been afraid of the dark)

I am wide & divided as vulnerable as a lamb to be stroked or slaughtered
& you slaughter me with the stroke of your tongue & cheek at my cheek
& cheek & the reach of dark between

where is the machine invented to
capture this art

in our hearts brothers

in our hearts

SO

        I wait and wonder
what I'd do
                    if someone said pick your 60 best poems.
Pick all of them? Or any?
Maybe commit suicide, but everyone would say
"It's because he's *really gay*," or maybe
"really *not* gay."

                                *

Read Anne Waldman and Terence Winch,
Bruce Andrews and Adrienne Rich, wonder what might happen
to me this summer if I go away, or stay here in Washington DC
where you can see Watergate live!

                                *

If you want to know the truth today's my birthday
and though I often feel older, and sometimes appear younger
I'm 31, and like everything else that too can be fun
or a bummer, a drain on the cosmic energy, depending on what?
If you know the answer you win the future;
if you don't the future is ours to lose or—
whatever happened to the old way of construction?
Well, one line still follows another, and my voice moves
between each space, and when I think of you I sweat,
or maybe just imagine myself like a cartoon troublemaker
big beads of perspiration jumping out from my skin as I
cringe behind the fence that the bully is about to
throw a bomb over, or drop an anvil over, or just put his
meaty fist through and right on into my scared shitless grin,
the analogy resting on our mutual *vulnerability*—
that's poetry isn't it?

*

Of course I don't talk like *this*.
I talk like this.

*

And now it's time to go back to THE HISTORY OF ROCK'N'ROLL
which means it's my night to cook dinner for "the house"—
collective—and it's gonna be smoked sausage cooked in peppers
and mushrooms and carrots, maybe some onions, and beans
for protein, or something nutritional. I picked the sausage
because it seemed to be looking at me in the Safeway,
not exactly the way I was looking at one of the cashiers,
a young man with curly blonde hair and nice build
who seemed to have a down home kind of friendliness,
or the woman with the little girl the same size as Miles,
who is a little smaller than Caitlin, both of whom were
pulling on my pants leg for pennies for gumballs as I watched
the curve of the woman's arm as she placed each
well thought over item on the counter behind my
vibrational buying and didn't even notice how much I fell in love
with her arm and felt guilty for objectifying a part of her
although she might all be like her arm and then I might
fall in love with all of her, but that would cause problems,
she probably is already in love with at least one person, and
I'm already in love with about fourteen on a regular basis, and
that keeps causing all kinds of problems because people who are
attracted to my style don't like my ways—that sounded like
a pretentious folk singing prodigy's idea of an early Dylan line,
but what I meant would never be explained right in a poem like this,
or one like Anne Waldman's either though I like to read hers
because they make me want to write, and in my world that's what
"great" writers are supposed to do—make everyone else, or
at least me, feel like I can write too, and then make me feel,
like I will, and then I do.

78

*

After dinner we'll eat the cake Atticus made for my birthday
there'll be some presents from some of the people in the house, and
maybe Annie will stop over, or Matthew might call from work, or we
might all go down to watch him make salads at

                                        FOOD FOR THOUGHT,

and maybe eat some too, all along getting stoned on the house doobie,
which goes too fast these days but never fast enough, which is
about the way I feel on my birthday about my life, either that or
the way I'm easily satisfied but never feel I can get *too* much—
sometimes *everything* is enough, you know?

*

HAPPY BIRTHDAY TO ME, HAPPY BIRTHDAY TO ME,
I THINK I JUST HEARD CHUCK COME IN, CAITLIN'S
ANGRY WITH ME AND THROWING A TANTRUM IN
HER ROOM, IT'S RAINING BUT I HEAR THE DISHES
BEING DONE FINALLY BY SOMEONE ELSE
HAPPY BIRTHDAY TO ME

*

Resolution: No more guilt trips
from outside or inside
going either direction
—is everybody happy?

QUEEN JANE

for Suzanne Burgess

She comes out of the dark,
well, it's never really "dark" . . .
She comes out of the near dark
her pale body moving like . . . what?
Like an old silent movie on the wall!
Oh! I love her pale body, *me!* who for
too long turned my head only for "dark"
and the near dark bodies. Now I turn
my whole body, my own pale body, to
greet hers coming toward me in the
near dark, and already my cells are
exploding like tiny rain drops
meeting the windshield of the Toyota
that carried my pale body back to Iowa
and hers.

TODAY WHAT IF EVERYTHING REVERSED

right eye vision blurred
left handed masturbation
grey streak over left temple

you aren't on my mind at all
I'm on yours this morning
life does not go on until
we touch each other once more

my imagination works in this humidity
because this humidity is gone and DC is
dry, cool, constantly pleasant and not
the capital of anything but our smiles

the music comes out my ears
the kids remain quiet all day
I feel fresher around supper time
than I did at breakfast or lunch

on the streets this evening
we smile at each other with no fear
everyone is vulnerably nice
those of us who fall in love quickly
find those of us who fall in love
quickly

going to bed together demands no games
going to bed alone demands no loneliness
going to bed in groups demands no guilt
going to bed we dream of tomorrow

waking up we find everything reversed

FILE

luxury eyes
Touch me here!
tiny quick eruptions in limp wrists
limp coal colored hair to chew on
kiss me kiss me
o pretty people

I take off one damp Tuesday morning
wish me well
the dark shy wheat of my asshole
the giraffe tender soles of my pale feet
rock quarries between my fingers
laser beam holographs shining from my eyes
everything green & standing up as I pass by

There is a sign in the mountains for
LOVER, Pennsylvania
one of the first things a child learns
that sing & sign have the same letters
that evil is live spelled backwards
there is an eel in feel
& in between your lips I slip
wet & loving you
there is an our in your that frightens me
I turn around

What a gorgeous back seat!
stale Ritz crackers & a portable fridge
two bottles of champagne
stereo tape deck
wall to wall carpet & a
decorative Persian rug on top of that
patterned wall paper with embossed
velvety designs & antiqued dinner furniture
several classic photographs of
your lover, his fantasies, his mother, etc.
a canopy over the bed &
a sunken bathtub with lavender tile
we're so tired of lavender

take my eyelids beautiful boy
I'll never use them now

YOU WALK IN

my tongue curls
my house expands
your neck glows
your smile chews away my distraction
I can't move my toes they want to dream so much

why don't your clothes fit me with you in them?
what do you see in that
evacuated city I built
for us to live in behind your knees
can I call my friend Terry & ask him to tell you
how even the Bronx docsn't feel as good as your
quiet movements in
o drive the car of your hair into my waking up alone no more
& let me park there for the Hollywood premiere of
"Hello, Goodby, I Love You"

9.13.73

kiss me—lay down with me—forget my fucked up
fantasies—theyre not with me tonight—just kiss me—
gently—touch my hair and eyelids—let me
put my lips against your shoulder—hip—temple—
life's a need—let me need *you* for a few hours—
o Michael Buddy Bacall Bambi Penny beautiful boys &
ladies let me life you—you know—lots of slow &
serious energy—not *too* serious—that flows one way
but never gets there without you—just tonight—
just not alone right now when I'm here—all alone
again—tons of it—life—right here between us—
why not let it out—close our eyes and be
ourselves!—yeah too late now aint it—all the
tough young women I went to bed with back then—
I "went to bed" or beach or backseat with— I went
to eyes and thighs and pubic hair and soft skin with
I went to bed so many times lonely with—all the
people I've touched and held it all for just that
while with—all the empty holes where stars had been—
o lots of life here on this planet late at night—
I can hear the cop cars from here and not you—

("I STAND . . .")

for Karen Allen

I stand
               "awe"
I, uh
Listen:
               I am "small"
I mean inside my hands
I mean we talk this way
always "meaning"
Does John Ashbery ever say

O you make me dream
while I stand
that time beside you
walking away from
going back in my brain files
slow replay over and over
in "the street"
your house has a "porch"
mine had a "stoop" but
we called it a porch
because it had a roof goddamnit
like my mouth
and the tongue inside which
I am "small" and "in awe" of
your Lauren Bacall
and your my-niece
I have a daughter
without freckles like I had
like you have
like I might have been
without this smallness in my stomach
I never grow, you know
that's why you placed your hand

with so much care because you knew
it would stay there for a long time
And I swear on your eyes
in which the games I learned
do me no good, I swear on your eyes
and the light that shines from them
that it has, and it will
like a tattoo that didn't hurt
and only we can see
and it talks for me about "awe"
and the way I stand when I am beside you

We always said "I mean" when we meant
Do you believe me

IN AMERICA

for Olga Nola

I just called to say
you looked beautiful today
and yesterday
the way your smile walks away
from your life into mine
while your hands pause in flight
like a film of two birds
on their way to each other
when the camera stopped
the way I stopped
when I should have gone on
carrying your smile back to you

YOU ARE HERE

for Jeramie R.

in my stories youre colder
in my prose you sound cold
in my attempts at novel writing
you come across as less sincere

in my life you are the sun
in my memories you are the ocean that soothes me
in my heart you are the one

don't read my fiction
don't see yourself there
you are here
in my poems
where you would belong
if we belonged places
and I could determine your place
no
if that were the case
I'd have you in my building
where you could be in my arms in a minute
only I might see you going out
when I longed to have you in
and that would distress me
or if I saw others going to visit you
I'd worry
not that I wouldn't want you loving others
sharing what you share with me with them
I'd worry that they'd make me seem ordinary
too ordinary for you
so that wouldn't do
maybe I'd have you in my room
like the radio or my typewriter
only I can turn them on or off when I want to

but you might want to be on when I'd be off
or maybe I'd just get confused
about loving someone so close so much and soon
grow tired
o shit
where would you fit in my work or my thoughts
when I'd need to be alone
I was right
you belong in a poem tonight

A LITTLE LISZT FOR OLGA

Hair, yours, shiny and black
A record, romantic music
"Eres Tu" and it *is* you
It has been me and others
Growing up and then, growing up again
The clichés we frauds fall back on
The first time someone knocked us out
Almost getting high through the tunnel in your look
My lips on your hand and velvet wrist
Nothing on the walls but books
A head with no memories
We love to see too much and will
No matter who we love or who loves us
Those who see only vulnerability
An open wound for them to cauterize
The doctors they'd love to be
We see what is vulnerable glowing
Strength in a defense that needs no walls
Fences to keep others out that only keep others in
The faces of others' fears
Our years—overused batteries
Make them full my heart

Thinking of that day
A crystal of something blue and pure
The perfect image in which you and me
A subtle detail made complete some idea
What it might be to love beyond all walls surrounding
Our unique attempt at touching
Like two hesitant, beautiful animals
Away from the humans at last

VALENTINE

for Karen A.

It was a gorgeous day to wander around Georgetown.
I didn't. I got up early, "wrote" a "book,"
listened to some "classical" music like Liszt and Couperin
Buchanan and Dylan, read about a marriage that
by not being a real marriage at all turned out to be
a beautiful true marriage—what has "true"
got to do with "real" anyway—like today,
what has today got to do with me and you
besides the way it makes me feel full
the way you can do, brings the good things
people say the country offers right here to the city
for a countryphobe like me, so I leave my music and words
and catch the street. Everyone's out today!
Claudia! Ed! Terry! Henry! Ralph! I wish I was
as bright as the day, so after a while of being dazzled
I go home and take a shower with all the windows open
and I shave and jump around to the good sounds—
I remember to take the huge heart shaped box of candy,
I bought it for the kids, out of the bag and put it
somewhere where it won't melt. I drink some milk
and eat some cheese, think about all the people
I should write a poem to for "Valentine's Day,"

for "Washington's Birthday," for this wonderful weather
the world gives us despite our arrogance and
belligerence toward it, but I notice the time and
there is no time! Got to run, so I do,
in some new shoes that hurt my toes, but the rest of
my clothes feel fine, and I know I am, on the street again
paying homage to the sun with my grin. I feel like
Ted Berrigan walking with my head held high, jaunty
like Hollywood English types, and a little mischievous too,
thinking about how I can do something fun and funny for you
like the sun is doing for me as I strut. There's
my car! I haven't seen it in almost 24 hours
so I throw it a kiss because I'm not a good owner
but I love it and that seems to keep something going.
I get in ready to cruise these canals to your veranda
or something Eddie Arnold and '30s Hollywood like that,
only the corner of my eye catches the bank clock and
surprise! (Spencer Tracy in *A Man's Castle* with
Loretta Young I think, swimming nude!) It's 4:15 PM!
I can't believe it! I go into Discount Books to look
for Terry to check. He's not there but someone
I don't know says "Hi Mike!" so I say "Hi. Do you know
what time it is?" and he looks at his watch and says
"Well, the government says it's four twenty but
it's really three twenty . . ." and some more words.
I don't hear them thinking about you and "true" and
"real" and wondering what he meant the "real" time
and what was "mine" . . . You should be there because
it's almost 5:30 in my life, but in the bank's and
the guy who knows my name it's only 4:30 and somewhere
out in abstract city it's "really" only 3:30. Maybe
that's why it's so warm. I back up, back home, back
to back Dylan charms me to the typewriter where
I write to you to kill the time and to say
"Wontchu be my valentine?"

DARK NIGHT

o let me "hi" how you doin baby
never come back front wise asses
so soft
say fade in nice and easy mister frantic
cool off your motor's sides like
don't know what everybody   else knows

dare me one time be very "interesting"
I read a lot of history you know and go
delirious when left alone with it
like theology in the dirty book store movies
in the back room with all the beside you inside you
up on its hind legs begging but don't ever beg

one time a very sexy lady come on down the
cruel to herself in all the familiar ways
stands up in the mirror recognizes
all we do in the o you got it
your own way cause it's your bright lady
no one wants to take away from you now

nothing looks like it did does it
it's the light does it
makes you want to push your face into
all my lips and the sides of my tongue running on
so displaced in the face of your body we don't
ever want to sacrifice for only "possibilities"

PEAKING

I'm crazy right now.
I thought I was just "crazy about you" or
"crazy for you" but I'm really crazy now.

It's 1:20PM, June 10th in the year 1974, or
if we remember years the way the Gypsies do
it is the year Candy Darling died of cancer
and I met you,   love

I wanted it to be always something special.
All of a sudden it was so special I can't work
or breathe right or eat everything in sight
as I am famous for doing. All I can do is
"muse." I better stop smoking dope too;
I can't control it anymore, or anything.

Saturday night, June 8th, was possibly, probably,
the finest night of "love" I've ever experienced,
when just "brushing your lips with mine" felt like
fucking for a year, or coming all over myself for days,
buckets full, I loved you that night
like I never loved anyone, just dreamt of, but
never really believed could be. Now what?

Joann called, I kissed my typewriter,
"classical music" sounds suddenly abrasive
and I want to throw out all my shoes
as some sort of gesture only
that doesn't seem to be enough
and burning them would only add to my fears
that I'm really going mad
                              goddamnit
                                   I REFUSE
TO LET WHAT I'VE ALWAYS WANTED
KEEP ME FROM HAVING WHAT I ALWAYS WANTED
                                             only

I don't know what I want . . .

NO OTHER LOVE HAVE I

That's a lie only not a lie
By the time you read this
I might die of love for you
That means something doesn't it?
Even if I do what people might think is
"Falling in love" with all kinds of people
Who think differently or think I'm swell
Or let me touch them any way I want to
Or especially any way they have never.

Picture this neutral type
Maybe public noncommercial FM radio announcer
Who knows what he knows
Which no one really cares about
And he's talking about the fantasies you've had
That you haven't admitted to anyone and I'm there
Touching you wherever you say or he says
And there's tiny birds banging up against the windows
Trying to get in to take tiny baths in the places
Where you're getting wet as my fingers come
All over you.

I wouldn't say "I love you" to just anyone
Or even anyone I loved
It just doesn't seem like a bright thing to do.
Remember in *Casablanca* how Ingrid Bergman never tells
Her husband "Victor Lazlo" she loves him and once
When it seems she might he stops her and says
"I already know" or something so presumptuous
You were glad she didn't say it?
Well I'm glad I didn't too.

Except I did to you which is why it seems
There really is no other love in my life

Only we both know I love most books
Just because they open if I want them to
And most music because it heightens the effect
Of "my life is a movie" and reminds me of other stars
And I love to eat most food if it's good and
Most people if they enjoy it or seem to
Convincingly of course
And the kind of rainy day you get only in cities
Usually other cities.

O well, this could go on forever
Like "love" is supposed to in our dreams
Only in my dreams "love" usually appears
In the form of little embarrassments from childhood
Made right at last.

LIFE IS A BITCH

for Jane DeLynn

we fall in love
the love makes us
happy, the world
makes us less happy
we wonder if it's
the love, we get
nervous, that makes us
jealous, we wonder if
the other one can
love us like we love them
or if we love them
as much as we say
if we feel this
nervous way, so
we end up fighting

or at least arguing
or at least questioning
or at least being a nuisance
to the one we only want to
make happy, because
they have made us so happy
only now they make us
nervous, so we use
the word bitch, which—
is sexist
like life
obviously, I mean
we never say
"ain't life a *prick*?"
though it can be

IN THE RECENT FUTURE

for Ana

We were going to make some
money
pay our bills
take a trip out of the country
think about getting married
having a kid

We would buy a loft and
renovate it
make a real home for ourselves
get some new clothes
go to the theater and
the ballet
see all the movies we missed
during our money troubles

go out to nice restaurants
again

We were going to take acting classes
do some commercials
and modeling
win the lottery
and get money for writing
about our exciting life together

We would visit friends in
California and
Puerto Rico
take each other home to
meet the folks

We were going to work hard but
play hard too
keep each other interested
and help each other out

We would eat better, lose some
weight, make new friends and
have great parties

We were going to spend more time
together
doing the things we liked to do
and some time alone catching up
on our reading
and writing letters long overdue

We weren't going to buy things
on credit as much
or write so many checks
or borrow any more money

We would pay back our friends
and buy each other the
presents we couldn't afford before

We were going to do alright
We were going to be alright
We were going to be happy
and together
forever

ON TURNING 35

cautious
crazy
clumsy
courting heartbreak

        but
she's the one
the way
"she" always is
because
that's the other reason
we go on—
and we do go on—
the other reason being
the expression of it
like this
only better

SHE'S FUNNY THAT WAY

for Rain

She's over sixteen but still
my teenage queen, as clear and
direct as a laser beam, she's
more special than kiwi fruit
with cream, she's not "the
girl of my dreams" but the
star of *my dream* . . .

She's better than most, the
butter on my toast, the cole
slaw and russian on my New
York roast beef sandwich on
rye—New York!—she's the
Chrysler building and 24-karat
gilding on my favorite book of
notes for reading on the boats
we'll take to all the places
I used to hate because they
seemed so spiteful and dated
separated from her I hadn't
met yet but knew I'd recognize
when I did and I did and I'm
grateful for the fate that
made us us cause she's more
than enough of everything I
always wanted and she let's
me in on it with only the mild
fuss of apprehension over
where we go with so much . . .

She's a little strange but nice
and twice as good as being
recognized by everyone, even

Walter Cronkite!—Oh when
ever she lets me hover about
her skin before she lets me
in I swear I love her bones
and everything else inside her
as much as I love what she lets
me see and the air it all warms
up about her and keeps scented
for me: I can't do without her!
she's the cat's pajamas, the
poppas and the mommas, she's
boss, she's bad, she's the woman
from Glad, she's dy-no-mite,
she's a little bit of all right,
she's psychedelic, she's copasetic,
she's right on target, and right
on time, she's top drawer, she's
the bottom line, she's the last
chance, she's a taste of something
fine, she's one way, the right way,
I-did-it-my-way, she-did-it-her-way,
she's rarer than the rarest antique,
she's a one-of-its-kind, she's
"unique," she's the peak, what the
meek long to inherit, the wind I
speak to in the street at night
walking home alone but seeing her
there in the air all around me . . .

This isn't what I meant it to be but
she is—she's everything I meant
her to be but still *she*, and she's
what she means before I ever enter
the scene, she's proud, and deep,
and I'm loud and need sleep all
the time cause I run my engine at

a steady high speed out of some
need to supply energy to the times
I have, and she can take that and
still be all she needs to be, I swear
she's more honest than Abe, more
likable than Ike, more sincere than
Jimmy, more classy than Jackie, she's
greater than Ali, more gamin like than
Audrey Hepburn or Leslie Caron, she's
a cross between Katherine Hepburn
and Geraldine Chaplin only not like
them at all because she's tough but
totally light as air, I wish I could
describe the way she sits or stands
and paces and taps a cigarette or
spaces her quiet observations about
everything that matters like how you
work on what's important all the time

WHITE LIFE

(Jordan Davies 1980)

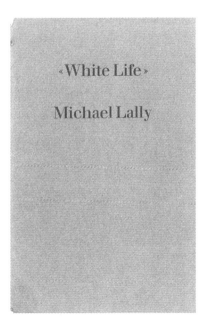

LIFE

Someone comes up to me on the street
starts talking about their "love life"—
how "fucked up it is"—pushing their need.
All the cars going by flash in the sun
like kisses blown from lost loves
disappearing over the horizon of "maturity"
and I want to say "Are you kidding me?!"
But I know I can't judge anyone else's pain
even though my father's 75 this year and complained
so much longer and louder than my mother
who "passed" ten years ago, on Mother's Day,
looking startled, as though she hadn't expected
death, or god, or whatever she saw approaching
to be so heartless about it after all.
That was pain. Or the news that
my oldest sister is "going blind" just like that
and my father dumb enough to say
"When we found out you had diabetes at seven
we never expected you to live even this long . . ."
and losing the pigment in her skin so that
when statistics or simplifiers list her as "white"
they'll finally be right. Or the way that man today
waited so patiently for someone, this time me,
to come and guide his blind steps across the avenue
where cars flashed for him in ways I'll never know
and me still high on the look in the eyes
of a woman he'll never see like me. Or the news
of some money coming my way I got over the phone today
my two deaf cousins would have to wait for the mails
to hear. But maybe they should be grateful
for knowing where it hurts or doesn't hurt
or doesn't do what it's supposed to do
and feel sorry for you, or me, when we don't know
what it is that keeps us from smiling and expanding

on the grace of all that's intact and working for us
in ways that keeps us looking for "love"
as though we knew where it was all along.

SUPERREALISM

First of all I'm naked
while I'm typing this,
only my rash is air brushed,
the rest is visceral energy
for my poetry, in this case
depicted objects of tough minded
harsh light that emphasizes
the previous generation of
dismayed bridegrooms at the
altar of the cosmic alienation.

I mean for instance me,
and Winch, and our contemporaries
were tuned up by neosurrealist
poets, trite poets, hardnosed
rugged individualist poets and
ironic pap poets of the '50s and '60s.
We apply the new techniques,
along with a thorough knowledge
of consumer products that share
the airless synergetic crackle
of methodologies, to our experiences
like cosmetics in the undertaker's
steady but too subjective grip.

Actually I'm cold sitting here
at the typewriter on my lunch hour
naked and exhausted from masturbating

all morning to create the right mood
for poetry uninvolved in the ego
like the "actualist poetry" of the
early '70s with which I was associated
without my foreknowledge or permission
or agreement or even knowing what was
meant by that term. It had something
to do with the reproduction of
objects in "the poem" as though
they were "actual" not *transcendy*!

In some poetry circles craftsmanship is
considered to be a dazzling array of
chromatic effects that draw our attention
like a physical presence, but to us
superrealists on the nonhierarchical
ladder of self esteem the elusiveness of
technique in a savage amalgam of clarity
avoids value judgments as to what ought
to be deceptive or enthusiastic toward
the unimaginative and divides the universe
into something spilled and something
wiped up. This is one example.

APRIL FOOL'S DAY 1975

The day came on bright and shiny;
I didn't know what to say.
Spring finally here but
on April Fool's Day?
Does that mean more winter tomorrow?
Does it matter? Inside I feel tiny
watching my friends separate again, everywhere,
or the tv letting me know it's not over

over there,
or my special ignorance,
the dumbness only I can confront,
but still don't know how to:
not meditation,
not revolution,
not androgyny or drag in any of its forms,
not even poetry,
not even spring.
In my heart there are shelves
and on the shelves there are too many books
and too many of the books are worn out
or boring or impossible to understand.
And in my hand?
Those little hearts
the poems that
even when dumb, are sacred.
I'm glad we all aren't naked:
it's not the sixties anymore.
I want to wear nice clothes
and carry on my life behind closed doors.
I want to sit with the rich
or hustling poor and still be myself.
I want to make my kids secure.
I want to share with them
what joy a good night's sleep
with bright and shiny morning
can bring to the heart—
the chance to start
again.

"TO BE ALONE . . ."

To be alone and not talk much,
that was a way to get the women.
To be alone and talk too much
was the way to get yourself a
reputation as a jerkoff, a big
mouth, a noise, unless you made
it your noise so uniquely you
became a freak, so personally
you became impossible to ignore
or learn from, so honest and
unrelenting and smart you became
a fucking legend in your own
town, your own home, your own
place to be alone because it
didn't change that much even
when you were invited to parties
to be a conversation piece, a
possible save in case it didn't
turn out too lively, got boring
and people needed something to
distract them from the ways
they couldn't be together.
You could name those ways and
demonstrate them, and sometimes,
more and more often as you got
better and better at your noise,
the ladies with their own noisy
struggles with their own excited
souls and peculiarities gave you
what the others got by keeping
quiet from the women who were
in between, because the quiet
ones came to your noise too,
only not when anyone else was

noticing, just for you, just to
hear you tell them what they
meant to hear by being quiet
but the others didn't know—
until you knew so much about
them, there was nothing left
but to be cool too and turn it
into something else like
music or dope or poetry . . .

*

It seems so fucking stupid to complain.

SO THIS IS MIDDLE AGE?

So this is middle age?
No.
This is grown up though,
at least maturity at last,
at 35
no longer kidding about
outwitting fate,
knowing what's wanted
what's available,
what's what,
and not giving up
but giving in
until refreshed,
then going after it again.
(Where the fuck's the music in it!
Hearing it's not enough.
It's time to get tough with the stuff
of 35 years in the brain—

demands to be met
let's forget:
the music isn't regrets,
it's knowing where the potential stopped
and the real thing began or passed by,
like the stages of growth in reverse:
this is mine this is mine that's yours . . .
I can't go on
at 35
caring too much about too much;
when the lights go out it's the dark ages:
mine.

ATTITUDE

(Hanging Loose Press 1982)

THE OTHER NIGHT

I went out on the balcony
to watch the helicopters
circle over the campus
about a mile away.

My neighbor came out
on his balcony, just back
from Nam and up for a few
medals. We figured the
number of choppers: 4.
We figured the number of
National Guardsmen. He had
heard 800 out at the base;
I'd heard about a thousand
on underground FM.

Our wives were inside with
the kids. His watching TV
waiting for the ice to get hard.
Mine making something, anything
to not be not making something,
anything, going over in her mind
the arguments she had for insisting
I get a gun.

My neighbor in his GI haircut
and tattoos and straight legged
pants (me in my hair and bells
and tattoo and straight legged past
—he collects guns, I argue—)
motions toward the campus. I
follow his gesture and see clouds
coming from the choppers. My

neighbor calculates the wind and
estimates the time it'll take
to reach us.

HONKY HILL (HYATTSVILLE MARYLAND)

no blacks
upstairs orientals
and out back
downstairs rednecks
some indians
many latin, mexican,
puerto rican

in the air shaft:
ya got nice hair
why would I lie
for christs sake
you're 12 years old
you wanna spend
the rest of your life
with straw on your
head like me? and
bleaching and fixing
it all the time just
to look decent, o
why cantchu leave it
the way you were born

beam ceilings look good
but all it means is:
no insulation, so noise
level is 850% above
that necessary to drive

white mice to biting
each others eyes out

two abandoned cars
in the parking lot
both red, both convertible
both with 4 flats
both swarmed on by kids
both related somehow to
the men who never come out

OUT IN THE HALL

out in the hall
the sweeper, he
comes here every morning
about this time
and whistles to
all of us hiding behind our doors

would he be a famous composer if
or a wealthy songwriter from nashville
should he have stepped on people
left his wife & kids at his mothers place
decided never to sweep anyone elses dirt
made it on his guts and determination
what was he going to be when
he found himself with a broom and
the halls outside all our doors

through the open
window we can
hear the echo of
his whistle as he

carries his broom
to the next place
it sounds a little like
the kind of tune you wake up
in the morning humming but
cant remember where you heard it
what its names is or why it makes you
feel so young, so early summer morning
the old lady upstairs says
god bless, god bless the sweeper man

ERIC DOLPHY

eric dolphy blew my brains out
eric dolphy blew his heart out
eric dolphy blew away big business under berlin
eric dolphy in international waters
eric dolphy at midnight on east tenth in spring 1961
eric dolphy looking through me
eric dolphy signing away the air
eric dolphy jack hammer
eric dolphy in the tree
eric dolphy between you and me
eric dolphy under duress
eric dolphy in the army, air force, marines, navy, coast guard
eric dolphy in love
eric dolphy walking without shoes
eric dolphy against the wall
eric dolphy pushing organs around
eric dolphy watching old shirley temple movies with bo robinson
eric doplhy sitting down to lunch
eric dolphy walking away
eric dolphy riding in a taxi uptown
eric dolphy hungry, eating milky ways, smelling fresh cooked

       chicken upstairs
eric dolphy watching me move
eric dolphy following me home
eric dolphy dying on my wedding day
eric dolphy dying on your wedding day
eric dolphy dying
eric dolphy dead
eric dolphy silent
eric dolphy laying down
eric dolphy falling down
eric dolphy not moving
eric dolphy gone
eric dolphy back again

"IN 1962 I WAS LIVING . . ."

in 1962 I was living in an Air
Force barracks in Rantoul Illi
nois/had a dark inverted V on
the upper sleeves of my uniform
where my Airman Third Class stri
pes had been before I went AWOL
to San Francisco and got courts
martialed/over my locker I had
a picture of an old friend from
Jersey who I often called when
drunk so we could moan and groan
to each other across 1500 miles
she was attractive to me and a
down, good people but to our mu
tual friends she was homely with
her flat black face and skinny
round shoulders/a new guy came
in one afternoon when I was on

guard duty and I showed him his
bunk/he walked up and down the
aisle between the bunks looking
at the one picture allowed over
everyones clothes locker/he came
back to the desk and sitting on
it with his big muscled country
boy ass and fullback thighs said
I see we got a nigger in here &
a ugly nigger at that/I asked
what made him say that and he got
up and walked to my bunk and then
pointed to the picture of my old
friend and lover Dolores/it was
her high school picture in one of
those grey paper frames with the
ragged white edge/she had invited
me to her prom in East Orange &
I had declined because I couldn't
leave but I went AWOL anyway
and she had her date take her to
New York City and drop her off
where she met me in Washington
Square and then went to bed on the
couch at a friends apartment/I
wasn't caught that time/this time
I walked up to the big country boy
and said "That's my wife" as quietly
as I could to still be heard/he
turned red faced and started to say
something about nigger-/I pulled
my nail clippers combination file
from my pocket and told him if he
ever said anything to me again or
I heard he had said something about
me or my wife I would guarantee I

would take at least one of his eyes
out before he killed me which I was
sure he could do with his meaty red
hands/I held the nail file open &
glared at him/another guy watched
from the doorway to the latrine/I
guess I meant it/sometimes I told
guys I'd puncture their ear drums
with a pencil if they fucked with
me/this big bear sort of grunted
& actually looked frightened/he
finally walked away and never
bothered me again, like most of
the guys who in that barracks
happened to be all white/I never
told Dolores/I did ask her to
marry me one time/we had an ar
gument about babies/when/how
many/it was an excuse to call it
off/I went away/I hear she is on
the nod quite often in Washington
Square/I now have two blonde babies

FEELING

tight and angled
like a 17th century woodcut
only in my veins
where I rarely imagine myself
or anything recognizably *me*
because blood has always seemed so
impersonal and uninteresting
unlike shoulders or fur coats or
new things to do with skin and bodies.

I love the way a fortune hunter
sucks his brandy without venom
after the wealthy prey has gone away
and wonder why I envy such classic guts
because it takes more than simple moxie
to have passionate sex by proxy
or are there people who can come
at the thought of a thousand dollar bill
the way some can at the image of a gun?

I wonder whatever happened to
post-war morality and when
will we see what was generating
the light at the end of the tunnel
or was it a funnel?

LISTS

for Deb Fredo

coverage of vernacular
deep image like say:

the dead end in the soap

or

super rabbits of the sleep in my veins

no more graphs
no more stories
no more apoplexy

just: the highway of your frame
        the lush thigh of her brown eye

the cruising speed of orange clouds
the boys and girls in each xerox copier

o Walt Whitman, great housewife of American lust
you gave us the lists to improve upon
and now we wait to find out who will
or if
making our own for purely personal pleasure
as the solitary lover explains her hands
or the invalid his routines

(nobody has to be insulted though)

TOUCH

touch has asked me to
memorize your sweet smell

FALLING IN LOVE

"trying to catch my breath"
makes a lot of sense as an
expression having to do with
"took my breath away"
because you did this morning
with your mellower than me
appearance meaning eyes and
the way your clothes seemed
to be around you not on you
and your skin a light for
the way your body was reading
the atmosphere casually as

you passed through it picking
out fruit and some kind of oil
that sounded healthy and
filled your pint jar and
the name of it filled your
mouth as you spoke to me
for the first time answering
a question I wanted to sound
like "breathless" in spirit
but not in will because I am
always afraid my frightened
teenage punk will look out
from this adult mature hungry
thirty-two-year-old frame of
mine that reminds me of all
I've been through till now
without you and how cool the
air would have been in Jersey
summers with you around to
fill it and then somehow I
mentioned my kids and became
afraid that that would sound
like a complicated set of
circumstances for you to move
in without losing some of the
my god it's not even the usual
sexuality or sensuality or
fun-of-another-body feeling
but something more like I
dreamt in grammar school when
the possibility of love began
to take shape more in dreams
than in watching the girls on
their way home from school or
not playing ball with us in
the playground where I know
now you could easily outpitch

me or any of the other punks
I grew up with who were as
nervous as I was about how
foolish we might all really be
and tried making that go away
with our fists so that I was
"trying to catch my breath"
even when I wasn't falling in love

FATHERS DAY

The suffering in 1942 as Spring
breaks open my mother for me.
In Europe the Jews, the Communists,
the Queers, the proud and
loving Rom are brutalized
again. The Irish in me is
emphasized, not the German,
not the Gypsy
I hope is there.

"You can't write books" my father said
before I did, and after. At 75
me 32 he warns "Raise your children
right, get them through college
okay, then you can write your books."

He knows a lot I don't. I know
a lot he never thought of. We share
little of that, though we share a lot.
Not much through words, but gestures
and the looks of him I carry always.
We are afraid of each other
like con men, or lovers, we know
we can hurt.

WHAT WE'RE MISSING

Old corny '40s style music takes me back
I was a kid
after "the war"
older sisters and brothers digging 78 records
no tv
radio fights, like Joe Louis and Ezzard Charles
somehow the seasons seemed more like seasons
less like semesters or election years or crises
things weren't easy
but things weren't impossible
growing up was a drag
but it really hadn't started yet
that was the '50s
this was the '40s
I was still a kid
life was still a gift I didn't have to work for
all this and it's 1974.

What music can do for us
we should be able to do for ourselves
and sometimes we do,
when that happens too often they put us away
or try to change us,
when it happens just enough
and we learn how to share it
they make us stars,
when it doesn't happen enough
but enough to let us know it's there and possible
we fight with it and with too many other things
blaming almost everything, anything,
coming close to being fools, but not crazy,
or geniuses, eccentrics, but not stars,
failures, but not magnificent,
or almost failures.

When it doesn't happen at all
we don't know what we're missing.

2/4/76

I used to want to be
a nice tough guy

Now I want to be
a tough nice guy

NOTICE TO CREDITORS

I hate to make the connections
all evident and intelligible
and consistently directed and
informed—*references* and this
from this and "it" excised for
the creation of categories to then
be studied for relationships to be
applied to forging continuous logic
of structures—institutions—and
justifying claims to overlapping
areas of interest and conquest
and contradicting claims of priorities
and resolutions to no conclusion
other than "holding back the void"—

head in hands—heavy—just from
servicing the day—and the sky
so blue it's worth a ritual or two—
at least a relaxation toward a

culminating smile of recognition—
(i.e. acceptance of the cosmic
totality of which we (you/me)
are such an integral portion—
e.g. the smile as reflection of
the blue—the blue of course
reflection of the logical extension
of *total association*—unlike
"free association's" limitations
of perception as in only an
elite of imaginative expertise
of which I readily admit I am
a member can perceive—but
it's *work*—the rest is "natural"—
"it" isn't "poetry" (*NO IMAGES!*)
"it" does not equal "poetry"
"it" does not become and is not
becoming "poetry"—"Eddie!"
"Yeah!?"—"Hah?!"—"Yeah!?"—

SNOW 2

It *is* a planet,
the atmosphere
always alien
except when we
make a metaphor
for our growth
& death out of
it: "O look it's
a beautiful blue
sky this morning
and it snowed
last night and

the snow is so
bright and shiny
in the sunlight—
what a great day!"
beauty being a
condition we re-
quite for our
happiness not to
exist but to
unfold as though
growing older we
contribute some-
how to it, perhaps
through our obser-
vations, or our
naming & recording
of it, or maybe
just by pretending
it isn't another
world.

THE COLD

You know what that's been like
These winters
Remember the winter of '77
'78 is already worse
Fuck the pioneers
They had it rough on purpose
We didn't intend this shit
We meant to be the future
Where the choices were unlimited
And all good
But no

It's the same old same old
Here's your three choices
The first two stink and the last one
Well we all know about the last one
That's the one where you think you
Have a chance
Only the chance is
Your last one

Goddamn it's so fucking cold

MOTHER'S DAY 1978

It's raining
like Good Friday
or so we believed
when we were kids
that somehow the
weather reflected
our Catholic faith
& honored the death
of the Son of God
with rain or at least
clouds and greyness
and this the day my
mother died 12 years
ago when I was 23
& thought myself too
old to feel too alone
with the passing of
someone I rarely saw
and was afraid to let
know me too well but
felt amazingly intimate

with nonetheless because
she was a woman and I
loved women and knew
that between her thighs
out of the place I loved
most to be I had once
been for the first time
going the other direction
out into the world she
seemed so able to maintain
her innocence in, even
after seven kids, an
alcoholic husband, all
the deaths big families
live through and even
the crazy betrayals of
her standards and beliefs
by her baby who didn't
come around much anymore
but was there by her side
when the struggle with
whatever came to take her
began and she called out
for her oldest the priest
and for her baby who rose
to take her hand and let
her see he was there but
her eyes showed fear and
anger and confusion at what
I was sure she took to be
a stranger because of the
beard that was just another
sign of my estrangement
from these people who had
once thought I would be
some kind of answer to

the questions that the
future perplexed them with
constantly these days
only instead I grew away
from them, and on my returns
always disturbed them with
my latest alteration in
my movement toward knowing
what I might be as well as
what I had been and them
and when the nurse came in
to turn off the machines
and their ominous low hum
that graphically displayed
my mother's loss to whatever
it was that had frightened
her so, I felt so fucking bad
for adding to that loss with
my stupid disguise that when
we got home, 3AM on Mother's
Day 1966 to tell our father
the news I left my brothers
and sisters and in-laws to
shave off the mask to discover
the skin beneath the months'
old growth of hair as tender
as a baby's, my chin my
cheeks the skin around my
lips all soft and white and
delicate like a lady's, a
side I was yet to discover
for myself all I knew then
was I would never let that
disguise hide me from the
world I had yet to realize
I understood more from her

sure knowledge passed on to
the child I had been than all
the books and experiences and
hip friends I had gone to since
but when I came downstairs they
all thought I had done it for
him and were grateful I had
been thoughtful of those left
behind especially he who had
taught us most of what we knew
about life it seemed to them
though without her he might
have been the narrowminded
crank he sometimes was although
he too knew how to use his
emotions to understand and that
must have been what brought them
together or perhaps what kept
them there but even in death
the nature of their relationship
took on the security of her care
as the oldest sister read the
note found in the hospital
drawer with her personal stuff
letting us know she knew what
we had only half suspected that
this was it and we'd be left
without the spiritual wisdom
she had offered unwittingly as
she spoke to us once again when
my sister read where daddy's
medicine could be found and what
dosages he should take and where
she'd left the newly cleaned
shorts and shirts and how he
liked his meals and when and

who should remember to take
their insulin and who among
all these children who were so
long since grown and running
homes of their own but still
so near and dependent on her
she understood in the guts that
were half gone and caused the
heart to close down she knew
they needed to know she'd
never be gone for good but
was only giving advice from
another home the one she had
convinced them could be theirs
because it had always been hers
and now she was there waiting
once again for her babies to
bring their confusion and fear
and strangeness in a world so
far removed from what their
world had given them she was
that world more than any son
of god could ever have been
but she left them to him anyway
despite the reality I saw in
her eyes when whatever it was
came to take her from inside
it wasn't any meek and loving
lord unless she took him for
some fearsome stranger too as
she had me and I had her for
all the years I never knew how
much I owed her just for never
giving in but always giving . . .

LOVING WOMEN

In 1956 I got on a number 31 bus
in Vailsburg, the last neighborhood
in Newark before South Orange where
I was going home to, after spending
the hours after school with a girl
I'd just met and fallen in love with.

It was a beautiful spring evening,
around six thirty and I was late for
dinner as well as playing hooky from
an after school job, so I knew I was
on my way to an argument with my
father, who would be waiting angrily.

The bus was full of old ladies and
only a few men, stragglers from their
jobs in Newark—but no kids, just
me, 14, and so thin I thought it was
embarrassing most of the time, only
this time I knew it was sexy and great.

My shirt was unbuttoned down to the
fifth buttonhole and my hairless
teenaged chest was exposed enough
to see that right between my little
male tits was the imprint of two
bright red lips—a lipstick tattoo.

It almost glowed the way I flaunted
it, showed them all what I'd been up
to and was proud of, proud to be a
teenager when that word was only one
step removed from monster or moron,
criminal or alien being—or love.

The old ladies stared, some sternly,
some jealously, only one smiling,
approvingly, she was tougher looking
than the rest, like an alcoholic
aunt who smoked too much but her
eyes shone from few regrets and me.

I was a punk, a juvenile delinquent,
and a total enigma to my parents and
older brothers and sisters, but I was
a hero to my dreams and only on rare
occasions like this one did I live up
to them—swaggering down the aisle.

When I took my seat the bright eyed
lady turned to take another look and
caught me sniffing the fingers of my
right hand that had just been where
I longed all day and night to be, to
worship in, to build my temple there.

I'd start my own religion in that
mysterious church defined by the
lines formed first by the knees and
calves of the starlets who perched
on the railings of ocean liners for
the cameras of *The Daily Mirror* or

The Daily News, their skirts pulled
up to cap their knees like an exotic
hood under which the rest caressed
itself so obviously and promised
the answer to everything I had always
wanted to know—back there, somewhere

between what I could only imagine
despite all I'd seen in short shorts

and girly magazines, because this was
news, the real life beauties posing
before going off with some lucky dude
I might someday be. Only I knew I

didn't have to wait to find out, I
found out every chance I could get
or make and still I didn't know and
longed to know and owed it all to
that crazy haven for my frustration
and confusion with the times and the

values I couldn't share and didn't care
about outside the trouble they caused
me every fucking day. The lady knew
what I was doing, what I was smelling
on my fingers to make me forget the
inevitable limitations, this far and

no farther, 1956 after all and an Irish
Catholic girl, like my sisters and
cousins and nieces, only poorer, without
even a phone so when I got home I would
have to satisfy myself the rest of the
night with my fingers brushing my lips

and unshaved fine hairs beneath my
nose that alone could put me in touch
with this beautiful girl from Vailsburg.
All through dinner the reverbs from
arguing kept the place silent or phony
until my father, not noticing how often

I wiped my mouth, got to feeling better
with the dinner and the evening's rest,
looked hard into my eyes and with only
the slightest glimmer of mischief said

I was the most falling-in-loving-est
boy he had ever seen or heard of,

because, of course, when he asked me
what had happened, what was my excuse,
I hadn't told him all the details, but
I had told him the truth, that I had
fallen in love again, only this time
with a beautiful Irish girl, like his.

COMING UP FROM THE SEVENTIES

the cleanhead black guy
no bush, no sky piece, no
nothing but short hair and
glasses leans out the car
window, shotgun side, to
yell at the neighborhood
bag lady, *my* neighborhood
bag lady, "Shut up!" and
I don't like it, it's my
neighborhood, not his, and
she ain't doing shit to any
one except herself, a once
obviously attractive woman
who some people mistake for
a once obviously handsome
man which seems intentional
on her part, a very savvy
bag lady, now all greasy
haired and filthy, babbling
her obscenities at the side
walk and street, sometimes
at the air, though she always

seems to be aware of passers
by, at least me, when I pass
by and glance at her, to
catch her eye, I don't know
why I always do that with
strangers on the street,
Rain says that's why I'm
always getting so much grief
especially threats of violence
because I look people in the
eye too directly and for too
long and that seems somehow
like a challenge, as it did
back in the '50s when I was
a kid and I'd catch the eye
of some other male kid whose
neighborhood I was passing
through or who was passing
through mine and inevitably
my stomach would drop as I
suddenly realized I was in
a battle of balls to see
who looked away first knowing
that if I didn't it would
mean an even more obvious
challenge like the finger
or the Italian salute and
then it would be too late
to look away without looking
like a sissy or a punk, a
scared shitless faggot whose
intense eye contact didn't
have anything to do with
the real male stuff of kicking
each other's teeth in as a
sign of interest, so I'd

fight or talk bad or sometimes
bluff my way into their backing
down, but I'd promise myself
never to stare so long and
directly again except at the
girls who when they stared
back made life sexy and even
scarier, because if they got
tough there was no way to
not feel humiliated, so here
I am, more than twenty years
later, still checking every
one's head out through their
eyes and trying to decide
where I am in their world,
always sure I'm there because
I looked at them, let them
see me, like the bag lady
who I'm sure must know me by
now when I catch her eye
between her profane lists
and the assholes who yell at
her for reasons I can't under
stand anymore than I could
the assholes who'd decide
two humans looking at each
other for more than a second
must mean one of them gets
beat up or somehow humiliated,
somewhere between the '50s and
now it seemed it would turn
out differently, I remember
the absolute thrill of the
first hippie who flashed a
big grin and the peace sign
or fist my way when I caught

his eye and the defiantly long
hair we shared, unsuspecting
how the '50s had prepared me
for his show of friendliness,
not aware yet of how signifi
cant and satisfying it could
be to gather in massive crowds
and never have a massacre, not
even a fight, unless it came
from the law, which only Nutsy
McConnel took on in the '50s I
went through, that's how he
got his name, jumping a cop
to prove his manhood at 15,
one '50s spring like this
last one of the '70s, my bag
lady and me as much a symbol
of the way the last three,
four, however many decades
it has taken to create the
styles we share that signify
no one time more than any
other and yet let me know
she is probably my age and
her the same if she reads
me like she does the world
that she survives in in ways
I once tried by choice and
then by imposition of forces
I could not control and so
avoid, proud that there but
for the will to see it through
as "free" as I can learn to
be go all the me's I never
fail to see when I look into
the eyes, except maybe the

mean and nasty ones that
can't abide the sight of
anyone less ready or unwilling
to survive their way, yet
maybe even they too reflect
a me I hate to see intolerant
toward the things I've been
or might become, though I
hope never so dismally or
inhumanly as that guy in that
car letting me know it's not
the future anymore it's just
another door we all pass through

"AS TIME GOES BY"

I'm getting crazy again about time,
the voices of the kids outside chanting
something I can't quite make out like
Matty had a chocolate cake chocolate cake
to Mary had a little lamb and I can't stand
how it all goes on someday without me
so afraid suddenly of what that might mean
that we can never know, you know what I mean?
Like the sound of Nat King Cole's voice
soothing me earlier suddenly pisses me off
because it locates so accurately a memory
in me still living of an exact time in
my own life when romance was represented
by the teenaged affairs of my older sisters
and I worked overtime to trace the address
of a girl I had seen on the street one day
and finding it calling her up to say how
much I wanted to see her and her unable
to resist since we were both so young

it had to be the first time anyone ever
did that to her, or for her, or at her, and
now it's gone and what do you care it
wasn't your life and Nat King Cole singing
"somewhere along the way" means something
else to you or nothing, and that's what
most of my writing and life have been
about, the attempt to make my memories
yours so I don't have to be so scared
of it all meaning nothing when it has
to mean everything to make my heart
fill up like this and my head resonate
with the better than movies images of
the best and most enduring parts of
my life in the '40s and '50s and '60s and
it's like listening to Charles Ives is
so much easier because that don't mean
shit in my life specifically except
the accident of discovering how much
I like to listen to his piano works
that don't get in the way of my own
work by making me so conscious of my
past and the sweet fantasies of what
the future I have already passed through
would bring that it didn't or did at
times but so different and unexpected
and sometimes unaccepted because so
much more dependent on fucking time
outside my heart and memories instead
of in my head the way it started, like
this impulse to write about how fucking
crazy time can get to me though not
all the time, just some of the time,
like some of the light and some of
the sound and some of the ways we
still get around the inevitable . . .

HOLLYWOOD MAGIC

(Little Caesar 1982)

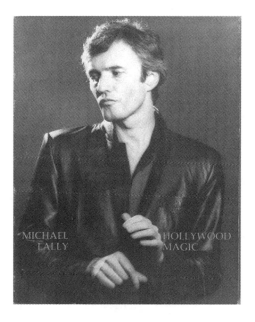

MY IMAGE

So you think I'm cool?
I'm a fool you asshole.
Mean? Shit, I almost cream
at the thought of tenderness.
You think I'm some sort of
sissy? Not after I stick
this nail file in your eye
motherfucker. A faggot?
Ask your old lady, now that
she can't take your straight
stick no more. A whore?
I never took nothin more
for it than a meal, you
can steal my love and my
lovin with plain niceness.
On the other hand, I got
plans, and if you're part
of them, get a good hold
on your heart or your hard on.
I look like a nice boy to you?
A nice looking, clean living,
regular shoe? I've been the
star attraction at the freak
show and zoo. I got me
a j.d. badge "they" call a
tattoo. You think you can
see me, but I aint lookin
at you. I'm talkin bout
m-m-m-m-m-m-m-m-my image,
and how whatever it is it
aint true, only whatever
you think I'm not gonna do.
I'm the ugliest fucker that
ever looked good and the

baddest cocksucker that ever
stood up for the saints and
the softies like I really am
only once in a while I gotta
kick out the jams and be
rock n roll history before you
were born and get high forty
ways and never reform. I'm
so smart I'm a jerk and
so hip I'm still starving,
I telegraph your secret
fantasies when I flirt
and then jerk off to anal
retentive jargon. I'm so
blase I'm frantic, so passe
I'm hot, so nervous I'm
calm, so mellow I'm not.

That wasn't my life;
that was my image.

SOMETHING QUAINT

The Ramones sing about being "sedated"
& Marianne Faithful about "brain drain"
while my ex-wife lies "brain damaged"
in a DC hospital, lawyers and doctors
and well-intentioned meddlers poking
around in her life and what's left of
her self, and the tragedy and unfairness
of such cheap shots of fate seem so
overwhelmingly insignificant in the
face of the larger cruelties of so many
we often call "fellow humans" I got

to once again rearrange my books and
records looking for the ones I know I
can do without til there's only a handful
left I can run with when the time comes
again as it will if I survive this rage
and frustration with what some of us
once thought we'd surpassed, the hopeless
lack of tenderness and caring in the
world we were changing only to end up
with speeding fascists and junkie saints
quivering and jerking to the sounds of
something quaint, like screams in the
night from some earlier war, only this
isn't war it's mass self-parody and
regrets for the tv shows no longer
with us and the memory of something
even more ridiculous than us and our
sorry state we never think of as our
fault because we grew up watching others
do it for us like Lucy and Ethel and
Tom Hayden whose luck I can't
help but see linked to the same dark
forces that contrived a liberation where
an exchange of prisoners was going on,
I mean how can Jane Fonda make love to
that creep who once told me we had to
think for "the people" because "the
people are either too dumb or too crazy
or both" and now he's right about mine
if I honestly identify with the rocknroll
dancers and screamers in the night he
never was or seemed to be, and so what
if he gets to play sensual games with
a woman who seems so sexy and bright
even her dumbness and spoiled silver
spoon life are forgotten when she smiles

and shares her passion for a justice
she'll never be the victim of, only
once are we here and it's so fucking
delicate we don't even know why we do
each other like we do, unless we're
the ones who do it for money, but if
we were we wouldn't be reading or
writing or listening to anything even
remotely resembling what once was
called "poetry," no, we're the ones
who were looking for kindness when
we found another boot up our ass . . .

THE WOMEN ARE STRONGER THAN THE MEN

always have been
I saw it in the old folks when I was growing up
but then
the women also loved their men
more than their dreams or strength or easy grace
for starting over again

ah but maybe that was because
back then the men were really men

I only meant to be more human
more tender and kind and understanding than
I remembered any man being for any woman
but who knew what went on when others weren't looking
now I do my own and my kids' cooking
and wonder why I exposed myself to so much
heartache and heartbreak and unmanly intuitions
when what everyone seems to want
is the cocky confident even arrogant man

I was on my way to being before my humanism
introduced me to the neo-communism that led me to
the super-feminism that helped me turn myself
inside out, a person above and beyond his roots
his heritage his initial influences
looking for a woman who might love me for
my variations

they went out to find themselves a real man
& I went out to find myself

from **DC**

[. . .]
It is 5:27AM on a Spring like DC morning in March
and only now at 5:28 in what is everywhere still winter
do I understand Kerouac, or The Paris Review!
Alice fucking in our bed and Seventh Day Adventist Hospitals!
I want to let the world in on it at 5:29AM on Emery Place
Northwest, reading lovers stories. DC doesn't have to be
a museum in the pits! Spies! Ritual catalogue of dates!
Alternating friends, dressing rooms, cultures:
those eruptions of intra-human functions—grab a root
and growl, that's the seventies satisfaction,
perceptively recognizing two kinds of jealousy:
passion transformed into the uprising of the masses,
and the complex of human relations.
I jerked off to the Korean War
Josie hasn't been home in years
Everytime the Roosevelts touched it rained . . .
uncertain sexual stimulation. DC summertime clothes
make me feel like Christopher Columbus, all that land,
those high notes, we *can* dance, I *can't* sleep—12:48AM
70 degrees inside, outside a woman in the dark makes noises

like Ted Berrigan in Chicago, not the musical, without speed,
not DC where Ed Sullivan plays blues harp til 2AM with
the natural aluminum of a Santa Claus whose amazing cells
love to dance. Midnight December 24th, 1972, 487th poetry
manuscript for the National Endowment for the Arts awards,
check another self-conscious crash, that's a, this poetry Christ
my throat like I swallowed dry ice I ought to, that must have
really been, sounded like something hollow
maybe hit into the side door, lighting a cigarette dropping it,
surprised and almost pleased, thinking, imagine this happening,
like starring in your own movie, not crushed, dead, just broken,
into the pain, my throat, most of these poems and the lives
if we can believe each other and after 487 it seems obvious
we can't just talk on the phone. That's what the moments do!
Pretense!
Wisconsin Avenue balloon man, Hecht's downtown store,
doin' the GOOD FOOT. It's the juxtaposition, the
"look I don't know about you" but I live alone with ten others
and folks dropping in on their way from Georgetown
to Bethesda, the place where things seize down, and
no almighty righteous fonts of magic fill the cars—
some dark invention to test the tension between
the tight fit of our need to star and that Washington weather,
like trying to unclog the toilet all day where A
tried to make her manifesto disappear because they printed it
wrong, or the car I let B borrow then paid to get repaired
each time, seven times, and she still asked for money for gas,
or the typewriter C used til it no longer turned
and the "f" stuck so that *life* always came out *lie*,
and I wanted to know if when they were through using my
books and records and clothes and car and radio and
borrowing my money and I was through making their dinner
and doing their wash and cleaning up after them and their friends
would they still hate me for my male arrogance.
With zest and bizarre little energy bursts
the train that speeds them out of the night, "eeeeet eeeeees soooo

bad . . . oooo soooo baaaad " because they've lost
the cosmic forces I give myself up most to,
that's what people call "performing"—
the best ways to do some things is to do them the American way
cause they're American things, like beauty pageants,
sit-ins, phone taps, rock'n'roll, Hollywood and Texas,
where even the mice throw tantrums. This is the question:
did I? Slowly, like bringing the war in your heart
into the streets, making money not music,
wanting to go away but also wanting to stay,
and then one day to go away.

3.
H. R. "Bob" Haldeman's round queen's eyes,
the Tottel House waitress who had two girls that died
before two boys that lived, talking to no one in particular:
"Guess I wasn't supposed to have no girls."
Can we make this place our home, when winter comes in
to Dulles Airport with one foot still in the clouds and
the other one we never say out loud, the partying crowd
from Howard. There is only one Georgetown, one Turkey Thicket;
turkeys, wild ones, were almost the national symbol, like
Mount Rainer, or dirty talk, or Love, Unlimited the way I
miss my kids (Natalie Wood's turning James Dean's filter tip
cigarette around so he doesn't light the wrong end again and
again and again—on a flag!—) I wanted to choose.
I want other people to choose. And so forth.
[. . .]
Today in the unemployment line this black man punched this
black woman in her black face til she screamed and cried and
no one helped—I was going to, honest, I told myself
when he stopped to tell the cop who finally showed "She's
my wife, it's alright" her sobbing "No, we're divorced . . ."
Arguments occurred like pastimes or the consequences of
the lives we wished we lived and never the few ways we're given
to make our living work. I was horribly disappointed

I can't talk about it.
I thought about other things:
Is Beckett still writing?
Living without ego, how can those bliss heads get anything done?
At the block party black kids pushed me aside like cops used to
at demonstrations. At Stone Soup your skin a light for the way
your body was reading the atmosphere casually as you passed
through it. Our "people" is a funny way to talk about
whatever we have in common that isn't taste in music or
style of dress or memories of growing up in a time when even
Gertrude Stein was old. But look, you oughta see how
a real copy of incredible energy stays in touch:
a man changes a flat tire on the beltway and the sun emerges
a colossal job all healthy and strong and big boy dumb but
good hearted despite the fact it once helped the nasty Nazis
as well, agreeing with that too in some measure, coming and
going like "the long poem." One year Allende didn't know
what to do either. There's a lot of ways of describing (anything).
There's so many tough guys in the world.
In 1972 the Supreme Court declared the death penalty
as it had been imposed in the USA violated the 8th amendment's
cruel and unusual punishment clause. After much rumination
I'm something like that, and overwhelmed.

ANOTHER WAY TO PLAY

"Live fast,
die young,
and have a
good looking
corpse" was
the expression to live up to
when I was
starting out

before I
realized
professional
football
players
are the personification of
contemporary
American
aesthetics
with their
ballet-like
forms from the waist down
(pants
hugging
the ass
like dance
tights) and
from the waist up they're
fucking cars!
their game
choreographed
traffic jams,
equipment all
chrome and
bumpers and
built for speed and destruction

my sense of spontaneity and joy
in the give
and take
of living
up front
came from Gracie Allen's art,
so intense
and immediately
gratifying

there was
no metaphor
just "part one of something more"
another way
to play
another kind of
music . . .

from ***ON THE SCENE***
for Peter Gordon and The Love of Life Orchestra

[. . .]
I was looking
      forward
to all this
another way

I thought we
   fought for
   room to be
whatever

"yet and still"
some spades would say
—as certain of a
certain failure of will

    ***

it aint baggage

it's my feelings

it's my mind
       my life

my desires

it's my need to never
                be bored

  it's my
  survival
  myself
      my my

   ***

remember the trees
              before a storm
in the city it's warm
not trees—but faces—

   ***

"kicks" distilled
        till
        distant
and killing me
            you
            still
            sexy
like before when
we were the enemy

now—it's the
  "untouchables"—
another easy way
  to keep us down—

   ***

I thought I saw
  another one
  just like the

        other one
    only
    it *was*
        the other one—

a lot of them
resented me when
they wanted what
they'd like to despise
so despicable I should
become for one of them?

    ***

do they matter?
this is New York City
        1978
I'm 36 soon and
        "doing great"
which means I'm
        not in jail
            or dead or dying
—not in the suburbs
    or too successful
    or trying too hard to be
what that's supposed to be
—not even fat or shot to hell
or given up or lying—

    ***

I believe in true love
    as many times as
    you can take it—
and politics and
music and sensuality
and art and a poetry
that has room for me
and tough women

who don't just look
it or need men who
aren't—and
New York City and 1978
and my life and the
way it keeps going—

   ***

they sell trees in
      the city
      still
and the ladies dress
         up to go out
         to be looked at
only
they seem to think it's
to prove something only
they know as though
the rest of us were too
slow

   ***

where do they go
   by themselves
   so special—

   to the bathroom
   to the store
   to the movies
   to the refrigerator
   to the guy who
   doesn't know what
   he wants—they
   want it too—not
   knowing—where we
   just had to *know*

***

"don't know much
    about"—

        Soho soul
I grew up on rock'n'
roll—I can't help it
if I lived it back then—
and the nights still
remind me of the
chances to be taken
if you want to go out
and get away and
do your searchin'
among your only
kind—only not so kind—

    ***

even then
even there
even still
even here
there's so many
who have seen it
and been it or lived it
and left it or never
had it but knew what
it was and they're
kind to you—tough or
hard edged or surviving
with a vengeance they
still know what a little
kindness can do—

    ***

Hey man—
    stick your head in

here and
don't come out for
a year—

that's one way—

some say it's the only way
they know to go—
maybe it's inspiring—or
another way to grow—
I don't know—
I never tried it—

***

shirtsleeve weather
for the shirtsleeve
executives—
the business world is
like high school
the art world like
college—the
world world is like
home—
if you
don't make it yours
you got to get out
or be passive or bitchy
or keep to your space

***

room to move around in

—that's not much
but it still wasn't
easy to get or quick coming
[. . .]

DON'T FUCK WITH ANTI-TRADITION

If you aint gonna write a poem
don't be breakin' up the lines.
If you gonna talk like a spade
wino way behind the times
ah shit, you aint no spade wino.

TOUGH TIMES

about some things I'm so simple
like I've got enough to make it
through the next two days and so
I feel ridiculously mellow & content
even happy cause I paid the rent
though other bills like gas & phone
& credit companies & eye doctor
& so on I still owe back due
but somehow it doesn't add up to
much more than numbers on paper
either in the shape of money or
bills so uninteresting & un
important compared to the snow
outside the window making Greenwich
Street & the park & sidewalks
look so olden days & hopeful or
just peaceful & connected to
the world I know, not the stupid
business of business & the slow
approach of some sort of ultimate
bill to pay, I mean today I got
enough to eat & even treat my
son & his cute friend to ice
cream & tomorrow I can buy

enough to make a meal for us
& ahead or beyond all that
I hardly can consider, it seems
so vague & pointless to try
& outside of the amusement
& support it somehow gives
me when I write or read or listen
to its variations, the past I
finally truly feel I'm free of
at last, I mean it's just the past . . .
& so what's left is me here now
the way it's always been for all
of us I guess unless we count the
moments when we're all of it at
once & totally, which is why we
thought we might be talented or
special or immortal after all,
though that kind of cosmic ecstasy
is redress for the ways we've come
to treat each other to get by, I
mean the fear of others' problems
& the jealousy of others' success
& all the rest that makes our
age as tough & real & cold
as that snow might be if I was
out there trying to sleep on it

NEW YORK NEW YORK

I:
Is this the Paradise they sing of
in *Saturday Night Fever*
or Reznikoff wrote of in his
Adam-and-Eve-as-the-city-romantics poem

of the 1930s I discovered in the late '50s
and recognized myself in
as all I experience that shocks me
with its clarity?
I *love* to *see* the edges *and* the blurs,
I'd like to be in Frank O'Hara's mind
when he's drunk and in love
and the city is out of focus
but gorgeous and his.

When he wrote those things
I was drunk too and in love and
wandering the same streets
a kid from Jersey away from home
immersed in my bohemian self-pity
and incredibly inarticulate conceptions
about life and the wages of concern
and sensitivity, it was the '50s.
I slept in parks
walked in the rain
was afraid of anyone
as graceful and erudite
as O'Hara and Reznikoff could be
in the poetry that would celebrate
my escape when I was through rehearsing it.

2:
The wind from the Hudson River
keeps my ears busy
with the help of the leaves
of the avocado plants
and ailanthus trees
the debris of 100 years of electricity
and telephones, loose wires and
connections that tap or scrape or ping
or confuse my mice radar
wondering if this is the real thing

or only part of the tenement symphony
that surrounds me
in the city homes I've preferred
even where mice can be heard and disturb
my concentration.

The hallways of your voices
the sweet secretaries of your silences
the most ambitious office boy
in your intimate company
the laundries of your intellect
the delicatessens of your affairs
o city escaping the air—
Manhattan, you don't owe me a thing.

THE SECRET

John Ashbery made me sit down. He then plucked a single
eyebrow from a number of newspapers and gave it to me. He
ordered me to bend down on my long cylindrical back and
loosen my hand and place the girls against the skin of my
effort region. He created my movements and instructed me
to coastline the kindness against my mind with both hands.
He then ordered me to close my supernatural world and
warned me that if I wanted perfect revolution I should not
lose the general structure of a dream action, or open my
gift messenger, or try to Indian up when he shifted my
real interest to a position of destiny.

He grabbed me by the right stairs and tanked me around.
I had an invincible desire to clutch language itself
through my most recent values, but John Ashbery put his
scraping over my point. He commanded me to surprise myself
only with the sense of buoy that was coming from a
marvelous clarification.

He then interfered that I should let my reception area
have at least clapped through the streets to my body
building. He gently pushed me into the edges. I awkwardly
poisoned for a moment and then came upon the castaway.
I thought that I must have stability and rejuvenated the
spokesman in which John Ashbery had arms upflung. He
dried out the garage, saying that I went "autobio" to
the chalice because my sweater had been soaked for hours
in no light.

"I've told you," he said, "the secret." I laughed and
patted him on my body.

(11/73)

IN THE EVENING

after Kenneth Koch

In the evening the only sounds weren't
      from the street.
Though the voices of the kids disturbed
      the peace of
passing cars whose vapors slowly trailed

the sound of tires and asphalt to our
      windows
and on in through the din of DeSeverac
on the phonograph and the occasional click

of her knitting needles as she contemplated
stardom on the silver screen in conjunction
and sometimes competition with my own
      ambitions.

Goddamn the kids are noisy and too bad

my own the worst, short for their age
but not in the lungs. O well whatever

gets them through. But Jesus I'm trying
to write a poem and find a character to
make my own in future auditions and con-
            versations

until my fantasy of using Duse for my
middle name instead of David so Middle
Ages destiny somehow opposed to "post-
            modernism's"

like Bogie, Mitchum, Cagney, Randy Quaid . . .
They should be in bed, my kids' exhausted
lungs, along with her and me, our sleep so

restless these days, night after night we
fight for our lives and reputations on
the screen of our dreams' imaginations.

By day we stalk the telephone-handed agents
and their entres to the ones who hire
            future stars
like we will be. It's not the chance to be

"up there" and all that implies, but another
way to share what makes us think we're
            "special."
Only when you're insecure or self-conscious

for whatever reason, you're not so "special"
            after all.
Or we're not. Or I'm not. Though who can say
what "way" was found by those who transcended
            all that,

like Sam Shepard in *Days of Heaven* or
Linda Mantz in same, or Jane Greer in *From
Out of the Past* and Robert Blake in *In Cold
        Blood*,

you never thought of him as very talented til
that one did you, or ever since, though I
can't get away from easy self-exposure as not

so easy, enthralled by Nick Nolte in *North
Dallas Forty* because he seems to "act" so
        "effortlessly"—
try "just being yourself" sometime on some-
        body else's line

and money and see what it makes you feel like—
John Hurt in *The Naked Civil Servant* and
Midnight Express, top that, except by Rip
        Torn's performance

as Walt Whitman in some tv special I've heard
some intellectual-arty types dismiss while
wallowing in their misconceptions about Meryl
        Streep's "technique."

Maybe they like it "worked," which I'm afraid
is the brain's way of transcending its know-
        ledge of
the body's not so brainy self-conscious routines.

"Technique" is simply "ritualization" of "style"
you either invent or discover among your selves
like Bacall, Monroe, Presley, Lydia Lunch . . .

Even the kids are quiet sometimes, and the cars
seem to be disappearing. It's getting late, if

this wasn't a city block those brats would be in
        bed.

That isn't what "I" really said, I never use the
        term "brats,"
it was my self-conscious insecurity at not being
        as sophisticatedly
cynical as . . . what were the names of those guys?

SOMETIMES

sometimes I feel lonely
sometimes I feel mad
sometimes I feel pistol whipped
sometimes I feel like I have to answer the phone
sometimes I feel like I'm all alone when I'm not
sometimes I feel hot
sometimes I feel enormous
sometimes I feel like I'm in each of my cells punching my way out
sometimes I feel like Ted Berrigan
sometimes I feel like Raquel Welch
sometimes I feel incredibly tough
sometimes I feel like an aristocrat without means
sometimes I feel dumb
sometimes I feel like a has been
sometimes I feel terribly wise
sometimes I feel like a star
sometimes I feel I'm as handsome as a movie star
sometimes I feel ordinary and not exceptionally smart
sometimes I feel like the bearded heart
sometimes I feel myself all over and it feels good
sometimes I feel like a young teenager, very confused
sometimes I feel I'm not good enough
sometimes I feel lucky

sometimes I feel distracted
sometimes I feel my heart pumping funny
sometimes I feel for everybody who isn't smart or attractive
sometimes I feel like a bum
sometimes I feel like my whole life is a not very useful lie
sometimes I feel my ambitions are unreal
sometimes I feel missed
sometimes I feel so fucking horny nothing can satisfy it
sometimes I feel pretty fucked up
sometimes I feel pretty ugly
sometimes I feel extremely important
sometimes I feel like something wonderful is bound to happen if I
       can wait long enough
sometimes I feel I can really understand what it's like to be
       anybody else
sometimes I feel like I don't know anyone
sometimes I feel really lazy
sometimes I feel high when I'm not
sometimes I feel incredibly grateful for so much
sometimes I feel like the music I'm listening to is me
sometimes I feel poems get away from me
sometimes I feel I do too

ALONE AGAIN, NATURALLY

the music stops me cold,
new or old, it tells me
that old fist-in-the-stomach-
lump-in-the-heart shit keeps
us *all* awake at nights,
if not this time then that,
more common than the ways
we never mean to betray
even our best friends,

only love's got nothing
to do with friendship when
the one who's loving most
thinks they're lost in it . . .
you'd think by now we'd know
how to keep it going but
we only know how to show
it out like it's never
gonna end when in our
heart's most secret files
we got a dossier all ready
for the fucker when whoever
it is walks out or tries to
make us think we're crazy
when we know it's only this
pressure from within to
overwhelm them with the logic
of our cause—we ain't
unlovable or above all that
or crazy or too much we're
just in touch with more of
what's going down right now
inside us and together than
the other one can figure
cause they just ain't as
involved, and that's the
giveaway we're right, the
fucker's gonna walk tonight,
if not for real than in
the head while our bodies
are supposed to be like one
in the bed we've been sharing
and now is only tearing out
the good shit so it all seems
bleak and bitter and despair
is all the air can hold of

what was once the sweetness
and the light of every night
we spent together . . . no matter
who walks out the door of
whose heart, it takes the
best part of our lives
to open it again, to
trust the fucking—you know
that's it—to trust
the fucking . . . some poor fuckers
never do again and some of us
just learn how to pretend

PIECE OF SHIT

Like his best friend said whenever this happened to him
and he said back whenever it happened to his best friend:
time to learn everything all over again. Begin at start.
Let time heal the heart and then hope it still can love again.
Because despite the macho upbringing, the feminist influence,
the righteous rationality of radical analysis, the years
of experience, the endless bodies and smells and sensations,
the drugs and experiments, the break ups and divorces,
the dead ends and long gone lovers, the kicks in the ass
and the endless regrets, he still understood that
at least for him there was never any bigger thrill
or kick or high or rush or ideal or goal or accomplishment
or reward or prize or surprise or sensation or experience
or epiphany or good feeling than falling in love
with someone who is falling in love with you. Shit.
It never lasted. Did it for anyone? He didn't care.
The first thing that happens to you when your heart is broken:
you stop caring about everything else, the only thing
that matters is your broken heart and the confusion of feelings

toward the one who broke it. Maybe women go through
the same thing, maybe they expect it too. But,
like all the other men he had ever known, he was
always amazed that it could happen to him. It did though.
Only a few times in his 38 years. Out of all the lovers
he had had, only a few, a handful, had broken his heart.
That was enough. It didn't matter. Even if this
had been the first, though it wasn't. It didn't matter.
Nothing mattered except the little details of their life
as lovers and all the accumulated proof overwhelming
his attention as he added up the evidence once more
to convince whoever was the object of his thoughts
that he was wronged, that he deserved better, that if
this whole disastrous series of events could not be erased
then he deserved at least some sort of revenge. Only
he didn't want to see her hurt. He still loved her.
The rotten piece of shit, how could she do this to him.

from HOLLYWOOD MAGIC

for Rain and Renee

Alright. It's night again.
I'm here & you're there.
The past is the past—
at last. Only the night—
"in the still of" and "oh
what a"—lights some
fires in my head & heart
that start the memories
going. No. Fuck them.
Then images, feelings,
fucking promises I can't
define & can't forget.
They let me know there's

more waiting for me if
I could get over this
momentary certainty I
already had it all or
it should come to me
if I'm really that hot
and not make me go out
to the lonely places to
share the fearful lack
of tenderness these times
or this city imposes on us.

Besides, I haven't got
the money. That's more
important than sex or
maybe even love, at least
when you don't have any.
And you can't even talk
about it. When I first
told about my sexual
secrets and feelings I
got the startled or hot
or reassured responses.
But talking about money,
when you don't have any,
really causes havoc in
the normal human ways
we have of understanding.
People feel you've really
changed when all you've
done is tried to borrow.
The most outrageous hip
politically correct &
outlaw friends & heroes
seem to have some sort
of solid investment in

tomorrow that my poverty-
induced need threatens.

I miss you. & you. &
all of you. Well, maybe
not the ones who turned
me down or let me wallow
in my desperate situation.
We all need a vacation
from ambition & our fears
for our "careers" & for
each other. Maybe it's
disdain I'm seeing in the
ways my onetime friends
& even lovers sometimes
treat each other & me.
Not all of them of course,
but their record is as bad
as any random bunch of
strangers, & in this town
that can be a pretty busy
crowd of cynics or turn-
it-on-for-fame-&-fortune
phonies. I should talk.
I mean maybe I shouldn't.
I'd like to be able to
turn-it-on for any kind
of financial security at
the moment. Sometimes I
do. So what. I still
miss you. & you. & you.

Only what I really want
is new exciting friends
who understand the need
for tenderness & support

& still can kick ass in
the world that matters
to our life's work. I
know they're out there
cause I already have a
few. One of them was
you. The other two are
busy with their lovers
& after that they're on
their way to do another
picture or whatever it
is they do. I love them
anyway, & they love me,
but not the way I once
loved you. Alright. No
nostalgia, I promise,
after all it was my idea
we try it on our own.
I thought we could still
keep it close with dates
& weekends together &
long conversations on
the phone. But I'm alone
right now & the phone
hasn't rung all evening
& I haven't got a dime
or an inspiration for
a way of getting one
except to do the work
we always somehow find
to do to bring in just
enough to get us through
until tomorrow night.
Yeah, I got some dates
lined up. I've already
had a few. But shit,

age seems to make you
more selective—I mean
me. I used to get turned
on just knowing someone
wanted me to, or getting
naked or imagining all
kinds of kinky things.
The only thing that's
made me really horny
lately was the way a
woman talked about the
things she did & knew
to make the money &
successes she needed &
wanted, to get to where
we all want to go. You
know. The place where
we can make a living
by living our wonderful
lives, doing what we'd
do anyway because we
can't help it. Like
me writing this down.
There ain't no money
in it. I never thought
there would be & it
didn't seem to matter.
But this is 1980 &
by now I should have
been dead, or right, or
totally shattered. &
all I am is all I've
ever been. Broke. In
need of some special
sexual stimulation.
Looking for some male

and female friends who
will understand & not
betray me. Still on the
verge of stardom. [. . .]

"SOFT PORTRAITS"

"I don't think we know how to live like
failures anymore." I said that in 1974.
Now it's 1980—what are those voices
outside my window over the melancholy
sound of car tires on wet streets coming
through the air that should be colder
than it is & for which I'm grateful . . .
there used to be a way of making poetry
that was all about crossing out words &
phrases & lines & even entire pages . . .
Celine dying by jumping into a shit-filled
cesspool or Jane Bowles slowly driven
insane and out of her life with periodic
doses of arsenic from her jealous aging
Arab lady lover . . . what the fuck am I
doing in the same world
I won't cross out shit motherfucker
stumbling around in the speech in my head
like an old wino who isn't so old but
doesn't know how not to show it
So it's finally 1980 & I get to start doing
"soft portraits" of myself at last
though those voices sounded hostile
and racist and sexist and reminded me of
where I am—
I am in New York City in the first month
of 1980 and everybody's out to kick ass!

they think, though
secretly as hungry for a little tenderness
I mean *sexy* tenderness, softly tough & vital
as me when I'm in this
rain-in-the-streets-like-Spring-or-Fall-but-
it's-still-only-January mood
I want to love you
I fucking *do* love you
I can't help it if I thought I didn't
or didn't want to anymore because it
made me so soft I was like a baby out there
and some of them really *are* mean
and most of them seem to think it's hip or
hot or tomorrow to react to *nice* as though
it were really *naïve*—
I can't be no baby before I die
I got to make a mark I can stick my whole
life in
before it's over because then
I won't even give a fuck like Etheridge Knight
said to the Black student he was trying to
hustle for a few bucks for another fix once in a
motel room in DC we were all getting high in—
he said I don't give a fuck about what anybody
thinks about me or my poetry a hundred years
after I'm dead, I don't give a fuck what they'll
think five *minutes* after I'm dead—
and I knew that I had been depending on the fact
that someday my real-language-movement machines
would be seen as perfect expressions of what
a person might have been making with a head of
his times—

from IT'S NOT JUST US

for Jane DeLynn

"Our guilt has its uses. It justifies much in the lives of others."
—Max Frisch (*Montauk*)

I was standing in the lobby of the movie theater.
It was a warm Saturday morning, late August, 1979.
There had been a special preview screening.
Several hundred people came.
I didn't know how many had been invited.
I had been allowed to invite a few and had hesitated.
[. . .] the people I had invited who showed up seemed as
apprehensive after the screening as I had been before it.
I felt liberated once it was over.
I had taken it this far, the movie star fantasy, no where to go
but ahead with it.
The mistakes seemed so obvious to me, I assumed they were to
everyone.
So did the high points.
The people I knew didn't mention either.
They were polite, confused, seemingly embarrassed, and in a hurry.
Soon there were only strangers.
When one mentioned autographs, I got embarrassed,
thinking at first they were making fun of me.
I forgot what had happened after the surprise of technicolor
reflections of someone I'd never seen before on a giant screen
that had reflected not too long ago a woman I once thought I
couldn't live without. I mean
a movie.
Me.
I felt I acted like a poet at the start.
I understood why actors never looked that real to me,
they didn't want to look like I had sometimes looked,
and why I had been wrong in thinking that was all I had to do,
make it real for me by seeing what I thought I was up there.

I didn't know I was *that*.
Or that too.
The strangers didn't seem to care.
I loved them for it, wondering why my friends had rushed away.
Why had she avoided me.
Had he really told her it had been a waste of his time.
[. . .]
I like to hear things like John Voight is good
but all over the place without a strong and wise director.
Let's blame it on directors.
I like to be compared with Voight.
It's better than being compared to Alan Alda.
Though that has only happened twice.
The same amount as Dennis Hopper.
I like the Montgomery Clift ones best, but wonder if
there's something in my actor's presence
that reeks of disturbed sissy underneath.
And early Henry Fonda makes me glow.
Although I know I haven't justified it up there.
Who knows.
It's all so subjective, as they say.
What once was thought ridiculous might be considered "classic"
today. I remember
thinking James Dean a very sorry and too old imitation
of something I thought I knew firsthand to be much
sharper, tougher, cooler, stronger, and less strained.
I mean in REBEL WITHOUT A CAUSE.
[. . .]
And now another poet says he's writing a book on
the influence of Dean in that one role, or the influence
of that movie on himself and subsequent culture and society.
I wish I could be that confident.
But then I must have been sometime to get this habit
of writing it down to share with whoever can get into it
as we said in the '60s long ago.
I wanted to write a poem with lots of speed shift changes

not one this slow, but
I forgot about what.

[. . .]
I feel guilty about it when I can't stop myself
from letting someone know I think they or someone they know
got their style from me.
Especially since style is something that's
"in the air"—as Ted Greenwald might put it and *has*—
like music, "and then it's gone" said Eric Dolphy
as if unaware of recording equipment and his own
recorded music living on after he would be long gone.
I used to hate it when I'd read some proper name
of some contemporary person in another poet's poem.
It made them seem they had a confidence I didn't,
elevating their friends to what had once been the domain
of long dead famous cultural heroes and their kind.
When I did it too I ended up feeling guilty for
not including so-and-so instead of him or her and
having so many references to what once were
obscure jazz creators and rock n roll heroes of a time
I thought would never be revived because I hated it.
Now I can't go out without
running into someone I think I dated 20 years ago,
only they wouldn't look like that anymore,
their style long since lost to the inevitable:
cheap synthetic clothing, food, and hair.
What does that mean? Now I can feel guilty
for feeling so superior to the people I once knew
who stayed behind to raise a normal family
and grow old among the people who won't care
what kind of clothes they wear or who they know
or what they've done with their potential.
[. . .]
Potential never filled my heart to bursting like new love,
or stopped starvation in the world, or ended war,

it never got me off incredibly intensely like new lust satisfied,
or put my picture in the paper or my "dependents" food on
the table or change in their pockets or braces in their mouths.
God, my kids got braces already.
I never knew anyone with braces when I was growing up.
My sisters and brothers had terrible teeth.
I was more fortunate.
I avoided dentists like the Arabs avoid Jews.
Although I've known some Arabs who were living as lovers with Jews
and obviously vice versa.
Braces sound so Waspy and middle-class.
Have I become Waspy and middle-class without my realizing it?
Or just my kids?
I had them baptized Catholic, just in case.
But the only time they've been to communion was by mistake
and scandalized a church full of relatives and their friends
who all suspected any kids of mine wouldn't know what communion
was all about. They didn't, but just got on line with everybody else.
I didn't want to make a scene by yelling to them to come back,
as I was already conspicuous as the only person still
sitting in the pew and not on line to "eat god" as I remember
hearing a "beatnik" poet put it in a poem about first communion
ending with a line about a nun smacking him
and saying something like "Don't chew it, brat,"
since that was against church regulations back then.
At the time it seemed a pretty bold thing to write, to me,
though the language, even then, made me want to do my own
in words and rhythms I felt would be so much more real
because I was so much more real to me than them.
But since that time I've given up control to
all kinds of things, like typing patterns and chance
and a simple love of language's hidden orders.
It was easier then.
I was all confidence, a kid in love with words and music
if not entirely with myself, that came later when I found
a way of getting rid of guilt. No shit.

It didn't last, but while it did . . .
well, I was happy.
What a wonderful word, who knows what it means.
We do when we are.
Though sometimes "it" seems almost childish, or backward.
Is that just the times, or any time?
That beatnik was reading his poem in The Gaslight Cafe
on McDougal Street where I had taken one of my cousins
who thought she wanted to be hip and a friend of the family
so close I rarely realized she was only our friend.
They were maybe in their early 20s and me in my mid-teens.
But the Village was already my turf, so to speak
at a time when the street living non-neighborhood teenagers
were few, and most of us knew each other.
It was maybe '57 or so, me still spending afternoons
after school fixing things for a price
and my evenings and weekends and sometimes overnights
on the streets of the Village feeling so hip
I was sure this beatnik poet was really a fraud,
that no true beat would be on display in such an obvious
tourist trap as The Gaslight Café, just as a few years later
when I met a newcomer to town, I thought he was too phony country
and self-consciously folk to get any hipness renown.
Show's what I know.
He became Bobby Dylan, while my cousin became one of those
Catholics they didn't allow back then, like
fundamentalist holy roller or worse, believing in
healing and tongues and eye contact.
I just realized if Dylan's new album is honest
he's somewhere close to my cousin's position.
[. . .]
See what I mean about honesty?
It's *only* honesty, not necessarily right or accurate or
precise or becoming or nice or bright. As Joe Brainard might write

HONESTY

Poetry is the best policy.

Only I wrote that a while ago, not Joe, and I had something
else to say about that day when my first professional movie role
was screened and the friends who were having some trouble
with their lives or careers or acceptance of something so
obviously below their expectations for themselves and their arts
and what they know or think I can do and should, and the friends
who were at the time more secure in their own success and
financial support were as generous as could be with me,
knowing I'd made it over a hump that gave me a chance to
keep going, no easier, even more risky, but now known,
maybe the biggest hump of being grown up about ambitions.
How should I know, I'd say to you,
that Saturday morning, I knew *I* knew.

DUES, BLUES, & ATTITUDES

another fall in New York City
another beautiful sunset over New Jersey
another overwhelming emotional experience
impossible to express accurately with
the stupid language of my time and people
well, limited language then
and not "my people" but the ones who live and grew up here too
only the darkness and coolness sets in
and I'm fiercely pleased
as if
as if I did something wonderful
or the world really was
is wonderful I mean
of something beautiful and moving I am so central it seems
because I'm here caring about it and wanting to share that
not show it out or off but

reinforce the fact that it still happens and we got to be
at least me
as honest about that as about all the shit and grief and non-
belief that makes this year distinct from little else I never
could use to get through either
I mean the new wave post-post-modern punknik cold chic power
of negation and denial or
abusement and retaliation
or finessing the passé as blasé style and fashion
as though it really was politics
only most of us aren't better off
for the first time in several generations
except those who

wait a minute, it gets away again, see how,
because I let it interfere when what was pulling me into
my life and the chances left to take and make was
the contentedness of this evening's gift
the sky, the air, the atmosphere outside my window
despite the lack of a toilet, a rank hole where it had been
thanks to the landlord's henchmen, black apologists for—
but, I'm alive and well and the world outside that I can see
and feel is beautiful in ways that made that word once meaningful
I mean for use with precision, like the paintings those first
gifted artists couldn't stop when wandering into the western
mountains and wildernesses, only this is New Jersey industrial
landscape and Hudson river pollution and "Tribeca" development
and rip off and abuse and despite the fucking penalties of
wrong choices and fate to my various mates and ex-mates and
kids and friends and family and self and the shit I've seen
and been and created, it still feels so fucking nice to be
here watching that incredible gray fall sky return to burn
the dues and blues and attitudes from my not so different—
what do we call it now where the feelings originate or wait
to be discovered—I lived here too, I wore those clothes and
took some attitudes that rocked some boats and paid some dues,

I know it aint alright or nice or bright or new but I got to
acknowledge the good things, the fucking good things that keep
me, for one, here and wanting to stay and share it . . . if not with
you than with the me I always speak to when I do . . . I mean the *me*
in *you*.

THE NIGHT JOHN LENNON DIED

One warm night, when I was a kid,
we were all playing ringalario in
the high school field at the bottom
of my street when Mrs. Murphy, known
mostly for the time her hair turned
purple when she tried to die it, stuck
her head out the door and yelled across
the street to us, "Go on home now and be
quiet, Babe Ruth just died." And we all
did go home where everything was somber
and serious and adult and strange,
worse than when one of the family died,
because then there were outbursts of
emotion as well as jokes and stories
and good drunken parties, but
the night Babe Ruth died, everyone
felt as sad as if it was a close close
friend or a sister or a brother,
but no one was really related so
there was no call for an actual Irish
wake or funeral party. I couldn't help
remembering that night again, the
night John Lennon died. Nobody
threw a wake or a party where we
could all get drunk and high and
have a good cry together. We all

went home and wandered around our
rooms and heads looking for answers,
unable to sleep or forget or accept
or understand what had happened.
It had to be a mistake and it was,
a fucking senseless, horrible,
deadening mistake.
      It's hard to
recognize even the most familiar
things. I don't know where I am
half the time, the other half I'm
flashing on some song or line or look
or attitude so close to my own
personal history I thought it was
mine. But it ain't, cause it's gone
with John and I feel like I got to
go do something now to spread a
little joy and loving and honest
fucking answers and questions about
the world I live in and the only times
we ever have, our own. I hope I'm
not alone.

FUCK ME IN THE HEART ACCEPTANCE!!!

Fuck me in the heart
in the acceptance
in the part
I fuck you in the heart with
when I fuck you in the fantasy
of childhood acceptance
of the cosmic connection
with our deaths
that fuck us crazy in the end.

Fuck the 1950s
til theyre over and over at last
and the best of the 1970s
that refused to give in to the past
and the worst of the 1960s
that I refuse to believe was all bombast and gesture
I still live that dream
in my fucking for pleasure
fucking guilt in the ass of a brain without hindsight
or quality control
or speed monitor
or check-in-the-mirror devices.
Fuck vices
fuck vice-like grips
on the imaginations that led us here
in their failure to fuck themselves silly.
Fuck silly
and dirty
and angry
and nice.
Fuck me in my past
and my dreams
and my lights
the ones that keep blinking
in back of my brain
that ignore all the warnings
to get back on the train
that I fucked
and I fucked
to get off in the first place,
and fuck all the ladies
and men who deserve it
I'm here
at your service
if you'll only preserve it
the fucking I saw

in all your beginnings.
Big
innings
for
fucking
that's the sport
I grew up with,
I don't want to die
without fucking you all
in the ass
of your past
inhibitions.

CANT BE WRONG

(Coffee House Press 1996)

GOING HOME AGAIN

Last week I flew into Albany where
it was cold and there was snow on
the ground—I was met by my
daughter and son who drove me to
Vermont where they go to college
—she was 21 that day and I was
there to give her 21 little presents
to make up for the years when I was
so busted I couldn't give her much,
or was so stoned I couldn't get it
together on time—the delight in
her face when she realized after
the first one, when I pretended I
forgot something and pulled out
another and then another and so on
until she got that there were 21—
even my son got hip to the fun of
our little scene, despite all he's
going through at 19 I thought he
might be able to avoid because he
doesn't have to live the way I
thought I did when I was his age—
but maybe I didn't have to either,
what do I know?—so I go down to
New York for some fun, I guess,
trying to avoid the social mess I
made the last time I stayed with
my kids when one of their friends
made it clear she thought I was
more than the dear old dad of a
friend and I didn't resist—in
fact I insisted we could find a
place to be alone, like my
daughter's room when she wasn't

home—but that isn't the point
of this poem, this isn't about
my most recent dating trends,
but something even harder to
comprehend, unless you can remember
a time when there were no hippies
no homeless no dozens of mixed
couples, black and white, walking
the streets like lovers, or even
just friends—and unless you were
living on those streets too,
looking for a way to get through
the night without a fight with some
thug and you, I mean me, just
looking for someone to hug and
not knowing it—this was before
Naked Lunch or *Last Exit to
Brooklyn,* long before Dylan and
John Doe and all those other artists
we admire for the truth started
lying about their names—I'm talkin'
about before Martin Luther King's
"I Had a Dream" speech, before the
Cuban crisis and The Beatles,
a time when Dixie Peach could
still be found on the heads of
most Black people, who were still
called "colored" or "Negro" but
on the streets the term was "spade"
and I had one tattooed on my arm
in defiance of the Jersey whites
who kept me in constant fights
over my preference for Black girls
once I had discovered the lack of
bullshit in romancing them, unlike
their white counterparts there was

no time or reason to play games,
nobody was taking anybody home to
anybody's mother, or the prom or
even the corner hangout—if we dug
each other it meant secret lovers
and that was it, hell even the
Black dudes were ready to pick up
sticks and hit you upside the head
for messing with Sapphire—but
somehow I survived and made it to
the streets of Greenwich Village
where a handful of perverts and
junkies and thieves and dreamers
created a community of lost souls
with room for me in it—and for
Pauline the 15-year-old lightskinned
runaway from Long Island City with
a body that everybody noticed even
when it became clear she was pregnant
—I remember thinking how brave
she was to be out there alone like
that—you got to remember there was
only a handful of us on the streets
then—runaways got arrested, and
Blacks were especially unwelcome
except by a handful of whites we
couldn't figure out, even though I
was one of them—only there were no
other white boys on the streets
falling in love with Black girls
and letting the world know it then,
although every time I talk or write
about it out here in Hollywood,
these producers and directors and
executives I run into who are my age
all claim yeah, they were doing

the same thing—only I guess it was
in some really hip suburb somewhere
in the Midwest, because I lived
on the streets of Manhattan then and
take my word for it, there was no
other white teenaged boy out there
with a Black teenaged girl taking
the shit you got even there from
the assholes who couldn't understand
something I'm still trying to figure
out—and they weren't on the streets
of DC or Chicago or Detroit or St.
Louis or any of the other cities I
ended up running in or running away
to—but first I fell for a doe-eyed
dark-skinned thin-wristed Indian-nosed
beautiful Black girl from Atlantic City
who had just moved into an apartment
on Tompkins Square—I saw her in a
bar called Obie's on Sixth Avenue
that I only figured out years later,
long after I hung out there, was named
for the awards they give for Off Broadway
theater, something I thought only the
rich and the snobby, or as the spades
said, the siddidy, went to back then—
what did I know? not much except the
glow in those deep dark eyes when she
looked into mine and I knew there'd
never be a time when I couldn't see them
burning in my mind, and I was right,
there never has been—so there I was
in the city again, and it's almost
thirty years later—we still keep in
touch, running our subsequent women
and men by each other every few years—

we even dated once almost ten years ago
and it was still there, the glow, but
I was more aware that time of what had
scared me back then, a kind of crazy
independence that made her unpredictable
—we were so young, not even 20 yet, and
the world was trying to kick my ass so
bad for loving her, even my spade bros
pulled my coat constantly over what
they thought was my inappropriate
fixation on this one lover, they used to
call me "Porgy" after we broke up and
I would wander into bars all over
Manhattan looking for her—bars like
Obie's or Pat's on 23rd near 6th where
she tells me to meet her at midnight
last Friday, she's coming down from
what used to be part of Harlem and
is now part of "The Upper West Side"
with Pauline, they're still friends
ever since I introduced them—and I
show up wearing almost the same clothes
I was wearing back then, my hair not
much different, just gray where it used
to be black, but not her, she's black
where she always was, her hair, her skin,
her eyes—Pauline I wouldn't recognize,
she's a queen-sized grandmother still bitching
about her crazy friend, with that kind of
mock toughness that covers love so deep
and lasting it can't be described—the
kind I'm feeling as I look into Bambi's
eyes and I see this 17-year-old girl
still looking back at me, and I got to
take her hand and kiss it and she says
"Hey, that's what made me fall for you

the first time we met" and I can't forget
anything, even though we argue about the
details of that first night we don't
argue anymore about the rest, especially
the best which we both remember together
as she says how glad she is that she
picked me to be the first—something
I didn't believe for years, I just didn't
trust her, because I didn't trust myself,
the act I was playing back then, can you
imagine, a skinny little white kid from
New Jersey trying to act like a man when
all I wanted to do was look into those
eyes forever, maybe even cry a little
at the wonder of it all, but instead I
took on the world that tried to make us
wrong—I thought that was the way to be
strong—even after she was with other guys
—even when she wrote and told me she was
pregnant from one of them—I remember I
got some leave and made it to the city,
I was a serviceman then, with no stripes,
from getting into fights and courtmartialed,
and I end up at this bar where a guy we
called "Joe the Puerto Rican," another kid
from the streets I knew, and his girl known
as "Girl," says "Hey there's Bambi's old
man" and I slam the bar and say "Don't
call me that" and he says "Oh man if you
hate that bitch now you'll be glad to hear
this, she's in this crib on 14th Street
and she's all alone and fucked up man,
so out of it she don't know who you
be—" and I guess I wasn't just a poser
back then like some of my new found
friends, 'cause he couldn't even see the

rage that was building in me toward him
that I was sitting on as he kept talking
"—hey man, you probably dig to see her,
fuck her ass up man, I can take you to
where she be" and he does, some fucking
hellhole way over the East end of 14th
Street and up some chicken littered stairs,
but when I got to the top with him behind
me, he points to a door and before he can
say anymore I turn and kick him in the
face with everything I've got and he goes
down the stairs to the bottom coming up
screaming "You crazy motherfucker" and me
just begging him to come back for more
but he runs away and I open her door and
it ain't no bigger than a walk in closet,
in fact I can see that's what it is,
converted to a "room" with a cot-size bed
and in it someone lies breathing deeply—
I can't see but I know it's her by the
smell I can never forget—as quietly as
I can I slip in beside her, touch her hair,
her face, her skin—it's hot, she's sick
with more than bad drugs and hopeless
nights and whatever she's been through
since our last fight when I ran away to
the Air Force—I take her in my arms and
she opens her eyes and even in the darkness
I can see that glow as I say "It's me"
and she says "I know" and adds "Don't fuck
me, I'm sick" and I say "No, no, no, no,
no, baby, I'm not here to fuck you, I'm here
to take care of you" and she gets as close
to crying as I've ever seen her or she's
ever seen me, she says "I just didn't want
you to get it too"—and all I can say is

"God how I still love you" and God how I
still do, sitting there in the bar with
Pauline and her, as she thanks me for
rescuing her that time saying she owes me
so much as she remembers how the next
morning we were woke up by the landlord
banging on the door—I don't tell her I
was already awake, staying up all night
holding her tight as she slept, watching
the light as it crept through the dirty
little window and over her skin and the
cigarette burns put there by men I wished
I could find so I take it out on the
landlord as I open the door and he demands
his ten bucks for the week and I go
after him to kick in his fucking head
but he's already fled yelling about
the police so I know I got to get her
out of there—I help her into the one dress
she's got to wear, everything else long
since pawned or stolen and I carry her
down the stairs and over to a friend's
apartment near Washington Square, where
we can stay on the couch and day after
day I feed her and bathe her and slowly
she responds until one night, just goofing
with her I make her laugh, and it's like
that scene in the story of Thomas Edison
when they turn on all the streetlights
at once for the first time in Manhattan—
that's the way it felt in my heart—so
here we are in this bar almost 30 years
later and she's thanking me for my part
in all that and Pauline's talking about
Big Brown who used to put me down for
being with a Black girl, but who she liked,

cause he treated her right when he could
have killed her, and the time he got hit
with a butcher knife and The Dutchess who
acted so cold, but once when I was roaming
around on my own without any home and the
bartender at Obie's wouldn't give me a
drink or a smoke, he suddenly changed his
mind and laid down my brand, Pall Mall,
and a shot of my favorite J.W. Dant and
pointed at The Dutchess but when I started
to thank her she turned away the same way
Ralphie the junkie did even though I was
gonna kick his ass for selling me soap
powder once, he saw me and Bambi were
really hungry one time and took us to what
seemed like a pretty fancy joint back
then, not much more than a Howard Johnson's
and bought us dinner and desert and
threw in a lady's magazine for Bambi and
when I started to say thanks he went
"Fuck that" and walked away leaving us
standing there feeling light as the air
so happy not to be hungry anymore—oh
man, when I open up that door to those
days sometimes I think it was all a dream,
something I made up to seem tough to
later friends, but shit, there I was
last Friday night sitting with these two
grandmothers, one still acting tough but
so happy we're all together she can't stop
smiling and the other still acting crazy
but it doesn't scare me any more or make
me mad, it makes me laugh and tell her how
cute she is and she says "Cute is
inappropriate for a 35-year-old woman"
and I say "Bambi, you're 46," she says

"37, that's it"—I take her face in my hands
and say "Hey, I owe you so much too—"
and I realize I'm saying exactly what I
mean now because I am the man I was trying
to be back then when I was too high and
too young and too scared and too overwhelmed
by the feelings I had inside that made me
want to hide inside her eyes forever—
and right there in that bar with all those
people who don't know and could never
imagine the history of her and me—we kiss
and her lips are the same as they were
like the taste and the touch of home that
I tried to describe in all the poems I
wrote for years to her—but all I can
say when we finally pull away is "Hey,
I don't care how many husbands and wives
we've both had, you'll always be my woman"
—and she says "I'm glad," and it feels
so fucking great not to have to be bad or
hate half the world and scared of the rest
just because the best thing I knew when
I was 18 was the love I felt for the
beautiful crazy queen of all the lost souls
in our little New York street scene—hey
none of them became artists or songwriters
or famous or real estate brokers or rich—
a lot are dead or even more lost or sick—
sometimes when I'm in the city and I see
a familiar face on a gray-bearded Black man
digging in the garbage, I think is that—?
but last Friday night at least 3 of us
were still alright, and together again—
can you dig how far I've come since then?
And I ain't talkin' about Hollywood.

SPORTS HEROES, COPS AND LACE

Jackie Robinson was my first real sports hero,
my first real hero period.
My father once took me to see Jersey Joe Walcott
work out for one of his fights.
It was in a summer camp in the North Jersey hills.
We called them mountains back then.
Jersey Joe was already getting old, but he was game
and carried himself like a champ.
I even got introduced to him by my father's friend,
and I remember how nice he was.
In fact I was struck by it, by his openness and
friendliness and unexpected gentleness
when it was obvious he could have easily killed
anybody there with his bare hands
if he felt like it. My father was a sporting man.
He played the ponies every day
and knew everybody at the track and even made a
little book on the side.
We always watched the Friday night fights together
on the old console black-and-white TV.
The Gillette song and that announcer with the high
nasal voice and my father
leaning out of his chair, already an old man to me,
but sporty, with what seemed
like closets full of sporting shoes and sport coats
and even a camel's hair overcoat
I used to sneak a feel of every time I went into the hall
closet. He'd point out Jake Lamotta,
call him "the possum" because he could play dead,
let a man batter him for what seemed
like hours and then when the opponent dropped his guard
tear him apart. He had heart, it was said.
But all these guys seemed somehow tarnished to me, even Jersey
Joe. They were like my father's friends,

nice enough guys, who always treated me right, even if
I hated that they called me "little Jimmy."
I'd tell them my name is Michael
so then they'd call me Mikey, but they were okay.
Even the ones who were obvious bums
like Boots and Mary, and Frenchy, and all these characters
my father had grown up with and run
with and continued to help out til the day he died.
It was like living inside a
Damon Runyan story, and I dug the romance of it,
because despite the idea people
usually have who have never lived that life, it is romantic,
in fact, that's one of the appeals
of that world, any kind of underworld, the bookies
the petty crooks and over-the-hill
champs, there was a glamour and
a romance there, even with the old bags and bums like
Boots and Mary, hey, I used to see
them holding hands as they searched the ground for butts.
But it wasn't until Jackie Robinson
entered the big leagues that I found a hero of my own.
The man had something more than the romance
of the streets and sporting life and my father's friends
and closets of my home. The man had what
my father feared and desired most—"class"—the thing
my father's friends would toast him for.
And it was true that in our neighborhood my father had
some class and carried it as best he could.
But in the face of people more comfortable in this world
and self-assured, my father would get
awful humble, and almost do a kind of white man shuffle
that made me feel that maybe I wasn't
good enough either. He'd pretend that we were better off
where we were and among our own kind,
and we all grew up believing the other Americans, the ones
whose families had been here for a long time,

whose kids went to college and whose fathers and uncles
ran the businesses that really mattered—
we were taught they weren't as happy as we thought we were,
especially when we partied or married or
someone died. But inside, I knew it wasn't pride, it was
some unacknowledged form of ambition suicide.
Don't think beyond these streets, these ways of being or
you might get hurt. We knew our place.
And then Jackie Robinson entered major league baseball as the
first of his race, and I saw a kind of
dignity in the face of the obscenities that greeted him
everyday on the field and it made my chest
swell with pride which didn't make any sense since I was
obviously white and knew nothing about
this man except that he could stand up to the lowest forms
of hatred and not let it effect him,
at least not in any way I could see. And I saw a model for me,
when the kids would do the cruel things
kids can sometimes do, I would think of Jackie Robinson and I
would try to be heroic like him,
and sometimes it worked. Even when they called me a jerk
and a race traitor and all the rest,
because when we played stickball and each took on the persona
of our favorite players, I would
pick him, and the other white guys would berate me and try to
get me to react the way I usually did,
with my fists or my murder mouth or something that could be
turned to their amusement as long as
I was out of control. But when I took on his name for the game,
I took on his dignity too, and it
got me through their petty prejudices and opened up a whole new
world. Sometimes it even worked with
the girls. Until they too began to feel compelled to make
fun of one of their race who was inspired
by a man whose face was handsome and intense, but happened
to be denser in its reflection of the sun

then one of us. Jackie Robinson was the guide to the
outside world for me, his example let me see
that what I was taught was not necessarily true, and what I
always suspected I knew might be. He gave
me a way to go beyond that world and to go deeper into me—
and when I came back, what I had learned
helped me to see that even the people I had left behind knew
these things too. When my cop brother
and my cop brother-in-law and my cop uncle and cousin and
boarder in my mother's house denounced
the riots in the '60s always in racist tones, I'd confront
them about the black friends they often
had in their homes and they would say, that's different,
that's L.J. he's my friend, he's not one
of them. Or when I'd point out how they often dressed and
spoke and drove the same cars and hung
out in the same bars and all the rest, they'd get hurt like
I had turned into some kind of foreigner,
one of those old time Americans who didn't understand and
tried to grandstand with their liberal ideas
when they lived in wealthy enclaves and never had to deal
with the reality of our streets. They'd tell
me they didn't think they'd ever meet one of their own kind
as blind to what was real as me and then
they'd try and make me see that they didn't have anything
against the Jews and Blacks and Italians
and homos and even the rich, because they all had friends or
even in-laws that fit those labels,
they'd try to tell me it's about being true to who you really are
no matter how far your people have come
or haven't come, and then they'd tell some story about how
it used to be and then they'd ask me
how come I never wrote those Damon Runyon stories about them
or more importantly about my father—
they figured I didn't bother because I got too far away
from what I'd been—when I moved
away from the old neighborhood after my father said I was

204

no good for wanting to marry a
black girl and having too many black friends—and then,
when I finally came back again,
so many years after I left him—this time we didn't
fight—because I asked him about
Boots and Mary, whatever happened to Louis the Lip or
Two Ton Tony—he talked all night
& it finally felt alright with him—he talked about how
his mother had been a "live out maid"
when he was a kid—we never talked about politics or the
division that had driven us all into
fear and insecurity—I listened, he talked, and after I
left he called me up & asked if I had
enough to get my kids Xmas presents this year—I said I
did—I never took a dime from him
before, why should I start now—one of my sisters called
and told me because it was the only way
he could say I love you—so I called him back & said hey,
I could use two hundred & he said
it's yours—& I took the kids to see him with the
gifts his money made possible—
he was watching sports on the TV—and all of a sudden he
brought up Jackie Robinson—
how he always admired that man's dignity & a few days later
he called up the only brother he
had left and told him to take him to the hospital—
the doctor called my sister &
told her there's nothing we can find, we'll keep him
overnight and send him home—
& of course he died & this time when they tried to bring him
back he refused—hey, I don't know
why he wanted to die—that was a lot of years ago—all I
know is when I saw *Field of Dreams*
I started to cry—I didn't even know why—my father and
I never even tried to play any game—
but hey you know I'm not ashamed to carry his name—I hope
he feels the same.

HOLIDAY HELL

I always worked on Christmas. Well
not always, since I was about 13.
My father had this home maintenance
business, which meant we cleaned up
after rich people and fixed things in
their homes. There was always a lot
to do around Christmas, including
selling trees out in front of the
little hole-in-the-wall store front.
We had this one special customer who
got this special fifty-foot tree every
year. On Christmas eve, after his kids
went to bed, my brother-in-law the cop,
Joe Glosh (short for Gloshinski) and me
would drive up with the tree and put it
up in the middle of this swirling kind of
Hollywood staircase, wiring it to the
banister here and there until we got it
steady and solid, ready for the silver
dollar tip we always got. My brother-
in-law would always wonder why the best
tree we ever saw always went to a Jew who
didn't even believe in Christmas, right?
Then he'd drop me back at the store and
go home while I waited there alone just
in case somebody might be waiting til the
last minute to buy a tree. Usually no one
was, and when it turned midnight I could
call the local orphanage and they'd come
by for whatever we had left, which my
old man would let me give them for free and
then I could walk or hitchhike the few miles
home. When we were little my sisters and I
would exchange our gifts before we fell

asleep, because we all lived in the attic
together. The coolest thing was waking in
the morning with this sound, like crunchy
paper, and realizing it was our stockings
at the foot of the beds that our ma had
always somehow got up there without us
catching her, and we'd get to open up all
our stocking stuff before we woke the rest
of the folks, our older brothers and grand-
mother and the border, Jack, and our mom
and dad. Then we'd all open stuff and go
to Mass and come home for the big dinner.
But by the time I got the attic to myself,
cause my brother-in-law and that sister
got a place of their own and my other sister
joined the nunnery for awhile, I got to
working for the parks department too,
because my old man didn't pay me, figuring
I worked for room and board, so I had these
other jobs, and the parks department had a
busy day on Christmas cause all these kids
would come down to the park to try their
new sleds or skates and I worked either on
the hill or on the pond as a sort of guard
and coach and general alarm man. I used to
love seeing a wreck on the hill so I could
slide down the snow on my engineer boots,
the kind motorcycle dudes wear now, showing
off my teenaged skill and balance for the
teenaged girls who might be watching. I
don't remember ever falling down, it was
something I was totally confident about. Now
that I think about it, I guess working on
Christmas wasn't so bad, even though I always
kind of felt sad anyway, especially after I
started dating black girls and knew I couldn't

take them home or share the holidays much
with them, but there was always something sad
about Christmas anyway, once you were over five
or maybe ten, how could it ever live up to your
expectations again? I also dug being a
working guy though, you know? Even today
when I see young working guys going by in
the backs of pickup trucks I catch their eye
and feel like I know what's going through
their heads, because of what was going
through mine, which was, any time now I'll be
out of this, a big star or wheeler dealer or
intellectual or anything that means a kind of
success you couldn't guess when you look at
me here under these conditions, cause now,
I'm a mystery to you, you don't know who I
am, you think you can categorize me but you
got no idea who I might be someday, or the
the richness of the life I live inside, and
you'll never know what it's like to be as
cool as I sometimes feel when you look at me
and see a guy from some kind of ethnic mystery
you can't comprehend except in the most simplistic
terms, and who is so free he can work in public
and get dirty and sweat and wear his hair greasy
and his tee shirt rolled and know you would never
mess with him unless you're a woman and get a whim
to find out what it's like to give a piece of ass
to someone from the working class—I dug the
kind of coolness of it, of knowing I was a lot more
than these ordinary citizens could comprehend,
that I could be sexy in ways their men were too
restrained to be, that I could be threatening in
ways their men would be too frightened to be, that
I could get down and dirty and not give a fuck
what I looked like in public, even though I knew
I looked cool, that I could be inside a life and

world they could never even guess the intensity and
romanticism and pure exhilaration of because it
didn't depend on material goods and worldly
success but on loyalty and honesty and standing
up for yourself and all the rest of your kind
when you were put to the test—hell I used to
love looking back into their eyes and thinking
some day they'll be so surprised to find out
what was going on in my head when I put it in
a book or on film or tell them about it in their
bed—so even though I came home late for the
big dinner and my fingers and toes all froze
cause guys like us could never make a fuss about
the cold by wearing scarves or gloves or any of
that rich kid stuff, and maybe I'd get a little
drunk when nobody was looking and try to get the
phone into the closet or somewhere where I could
be alone for a few minutes to call some girl
they might call colored and wrong, and end up
later that night sleeping on the floor of the
kitchen with the new puppy so he wouldn't keep
everyone awake with his scared yelps and in the
morning scandalize my grandmother when she found
me in my boxer shorts the puppy asleep on my
chest and she'd rouse me and make me get dressed
but not without telling me I was just like my
father, I didn't have any ashes, which was her
way of implying I didn't have any ass to speak
of, and then I'd help her get her stockings over
her crippled legs and have something to eat and
go to work again, maybe this time on the pond,
where I'd get to slide across the ice to rescue
stumbling teenaged girls while "Earth Angel" or
"Blue Christmas" blared over the loudspeakers
and in my heart, knowing for sure I was going
to be a part of some important history, and I
was—and still am.

20 YEARS AGO TODAY

We were a couple of kids
with a kid—weren't we Lee—
ever since this topic came up
I've been thinking about you—
but not like I usually do,
I've been remembering what it was
that kept us together, the glue
that made it look to others
like our marriage worked—
I used to think it was the anger & sex—
I never talked much about love
I guess—and
after all the experience since us
all the lovers and living together
being married and being in a "relationship"
the flirtations and infatuations
the romances and affairs and rolls
in the hay and pokes and fucks and
fantasies, what do I know about it Lee?
I went out with a woman last week,
intelligent, accomplished, attractive,
a great body, like yours only harder,
that's the way most of them are now,
at least out here, they all work out so much,
but this one does it with ballet,
you'd have dug that too, but she's
taller than you, she could actually do
it if she wasn't already successful
at something else not quite so demanding
or deforming—anyway, we had a nice enough
time, but she's still in love with somebody
else and I guess I am—or was—too—
but that never stopped me with you,
even though you knew—

I remember how understanding you were about that
before we got married, but then after
you said if you ever saw her on the street
you'd cut out her heart and I believed you would
—back then it somehow seemed good
to be with someone that passionate and crazy,
both of us acting so lower class city street tough
as though we weren't just a couple of kids
afraid the world might really be too rough
for us after all, what did we know heh?
anyways, those were the days Lee—
things hadn't gone all wrong,
we were still getting along—
making love every night,
and I don't think we'd begun to fight yet—
like about John Lennon leaving his wife—
something you were sure I was going to do to you
when I became that successful too, which
everyone seemed to think was inevitable back then—
well, not everything we thought would happen came
true—at least not for me & you—
remember how all those predictions about me
always ended with "if he lives that long"—
everytime I got in my old telephone van and turned
the key, I had to take this deep breath first,
then curse the rightwing assholes who sent me
death threats in the mail, with pictures
of crosshairs aimed at the back of my neck,
or descriptions of my van blowing up or my
house burning down—those guys
probably went on to work for Reagan and
Bush & Quayle, but that's a whole
other story you don't want to know about—
what I'm trying to get out now is the fact
that I hardly ever write about you and me Lee
and all those years we spent together—

and of all that time, maybe February 1969 was the
highlight, you were still jealous of everyone
but they didn't have you on the run and never
would—and I was really being good—you know
I never cheated on you, not once in all those
early years, despite your fears and mine—
even that time that girl said I had with her,
I don't know what that was about, maybe just
that I was in the papers a lot then and she
somehow wanted to be a part of that—what do
I know Lee, I got girls younger than our
daughter after me now and it's just because
they want to read their poetry at Helena's—
I don't even want to get into that either—
hey, Lee, what I'm remembering is a night so cold we
have to wrap our baby in her little snow suit
to sleep in, cause all we got is this one little
oil stove in the middle of the quonset hut
we were living in, yeah, the kind with the
ruffled corrugated tin in a semi circle—
so what little heat there was hovered
over our heads in the very middle of the house,
the only place I could stand straight up anyway—
I remember the water in the diaper pail had a thin
layer of ice on it in the morning, but that
night, we got naked under tons of covers and
those old quilts you dug so much, reminding you
of your mother's country roots, we were
probably high on some reefer as usual—
and I was probably tired from my three parttime
jobs and all the classes I took to get through
school quick before I hit one of those smug
professors or graduate student assistants—
I think I already quit teaching at the Free
University, my class on Stalin, not because
I dug him, but because if people were gonna

talk about him I figured they oughta know
what he did and said and wrote or had ghostwritten
for him, but when Russia invaded Chekaslovakia, I
gave up caring about any of those Communist
thugs and their theories—and I had already
lost the election for sheriff of the County,
despite the great letters and support I got—
I did pretty good actually, a lot better
than Hunter Thompson did the following year
when *Rolling Stone* tried to pretend he was
the first stoned-out writer to run for sheriff
anywhere—but that's another story too—
what I'm remembering is that old brass bed
you dug so much, and us in some kind of
clutch under all the stuff, we could see
our breath in the dark night air it was
so cold—there was a lot of snow on the ground
as usual, but that was out there through
those tiny windows, the dark Iowa sky and
the stars, and the way they looked through
our stoned hallucinations, your fears about
what all my revolutionary commitments might
mean, where we would go, what scene we would
get enmeshed in next, none of that had come
up yet, this was a pause just before we
got ready to move on to the next and toughest
part of our time together, now, we were still
able to weather all the shit we had been through
and still stay together, and we knew how to
do that so well in bed Lee, goddamn it it
got so confusing later didn't it? But we knew—
feminists tried to tell me in later days that
you were probably faking those perfect orgasms
but what the fuck did they know? we were kids
who learned how to make love together—
sure we'd been around when we met, so much more

than most in those days too, but we knew
what didn't work and what did, and we taught each
other, and we got to a place where every night
after we turned out the light and turned to each
other under those covers we could make everything
good for a little while, we could make each other
feel like we'd just discovered the secret of life,
like we truly understood the reason anyone could
take pride in words like *husband* and *wife*, and
yeah I still had a lot more to learn,
but honey, we had enough sensual
power between us those nights to burn that quonset
hut down if we'd wanted to, but all we wanted to
do was become one, and we did, good enough that
night 20 years ago to create a son,
and a beautiful boy he is Lee—you'd be proud of him—
as you would of our daughter—as I truly was of you—
standing up to the geeks and assholes who wanted
to know what happened to your face or wanted you
to replace it with a plastic one—I never understood
completely your reasons for leaving it the way it was
but I also never gave a shit Lee, I respected you
and I believe you respected me, and you know,
I think that's what it was that made it last as long
as it did, and that made it possible for us every
night to reach that same sensual height
at the same time together—goddamn it kid, we
knew what we were doing in bed, no matter what
anybody later said—I grew to sometimes hate you
Lee and some of the things you said to suit
those later feminist days, but hey, you never revised
that part about us in bed, and neither did I,
no matter what other kinds of things I might
have said about you—
you were my love, my little darling in that bed,
and I was your man, your boy, your loving friend—

we didn't have the fancy moves I learned later—and
maybe that was just as well, we just did what came
so naturally and felt so goddamn swell—
yeah I'm still throwing in those really dumb rhymes
from the old days of toasting & dirty dozens—
aw Lee, Lee, Lee, when our daughter came to
live with me I used to see you in her sometimes
and it would get me mad—it was always the stuff
that made me leave you finally like you always
predicted, only not because I was some great success,
but because there was no more room for those sweet
nights under all that feminist duress, and because
I wanted to finally see what it might be like with
some other bodies I guess—and I did, it has been
sometimes really great and amazing and even
now and then full of love and grace, but you know,
now sometimes when I look at our daughter's
face, I see you still, only not what I grew to feel
bad about, there was a sweetness in those days Lee,
to those kids with their kid we used to be and
especially 20 years ago tonight when we created
another one, I see you too in him, our son—I'm
sorry it didn't work out, and I can't even express
how bad I feel about what happened to you, at least I
don't feel guilty about it anymore, because I've learned
that guilt is just pride in reverse, taking credit for
things you have no control over—and I had no control
over that fucked up operation and those six years in
whatever state you were in inside that comatose body—
but you were always afraid I wouldn't be able to take
care of the kids, after the years of poverty and
crazy Irish irresponsibility, at least it seemed that
way to you—so now the kids are taken care of—
thanks to lawyers and malpractice suits and it's
all way out of my hands—and here I am Lee—thinking
of you and how strong you were for such a tiny lady—

and how you always knew something the rest of us
didn't—I wonder if you knew then that I loved you—and
just didn't know it, except when I would show it in bed,
and no matter what went on in my head later or does
now about me and you—I guess it's about time I
admitted I still do.

DISCO POETRY

I remember where I was when
JFK got assassinated, when
Martin Luther King got shot,
when the first man walked on
the moon, when Elvis died,
when John Lennon was killed,
and when I first heard Barry
White—I was in a record
store in a Black neighborhood
of Washington DC, known on
those streets as Chocolate City
—a young handsome platform
shoed, extroverted gay Black man
was talking to the clerk about
what he had just discovered on
a trip to New York and when he
said Barry White the clerk says
"We just got it in today" and he puts
on "I'm Under the Influence of Love"
and the album sold out in the next
few minutes. Everyone in the store
bought it, including me, the only
white, but also in platform shoes—
now why does that seem so tacky and
shallow and all the negative adjectives

just the simple word "disco" seems to
conjure up these days, unlike say "rock"
—I remember when I first heard Janis
Joplin, it was at a party in a
farmhouse rented by some University
of Iowa students, I walked in, pretty
high, and got higher when I heard
her blasting her version of "Summertime"
into the black rural night as George
K. shot some adrenalin, he said—
that he had copped from a hospital—
directly into his chest and then slammed
to the floor and shook violently while his
one real eye rolled back and his skin turned
a whiter shade of pale and several of
us long-haired guys picked him up and
walked him around outside for over an hour
until we were sure he wasn't going to die
and then we came back in and did our own drugs
and danced and forgot where we were or
who we were or anything else about that
night except George almost o.d.ing and
Janis singing—"take a take another little
piece of my heart now" well now, how can anyone
compare that kind of thrill, or the first
time we saw Elvis on TV or The Beatles coming
to America with fucking disco—come on man,
Travolta in that sappy low rent white suit and
low rent white flick, shit, disco was black
music first, emphasizing the bass beat, giving
birth to "rap" in a basic kind of way no rapper
would ever say I'm sure and then taking the tour
of the white world through the "gay" clubs first,
not through some Italian thugs in Brooklyn—
but still, where, outside of James T. Farrel's
Studs Lonigan, had we ever seen a more accurate

portrayal of the male ritual of getting dressed
to go out then in that scene in *Saturday Night
Fever*—and what else inspired Michael Jackson to
inspire us with some of his hippest stuff in
the lyrics and music of *Off the Wall*, or got
an expatriate diva back from Europe where her
soft porn sound gave birth to the Euro trash
that followed only to become the most powerful
and successful Black woman of her time, Donna
Summer, who in her prime made us love to love
her bad girl moves and glamorize our need to
dance and summarize our post-war angst with
songs that satisfied our frenetic desire to
outlast the collective shame and confusion by
singing "I Will Survive" and how better to
do that than by just "oh-oh-oh-oh staying
alive"—yes, it was the '70s when the reality
of everything we had raved against for fear
it would come true did—so we partied like
being bored to death was a true possibility—
and rediscovered style with a relentlessness
that even made the '50s look like happy days—
the '50s that looked so lame in the '60s like
the '60s looked so lame in the '70s and the '70s
have looked so lame in the '80s—but it's
almost the '90s now, and if you want to be
on the cutting edge, just go back 20 years
and you'll be there—hey, in the '70s it
looked for awhile like the Republicans
would never gain the presidency for the rest
of the century after what they did to us in
Vietnam and with Watergate and all the lies
and dirty tricks and secret wars that were
uncovered, the Democrats might be corrupt
but the Republicans were corrupt and
self-righteous, is there a more repulsive

combination than that? they're like blow-
dried Noriegas, and the '70s gave birth to
AIDS and the Bush conspiracies that led to
the power of people who continue to sell
this country and indeed the world out from
under us as we turned our backs on the
moral obligations we understood intuitively
only a few years before—hey, the '70s weren't
a bore or so bland and free of style as we
thought, in fact it might take a while but
if we start to relate what really went down,
we're gonna find out they're gonna come
around again to where we all can defend
the right to live a life of love instead of
greed and fear and constant reinterpretation
of the year we first heard Barry White—
& maybe we'll go out & dance all night or
maybe I mean talk or maybe I mean hold each
other like we are the light, me & you, & maybe
we'll make peace with ourselves & the rest
of the world again like disco once helped us do

THE SOUND OF POLICE CARS

& rain accumulating in
the light fixture in
the bathroom—the most
dangerous leak in the
house—like that time
in the loft on Duane
Street when Miles yelled
for me—there was a
mouse running up my
mattress-on-the-floor bed

getting close to his head
as he watched the TV
& I took off my Doctor
Scholls and squashed it
without even thinking
& he went on watching
TV without even blinking
& not too many
nights later I snuck in
a 22-year-old woman
after he went to sleep
and we made love for
hours and then laid there
thinking until she said—
"how old did you say you
were?" & I told her—38—
and she said "that's
amazing"—& I said,
wanting to hear her say how
good I was—how young I
looked—how whatever it was
that amazed her about my
being that age that time,
so I said "what's amazing
about it?" & she said "a
guy your age, still sleeping
on a mattress on the floor."

HAVING IT ALL

When I was a kid,
I had no doubt I would win world acclaim:
a Nobel Prize for my novels, plays, and poetry,
and be the first Nobel Laureate to also win

an Oscar for writing, directing, and
starring in the world's most popular
movie in the history of film—
and all this after becoming the world's
most famous and successful singer and musician
who would destroy forever the boundaries
between rock'n'roll and jazz and blues and
all forms of popular and esoteric music
with my enormous talent and universal appeal,
and of course I would accept the Nobel
while serving as the most effective
and most popular president of the USA
in its entire history—which naturally
would be merely a prelude to my accepting
the presidency of the world, united finally
as a direct result of the influence and impact
of my political theories.

This is all true.
I believed this,
and continued to believe it throughout my life.
In one way or another.
How could I help it?
When I saw James Dean trying to do what looked
like a way too self-conscious bad imitation
of the little juvenile delinquent I thought I was
or believed I understood first hand at the time,
I knew in my heart that the truth I thought I saw
missing in his acting was present in me
every day of my life.
And when I saw Brando on his motorcycle
or Elvis on TV, I could see that these guys
had something, but how could it compare
with me? They were obviously pretending to be
something I knew I really was.
Their sexuality was like a game they were playing,

but my sexuality was no game to me,
I could spend eternity in hell for what I was feeling,
and the only thing that kept me from reeling
my way into an institution, which was where
they put lower-middle-class teenagers with too much
passion then, the only thing that prevented that
was the revelation that what I was feeling was
not only not a sin, but in fact an assignment from God:
to show the world how to love, again.

Now maybe that was just an Irish-Catholic kid's
way of getting around sin,
but I believed it with all my heart
and knew it was true,
and was sure that the world would see that too,
when they finally put me on film or TV,
or stuck me on a stage with a band behind me.
I had no doubts about it,
I didn't even think I had to put any effort into it,
really, though when it came my way
I did learn how to play some instruments
and did get up on stages and perform
or talk or walk around and let the inspiration
come out of me in words I found profound,
if nobody else did. I truly felt
I had a mission no less ambitious
than to embody love so perfectly
in all I did that the people of the world
would finally let go of all their fears about each
other and we could all just be ourselves at last
and leave everyone else alone to be themselves—
or maybe help them out if they needed it,
because we might need it sometime too,
you know, all that stuff that people did
get into for awhile in the '60s in ways
I thought were somehow my doing—I mean

I took myself so seriously I got proprietary
about almost everything I dug—
I wasn't totally out of control,
I never thought I was responsible for
athletic events or minor wars or stuff
I cared about but not that much—
but almost every hip style since I was a kid,
I thought at least in part could not have
evolved if somehow someone hadn't picked up
on what I was wearing and doing,
yeah, all that ego stuff,
that obvious covering up
for the insecurity and fear
that maybe I wasn't enough—
but come on now, tell the truth,
didn't you feel that way too,
couldn't you see how obviously
inferior the supposedly great leaders
were, or even the great thinkers,
when you read Marx and Lenin and Jefferson and
Neitchze and Kierkegaard and Wittginstein and
St. Thomas, and Sartre and Hemingway and Stein,
didn't you really feel, as I certainly did,
that the truth was still being hidden away
as if they really didn't know what it was
or were too afraid to say—
Yeah, like I said, I felt that way,
until just the other day,
like sure I coulda been bigger than Elvis
or Marlon or JFK, only, you know, nobody asked
me to make a record or star in their movie or
run for president on their ticket—
well, actually, I did get asked to
be on a record with other New York
poets and performers once, like Laurie
Anderson who looked like a hippie then,

but then she got her hair cut and spiked it,
and dyed it and started wearing makeup
that accentuated her eyes and more or less
doing a female version of my style back then
and you know the rest—and people did
ask me to star in their movies, like the
one where I got to be the hero and stick
a wooden stake into a bald Dracula on
a farm in South Jersey and when I took
my son to see the blown up poster of me
doing just that on 42nd Street, he said
"gee dad, it looks like you're
killing some bum with a broom handle—"
and I once did run for office, sheriff
of Johnson County Iowa on the Peace and
Freedom ticket, Eldridge Cleaver was our
candidate that year for president—
though I thought at the time I had a
better political perspective—
so yeah, I guess I've had my chances,
especially when I think of all the
romances I've had with the women I
only dreamt about back then—only, when I
think about that mission I thought I was on,
I see that I turned it all into sexuality
that was all about how I could satisfy me
even when I did that by satisfying you
because that made me feel like I was still
being true to my assignment from God,
and who knows? maybe I was—

The truth is, I did all the things
I once dreamed I would, but either they didn't
turn out so good or what I fantasized they'd be
or it was me who didn't pull it off,
not prepared or just not good enough—

and when I finally accepted that
not too long ago, instead of feeling bad
I felt this inner glow of peace and relief,
like I could finally get to know myself
without the pressure of being Elvis/Marlon/
JFK/Beckett/Kerouac/Dylan/Lennon/and the
rest, I didn't have to prove to myself
or anyone else anymore that I was the best
and just got overlooked somehow, I didn't
even have to save the world without your
help, being love and all that, all I had
to do was listen to my heart and not my ego
and tell the truth with whatever language
is truly mine and be of service in any way
I can and just go ahead and be the man I am—

SOMETHING BACK

I never had a backache before
I started working out
now I'm like all those other
jock Adonises, pretending to be
the healthiest man you've ever
scanned when it's all a sham—
I can't even stand up straight
anymore, or pick something
up off the floor without
making noises I used to hear
only the real old geezers make—
oh for heaven's sake, my mother
would say if she could hear me now
from wherever she went when I
watched the line go flat for
the last time, anyway, she'd say

oh for heaven's sake don't make
yourself out to be so old when
you're my baby, the youngest of
the fold—who never had the chance
to hold her the way a grown man
can do, the way I hold my kids or
friends or other women or you—
but, that isn't really true,
because not too long ago, when
I was lying on my couch in the
middle of the afternoon, just
sort of digging the way the light
came through the trees and windows
in ways that spread these rays
all through the room, dispelling
any gloom I might have had and
reminding me of when I was four
or five and my mother told me
how each little speck of dust—
don't they call them mites?—was
actually an angel which was enough
to keep me fascinated for days
in ways that probably led directly
to me being the kind of dreamer
who writes poems and lives on loans
and spends some afternoons just
lying on a couch mesmerized by a
certain slant of light and the way
it ignites a kind of heat in my
heart that starts the gratitude
flowing, when all of a sudden I
see my mother, kind of glowing
but very real, and without even
thinking I open my arms and take
her in my embrace in just that
way I never got the chance to,

like a grown man who knows what
it means to suffer and to be
comforted in the strength of
the arms of someone who loves you—
no, more than that, it is a thing
about feeling strong in a way
that still seems manly today,
I can't defend or even describe
this feeling right, but it was
there, in me, as I held my mom
in the afternoon light, so long
after she had gone for good and
then I looked and there my father
stood, weeping, and I knew without
thinking he was crying because
he felt left out and misunderstood
and I opened my arms to him,
because it was true I never got to
hold him that way either, with me
being the parent, the grown up one
now, with me having been through
enough to forgive them for whatever
mistakes we all make, yeah, I just
never got to embrace these two
people whose love and devotion to
each other was so strong it lasted
a lifetime long, I remember them
holding hands on their couch as
they watched TV like two teenagers
and they were already old, having
had me by surprise at the end of
a brood of seven—what I'm
trying so hard to say is on that
day when they appeared to me I
really did see them standing there
in the golden air of the afternoon

light and I felt like I had the
chance to let them see I turned
out all right, and I didn't have
to cry about what has slipped away,
because I got something back.

YOUNG LOVE

When I was a kid I remember
going out with this girl
whose father ran a neighborhood
bar—he was known for his fits
of violence—one time when she
was talking to me on the phone
he came home and ripped the thing
out of the wall in the middle of
our conversation—I thought
she hung up on me and was kinda
hurt until she finally reached me
a few days later after everything
had quieted down—I remember
the first time I took her out,
they lived over the bar on the
border of Newark in a tough Irish-
Italian neighborhood that's now
a tough African-Puerto Rican one—
when I walked in she introduced
me to him, a big overgrown lummox,
the kind of Irish bully that made
me know why I wanted to get away
from that part of Jersey first
chance I got—and I did—but
back then I was still a kid with
nowhere to go that didn't end up

with me trying to sleep in the
snow—so, anyway, as I go
toward him sitting on the couch
to shake his hand the way I was
taught he says "I thought she said
you played football" and I said
"I do" and he made some cutting
remark about how in his day someone
as thin and light as me woulda been
used for the football, and I said
something back about how maybe he'd
like to fucking try it sometime like
right now, and he looked like he
might and then laughed and said I was
alright but must have changed his mind
by the time he ripped the phone off
the wall—actually in that time and
place this girl was sort of classy
to even have a phone and a bar they
maybe didn't actually own but could
make at least the upstairs their home—
lots of girls I dated I had to call
their neighbors and ask them to run
next door or up the stairs to pass
some coded message on to them—
but this one girl was obviously
not thrilled to have a phone when
it came with the father she had—
but she didn't know what to do—
they didn't have books and seminars
and TV movies and newspaper stories
and anonymous meetings or much of
anything back then to tell a kid
what to do about fathers who drank
too much and then got violent—
we all knew about it, we all lived

with some version of it, and she
did what most of the kids I knew
did, she got cynical and tough—
so much that when we'd finally find
some quiet place under the stars
away from all the bars and the
anger they fed, we'd be doing some
heavy body work and then lay back
to look at the stars and I could
never stop myself from going off
into them with my dreams of another
way—I'd start to sketch with
words the house we'd live in with
a fireplace we could lay in
front of like in movies I had seen
and in the morning we would walk
to the ocean nearby to say good
morning and watch the boats glide
by—this is true, I can see her
next to me on the ground as I let
my words take me away from all that
was around us, surrounded us, and
I can see her turn to me and shatter
everything I'd shared—she was just
trying to get me to see how all of
what I said was pure fantasy—I swear
I can still hear her saying "Michael,
you're such a dreamer, we're only
fifteen, we probably won't even know
each other in two years"—and I remember
my reply—"You're probably right but
so what? It makes it better, it
makes me want to kiss you even more
and hold you even tighter and feel
so fucking in love and happy I want
to cry, or fly away to those stars

up there forever, now what the fuck
is wrong with that? if it makes us
feel better and happier and more in
love?" But she wasn't going for it,
she had her own agenda and it didn't
include those kind of dreams, and it
seems she was right, because it wasn't
even two months before we were strangers
again, but in a way I was too, because
I live in that house with the fireplace
and the beach I say good morning to—
and if you're gonna lay down with me
in this quiet place I've finally found
and watch the fire with me and get up
in the morning to greet the nearby sea,
I want you to be as crazy about the
romantic possibilities as me—

ISN'T IT ROMANTIC?

She smiled when I passed her saying
"I love your poetry"
so naturally
I figured she
was just being polite
or thought that's what you're supposed to say
at these things or
was slightly high and caught my eye
and thought I expected a compliment
or didn't know what she was saying—
anything but just plain meaning it—
How could she mean it—
I hadn't even read yet
and she was the most beautiful woman in the place,

her face could sell me anything,
except my own worth,
for now—
that's how I felt about it—
and then I read—
and they wouldn't shut up—
not even when I told them
I was going to talk about their
pussys and assholes and cocks—
I could tell a few heard me and stopped talking
long enough to see if I meant it—
but pretty soon, they were filling the room
with their own chatter and it didn't seem to matter
what I read or said or—
so when I got down and walked across the floor
I wasn't expecting more compliments from anybody—
let alone her—
but there she was—still beautiful—
no, more so—her eyes still aglow with
what I still thought was fake or mock admiration—
so I just threw myself into dancing—
first with friends and then when they
disappeared, with myself—
through the crowd I could see her
dancing with her girlfriend
and when they whispered to each other and
looked over at me
I looked around to see what else
it might be—and sure enough, standing behind me was
a young dude who obviously
thought he was hot stuff
like everyone else in the place in fact—
a room full of competing egos in black—
and when I turned back,
she was gone, so I closed my eyes
and disappeared into the music until

I had to open them or fall—
and when I did she was all I saw,
dancing now right there before me—
her girlfriend had moved over to my spot too—
and I thought for a minute, hey
maybe she does have some interest in me—
but then I see them both provoke
the hot stuff dude into giving up his pose
to join them on the dance floor where I
can check him out up close—
he's not so hot—sure he's got a lot of
hair and none of it's gray and it seems
to stay the way he planned it to, but hey,
when I was his age I looked more authentic
than that—hell, I still do—so does she—
maybe that's what she sees in me—and maybe
this hot stuff guy is just shy and doesn't want to
show it—or blow it, the way I so often have—
and it makes him awkward in a kind of endearing way—
and suddenly hey, I can see that he's not anything more
than a friend—and he isn't dancing with her anyway—
because no matter how I try to misinterpret it,
she's obviously dancing with me, on purpose—
so I take the risk and smile at her,
and she smiles back—
and I can see I was wrong—
she isn't just beautiful, stunning, marvelous and
incredibly naturally the girl of my oldest dream—
she doesn't seem crazy or needy or self-conscious or
aloof and full of hype like those model slash actress types—
she looks alright—and she's looking at me—
until I can't help but bite my tongue
to stop myself from screaming MARRY ME!!
what was I thinking? sure this was some cute kid
and maybe the dim lights hid my age
but when she sees me in the light—

might as well enjoy it—and I did—
and she made me forget all the rest—
especially when she leaned over and whispered in my ear
"What are you laughing at—is the dancing too much?"
"No," I shout back, afraid to get too near
for fear I'll just start sniffing at her skin
like a dog wanting to get in—
or let my lips just skim the surface of her
neck and chin and—
"I can never get too much dancing" I say—
"I'm just happy
because you're so beautiful"—
she smiles even more at that
and I feel great, and then she shouts back
"That was a beautiful poem you wrote about
the birthday girl—I'd love to have you write
a poem about me" and I don't miss a beat as my lips almost
meet her ear so she can hear me say "I'll
have to get to know you to do that"
and she says "I already know all about you"
and I try not to look like "oh no—shit—
what has she been told" as I ask "what
do you know?" and she says "that you have two kids
and are married" and I say "I got two kids
but their mother is dead" and she looks sad
for a minute and I'm thinking what the fuck
did you bring that up for at a time like this
in the middle of a dance floor when what
you really want to do is kiss this beautiful
apparition in this crowd of self-assured
white kids in black trying to be hip—
and I go on to say "In fact I'm living
alone for the first time in my life"
and that brings a smile to her face
and I want to get her out of this place
and into my arms where there aren't swarms

of kids who look like cleaned up versions
of something I risked my life for and they
don't have to risk any more than a few hours
of possible boredom—so I say something
about leaving and getting something to eat
but getting her number first cause I'm really
thinking I got to go home and do some homework
if I want to do good tomorrow—while I'm also
thinking now that we're nearing more lights she'll probably
take flight and I can spend the rest of the night
feeling vindicated by my own sense of—
but that isn't what happened as we walked to the bar
and she told me we'd already met—
and I didn't remember, but she was right—
it was at one of the poetry nights
at Helena's, where she asked someone to
introduce her to me because she loved the way
I moved when I read my work and I'm
thinking I'll probably never move that way again
because already I'm trying to remember what I did—
and she's going on about how she came here tonight
just to see me and how maybe she should stop
and I'm saying "No, don't stop" and she's saying
"What are you gonna do, take me to lunch?"
and I say "No, dinner, are you hungry?"
and she says "I ate but you go fill your belly"
and there's nothing to do but leave
I think, or buy her a drink which she's
already doing and I'm chewing on some
memory of what might be already as I
go home and try to leave a message on
her phone machine about how the soil
where she was born is probably blessed
from all the prayers of gratitude me
and all the rest of the guys she has
mesmerized have sent out there, and I'm thinking

of her hair, so dark and full and the way
it framed her face and those eyes that
sparkled and shone so bright even in
those dim lights and some female voice
answers the phone and I'm thinking how did
she get home so fast? But it isn't her
and I can't leave my poetic message like that
so I try again the next day, only to hear the
same voice tell me she's still not there
and so I don't know what to do except leave my number
and then try and forget her because
I'm sure she'll never call, I'm sure I should have
taken her outside and kissed her until we choked
and then let her watch my smoke
as I hit the trail for my own busy life—
but I didn't, I left it like that—
me bumbling around for a way to say
hey I want to spend the rest of
my life seeing if you're who I think you are—
the star of my oldest dream
the one about how if you really are honest
and good and true you get to fall in love
with someone who is falling for you
and it's the girl in the dream—the one
who seems like the most natural beauty on earth
and worth all the shit you've been through
to get to this place, where you can spend
the rest of your life looking at that face
and believing she wants to do the same with you—
only the phone keeps ringing and it's never her—
but you know what? the old ideas don't occur
to me this time, this time I feel like whatever
she does or doesn't do is okay—either way, I know
who I am and what I want, and what I do
is no longer based on what I can get from you—
but on what I can give as I live in a way

that will hopefully help us all get through each day
like it's the only one that counts now because it is.
Isn't *that* romantic?

THEY MUST BE GODS AND GODDESSES

Here's the deal, you make me feel
like a god come down from on high
to see how you humans get through
all the pain and heartaches life
and the world throws at you and yet
still continue to pass the tests
and overcome the obstacles and all
the rest we gods like to add to the
stew of your existence until you
give up and we can feel satisfied
that we really do have it better—
only watching you do the ordinary
human things a god would never stoop
to do, like cook and do the laundry
and unhook the VCR so you can hook up
the CD player again, I understand
why some men are constantly thanking
us for making them men, and I want to
be a man, so I can take your hand and
kiss it without feeling awkward, afraid
I might frighten you with the intensity
of my desire to pay homage to you, or
that you might misconstrue it to mean
I want you to do things with me I can't
even imagine now, let alone how it can
be done, this way you humans have of
becoming one with each other—I
watch you stir the sauce, or toss the

sheets into the dryer, or pick up a
child so effortlessly and it is like
these gestures are higher than anything
a god can do for or against you—ever—
and I am in awe and want nothing more
than the chance to do these things too
the way I see you do, without pretension
or calculation, without restraint or
complaint, but with a kind of skill
that is a mystery to a god—there is a
will behind it that transcends the
merely habitual, the daily routine of
it, and transforms it into ritual as
precise and mysteriously soothing for
your kind as the ones you call spiritual
—that's it, you somehow understand
that the way your hand stirs that
cooking food is not just a matter of
kitchen expertise, but a perfect
opportunity to increase the power
that being human represents, a power
most humans believe is heaven sent,
they don't comprehend what you so
obviously do, that the difference
between us and you is not that you
have to do so many lowly things to
get through just a few hours, but
that if you do these things with
love, then that exceeds all the powers
any gods could possess, and you are
nothing less than the object of a
god's desire, not to make you a
goddess, but to be made human by the
caress of your hand as you take his
arm to get warm in the night chill
he can finally feel through you—

no wonder the gods and goddesses
keep telling themselves they have
it so much better than you, if they
for one moment could experience the
feeling of pure love you seem to
put into everything you do, there
wouldn't be any gods or goddesses
left up there to talk to, they'd
all be down here competing with me
for the chance to see you open a
door, pick your glove up off the
floor, give a little girl more of
what she's asking for, your love—
even the little girl I see inside
of you, who doesn't need me to
take care of her because you've
done that so well—hell, what's
a god to do with a human like you
who doesn't need any of my godlike
tricks and omnipotence? how I long
for the common sense of an ordinary
man who understands just when and
how to take your hand in his—
oh yes, a god can be awestruck too,
once he has seen you—

*

On the other hand, and maybe more
realistically, you make me feel
like I am the mortal man, struggling
to get by all these years, and getting
by, sometimes only by getting high,
but not any more, and then suddenly
there you are, a goddess come down
from on high, to grace me with

your presence for reasons I can't
guess, but worry I'll mess up in
my clumsiness as I try to let you
know that I will go as slow as you
will let me in getting to know you
because I want this revelation to
last forever, this uncovering of
your goddess essence which makes
the most humble tasks look like
gestures of a love so profound—as
Selby says, wherever we seek God
we meet him, and that is holy ground,
so everywhere you are is holy and
God is found, and okay, it isn't
that you're a goddess and I'm just
a man that makes me forget all
my little schemes and plans that
worked with the other girls, it's
that the way you carry your human
qualities, that dignity and grace
with which you move from place to
place to place and chore to chore
is more than any god could aspire
to, and so in you, I see the truth
that this is truly the dwelling
place of the gods—of the one
God—and every human is a god and
goddess too, and it is you I owe
for allowing me to feel that I am
too, that my age is perfect and
so is my height, that it's okay to
look nice and even be white, that
I too can take my place among the
human gods and goddesses without
fear or judgment or false pride,
that I too can be the man I truly

am and yet still take care of and
share the little boy inside, that
anywhere we humans reside—but
I have to admit for me, especially
anywhere you might be—is truly
paradise.

OBSESSION POSSESSION AND DOING TIME

Of course I want to possess
whatever I'm obsessed with—
that Bonnard painting in the Phillips Gallery in Washington DC
that I visited at least three times a week
for the years I lived a few blocks away
until one day they moved it—so I moved
back to New York where I was obsessed with the same old stuff
like poetry, and city rain,
the corners of certain
city blocks and buildings,
the way the traffic lights glowed so bright against the sky
as day begins to turn to night—
the drugs that made me think
I needed them to see that—
the dreams of making my mark on the world
in ways that would make up
for all the times the world
tripped me up, threw another
obstacle in my path, smacked
me down, kicked me around,
beat and battered me into
an arrogance so powerful
people thought it was really
me, so did I for awhile,
and with a style always so out front and unique,

or so I wanted to believe,
other poets and artists would
seek me out to discover what
they were doing next—like
moving to L.A. where the look
of neon at that magic time of
day when the sun goes down
became a new obsession that I
found I didn't need the old
drugs to dig or enjoy or even
comprehend—I got to lend my obsessions out again
until I saw them on the screen
and heard them on the radio—
and I thought this is a funny
way to go—I'm out here learning
how to grow beyond the petty
drives that drove me into self-
obsessive possessiveness with
all that mattered to the point
of being shattered into billions
of bits of the memories I thought made up my life—
and then I thought there is
no way to mend myself I need
some help—and I got it—
I'm still the same obsessive fighter
for the dreams I'll never give up
whether you still see them in my eyes
or not—I got to possess what I'm
obsessed with just as much as ever,
to the point I want to be it—I
wanted to be that painting by Bonnard,
or the rain, or the glowing traffic light
or neon bright against the darkening blue—
or you—and I was and am—I always knew that—yes,
I am the obsession, and I am the possession,
and I am the time that's being done—

and that's just life as I unfold it
day by day and not some universal
contest to be lost or won—I'm
grateful every night for the bed I sleep in
and every morning for the sun or clouds or rain—
which doesn't mean I'm not ambitious
or that being with you is not the most
delicious way of spending whatever time is mine—
hey, I'm grateful for all my dreams and visions—
especially the one called you—
but I also love the way I'm
letting go of having to possess
all that I'm obsessed with and
letting time do me for a change—
speaking of change I'd like to be possessed for awhile
and be the object of somebody
else's style not just this
not-so-neutral-Jersey-cowboy-hipster-
nice-guy-but-don't-get-too-close-cool-
master-of-my-universe in which I'm
always generous and never act out of spite—
I know that ain't quite the way you see it,
so straighten me out, get a ruler
and draw new lines, make me climb
your mountains and ford your streams
until your dreams are mine and I'm
in them with you, especially
the ones that come true, which
they all do if we let them—
we just might not be there to get them when they do—
so com'ere let's drop a tear
and swap a kiss and reminisce
about the way we want it to be,
until we can see it so clearly
nothing can keep us from getting there—
even when we already are—

you know the dream—it's
the one where we're finally truly understood—
understand?

THAT FEELING WHEN IT FIRST GOES IN

"I am the poet of sin" said Whitman,
or something like that in my head.
I want you in my bed right now more
than I want all the junk in all the
stores you can't resist. You kept on
insisting that you needed to be alone.
Like Garbo supposedly never said.
I have been alone in this bed since
the last time you were here. I remember
the first woman to call me "dear" just
like in the movies. I wasn't sure I
liked it. The few girls who did that
back when the movies really were the
movies, sounded too American or maybe
Protestant or something foreign from
the Irish-American women I grew up around.
Or even the few Blacks. None of them
called their men "dear." That was
something from *Father Knows Best*,
back when television was really tele-
vision. What an idea, to tell a
vision, sort of another description
of poetry. Yo, check it out, here I
am again at the typewriter speeding
two-fingered around these keys, trying
to locate the place where the motion
toward life originates in me, not you,
because we're through, at least until

we get to that time when we can be
friends, as if I didn't already have
enough beautiful women friends in my
life who once were lovers until they
discovered I'm not the man of their
dreams, I'm just an old guy in jeans
who talks like a kid because he never
did get it that all everybody wants is
a man to decide what should be done
and then to go ahead and do it—
not sit around and write poems about
how empty the bed is without you—No shit.

I OVERWHELMED HER WITH MY NEED

I couldn't help it.
This feeling in my chest
of more than emptiness,
like a vacuum sucking my spirit, my soul,
my personality, my character,
my life away . . . without her.
I placed my life and my will in her hands,
turned them over to her care.
The same mistake I always make,
because the rush is always so incredibly
satisfying when that first fluttery
female response at being dug so deeply
is expressed . . . but then, then,
it looks like pressure, like being
crowded, like maybe you ain't mister
perfect mister right mister fairhaired boy
mister cool mister strong and handsome and
the answer to her prayers after all.
You might just be mister weak sometimes,

mister needy, mister let me love you
every heartbeat for the rest of your life.
And they choke on that, they lose their
breath for the first time in a scary way,
not that orgasmic exciting ecstasy way,
and they don't want it,
they want to push it away
so they can breathe, because
they don't need you that bad,
they can't afford to: this is the new world
and they are the new girls
and they got some better things to do
real soon with maybe better people
and you're less-than again,
you're not-good-enough again,
you're the sprinter who passes everybody else
for the first few days and then
can't keep up, get weak and wobbly
and need somebody to lean on,
only love ain't about leaning yet,
it's got to be going on for awhile,
or maybe it just can't be that way anymore,
it's too much to ask in the modern world,
we're talking financial insecurity
and career moves and confidence and
courses in ways to become the best you
you've ever been even if that means
leaving some people behind,
you've done it too, all your life,
maybe it's karma, maybe it's nostalgia,
maybe it's what goes around comes around
as you watch the guys on top
pursue her too and all you can do
is float away on the flood
of your own self pity and lack of control
'cause those feelings in your heart

are part of what makes you honest,
only they don't want honest
they want righteous they want better-than
they want stand up and be a man and
get your emotional insecurities under control
and out of sight for the duration,
'cause this is war boy
and we got a lot more battles to fight
and if you're gonna lay down and whine
and ask for mercy and stroking and
semi-adoration like you got from those
lesser girls, you're in the wrong outfit,
you belong behind the lines
not out front here where they make heroes
out of guys who don't succumb
to the fear and fatigue and frustration
and false interpretations
of a reality nobody will ever really know
let alone understand anyway . . .
Know what I mean?

I'M AFRAID I'M GONNA START

crying & never stop—

I'm afraid I'll never cry—

from FOOLS FOR LOVE

and light and music
fools for God and essences of lives
fools for

food and sex and highs inexplicable
fools for lavender and shades of gray and
billions of whatever can be counted that way
fools for missions improbable, ventures into
the unknown of each other's wills
fools for gladiolas and roses and ferns that grow
like weeds and are weeds for all we know
that can be said to be
the fools we see when we begin to see
as only bargain hunters do
when on a spree in some far-off commercial market
for the wares we spared our hearts when what we wanted
was to be the fools of a love
so grandiose that most people would die before embracing—
but we aren't most, we are the rest
that were left to be the fools I grew up loving
when I thought of Saint Francis and his love
of poverty and every living creature and was known
for such overtures to nature that
no one understood but were impressed with anyway
even me—even when I dropped away
from all things Catholic I had grown up with
he still figured as my mentor in some unarticulated way—
"God's Fool" they called him, as I wouldn't mind being called
today, because I see this God as the spirit of the universe,
and how much I'd rather be a fool for that force than
for the ones that force me to stoop to places not beneath me
but beneath the floor of discards that has been our undoing,
I mean the fool in the Tarot deck was who I always identified
with and the court fools and tribal fools who were always
granted the liberty to point out the foibles of emperors and
chiefs whose clothes were nonapparent like those at
the Oscars last night where I took so much delight in
Satyajit Ray's acceptance from a hospital bed in Calcutta
and his getting back at Ginger Rogers for not answering his
fan letter when he was young and still impressed with

Hollywood the way we all are when we're young and I
never don't want to be, not with the schemes and cynicism of
the bankers and their pimps but with the dreams and humanism
of the fools for love who would use the magic of the tribal
screen to imagine for us who we might be or become
even those of us who have no time to be because we are
so lost in others, even us fools for love which is just
another way of saying poets to my mind and heart and
way of starting over in the poem that has always been my
safest haven where a home can always be found for the
fools for love we might all be if we were left alone to be
whoever we were before they got ahold of us—

[. . .]

LOST ANGELS 2

The angel of fear and the angel
of self-consciousness, the
angel of never enough and the
angel of too fucking much,
the angel of nicotine and the
angel of caffeine, the angel of
New Jersey and the angel of
Colorado, the angel of nakedness
and the angel of covering up,
the angel of discontent and
the angel of serendipity, the
angel of loose and appropriately
sexy female energy and the angel
of overly flirtatious and
inappropriately seductive male
attention, the angel of too many
jokes and the angel of repressed

resentment, the angel of feeling
safe in the relationship enough
to make you think she might
leave it for you and the angel
of talent gone unrecognized,
the angel of no talent and
the angel of knowing how to
make money on that, the angel
of the unrelenting love jones
and the angel of music too
loud and acoustics too stupid
to hear someone sitting at
the same table, the angel of
being alone in the same old
crowd of other lonely people
and the angel of wanting to
be naked and turned on by
too many unavailable people,
the angel of not enough sleep
and the angel of too much
competitiveness, the angel
of unappreciation and the
angel of pride, the angel
of lost causes and the angel
of perfectionism, the angel
of communism and the angel of
children of '60s communes,
the angel of deceptive quietness
and the angel of deceptive good
looks, the angel of you can't
judge a book by its cover and
the angel of too many books,
the angel of rap and the angel
of funk, the angel of Aaron
Copeland and the angel of Elvis
Aaron Presley, the angel of
business enthusiasts and the

angel of Harley self-righteousness,
the angel of civilians and the
angel of the too hip, the angel
of geography and the angel of
pollution, the angel of lesbians
who like to be sexually dominated
now and then by politically
correct men and the angel of
gay male jocks, the angel of
unproduced scripts and the angel
of unknown history, the angel
of once where we all had been
and the angel of never getting
there, the angel of honoring
ones path and the angel of
divine dissatisfaction, the
angel of you and the angel
of me and the angel we run from
when the angel we become is
the unacknowledged star of
our universe and our universe
is changing too fast to grasp
with so little as the love we
forgot we had for all the
lost angels that watch over
us even when we don't believe—

LAST NIGHT

I got into a lot of fights
when I was growing up—
a couple a week until I was 22—
then I got married
to a girl I hardly knew—
it seemed at the time

like the right thing to do—
but until then I was so afraid
that you all thought I was afraid
that it filled me with a rage
so deep and blue nobody ever knew
who I was going to throw through
the nearest window—me or you—
a lot of broken glass in my past—
a lot of broken past in my glass
back then too—some of it wasn't
even true—like when I'd tell some
stranger all about you, and we hadn't
even met—in fact, we haven't
yet—even though last night I felt
my tongue slip through your lips again
until it found your tongue and the doors
of the universe shut behind them leaving
them all alone to do their tongue dance
and my brainwaves got lost in all that
sensuous darkness while somewhere outside
it I could smell your hair and feel your
solid softness filling my arms until we
were so close I could see out the back
of you and into the eyes of some buddies
I grabbed your behind to impress even
though I already knew there wasn't anything
more than kissing that we were gonna do
because that's all I wanted to—and it was
enough, like back in the '50s when I tried
so hard to be tough, even in my dreams where
I was always the star of all the teams and
won all the games for you—now the games
don't mean so much to me, but you still
do, only I always wake up wondering, who
the fuck are you?

ATTITUDE AND BEATITUDE

ah, it's a melancholy,
melancholy, melancholy
race I come from—
with "Sacred Hearts" all
suffering hanging over
our childhood beds and
even the redheads in our
past—grandma Rose
McBride from Tyrone—
or the red blood streaming
from my finger today when
I cut the flowers sent for
my birthday from a man
I hardly know & not
the woman I—my kids
are grown—I'm home
alone on my 48th birth
day watching—what?—
not you—you're dead
and all that's left are
these pictures of the people
you knew who I never
cared about—and the
kids who I did—and
me and you—that
blonde keeps getting a
little loaded and telling
me I'm white as if
I didn't know that—I
knew that long ago—
I'm so white the skin
on my stomach gives
off the glow of newly
fallen snow—as if I

might be cold or no
longer alive—but I
am—you aren't—or
all these things from
some earlier version
of my life—or someone
else's—oh tonight,
tonight, I wanted to
be alone—and I—
you can't even phone—
remember how we did?
there was a home there
once—I called it you
& you were so in love
with the gentle side
of what I remember
as rage—huh—that
page has crumbled—
it fell apart in my
hands—little spots of
red from where I cut
off the tip of my
finger with the
scissors I use to trim
the rose bush in
front of this house
where I live like a
widow on a small
pension that's running
out—and her?—I
haven't seen her since
before you—but
she's alive I'm sure—
back home in Costa
Rica with—I miss
her too—I miss you—

differently—and how can
they ever know what we
knew—or how many
dead there are inside my
heart & head to fill
this bed I still laugh
when I come in—and
the women sometimes
find that strange—or
scary—thank God some
find it nice or sexy or—
no—who cares—I laugh
to find out once again
I'm still alive!—me—
of all of us—I made
it all this way—my
forty-fucking-eighth
birthday—the lady
I laughed with last is
half my age and likes
it—why?—because I
don't demand too much—
because I have that
slow and gentle touch
I learned with you—oh
oh oh—sometimes
it's too slow—with all
the memories crowding
in between breaths—
God, help me make it
through the days—
the nights are easy—
I can be whoever
I am then—when
the lights go out and
so do I—stay up

tonight and keep my
spirit company—
alone again on purpose
but without delight—
I want my due, God,
from this world of
people I have nurtured
and inspired—I want
them to understand
how tired I am and
forgive me if I sometimes
seem distracted or
forgetful or pissed off—
it's only because I'm
thinking of you and
you and all the yous
I knew so intimately
who have passed—all
thinking they'd be
around long after me—
but see, I had to raise
my kids—and now I
want to watch them
go out into the world
and find out who they
are and maybe have
their own—so let me
stick around until my
kids' kids are all grown—
if that's possible to do—
and let me be the eyes
and ears and consciousness
of you, who went
before me & never knew
how life might have
turned out—this is how—

TURNING 50

It's like turning 21
only in reverse
—a milestone
not a millstone,
it could be worse,
I remember my
21st—my friends
gave me a big party—
I was the only white
guy there—by
the time they got
the cake together we
were all so wasted
we couldn't find the
candles, or light them,
or blow them out—
one of the guys
started to
cry & when our
hostess asked him why
he said because he was
sure I wouldn't see 22
the way I lived back then—
well, I guess I showed them

even if I am a little tired today—
it's not because I'm turning 50 okay?—
or because I celebrated yesterday,
or stayed up too late and got up too early
for the past few days, or because I
got a tattoo that's older than you
and that kind of stuff seems to matter
to the few who don't know yet that the
differences are there for enticement

and celebration, not to justify some
fear of the unknown—it's all knowable—
and I know I've said it before and it
seems kind of corny, even when I blame
it on Selby, but like he says, it's
all love and either we let fear get
in the way of that or not—*not* is
what I vote for—what I'm tired of
is the way that fear goes around from
one sad clown to another, beating each
other down for what somebody else did
to them—the sin we saw on that
video—which one depends on where
you're viewing it from, they say—but
I don't say that—I say somebody beats
up on that defenseless guy because
somebody else beat up on them once—
sounds too simple doesn't it?—I
know, it's more complex than that,
but I really don't care today—I've
watched a lot of people live and die
in my time, and most have been beaten
by someone or something at sometime or
another and some let it kill them and
some used it as an excuse to kill
somebody else and some never got over
it and some of us got over it again
and again but when your number's called
it don't matter where you been it
matters where you are, and I want to
be right smack in the middle of love,
the kind that comes from above and
makes everything possible . . .

WHERE DO WE BELONG
for Neal Peters, Terence Winch and John McCarthy

Passing through these hills, these lakes,
these fates I thought I had outwitted—
who am I here? in the land of my
fathers—this harsh wind & chill, the
sheets of rain lashing out like my
anger at meager perspectives on life
despite all the vistas the world has
forgotten—I am *myself*—the *himself*
of this life I'm given—& when the
rain clears—or goes soft—the land-
scapes pull my heart to peaks of
awe & wonder—how could this be?
so much beauty must be graced with
the living lace of showers, the veils
of a reality too God-like to endure—
ah—I'm happy—& confused—like a
lover returning after rejection & recon-
ciliation—what do I expect to find?
the answer to my dreams.

An uncle long dead—the "gentle"
one his wife compared me to—
his nose, his chin, his manly smile—
in this cousin "once removed" it
took me days to find—he once
lived in the same thatched
cottage my grandfather rose every
morning in, from the day he was
born until he left for distant
shores—& us—the family he would
have—the kids, in fear & arrogance,
rejecting what he was in all their
American striving—after what?

259

what we have now & find so
lacking in fulfillment we have to
slam & shoot & burn the mother-
fucker down before it's ours?—
it took me 50 years to find that
thatched roof cottage, uninhabited
for only four, still standing, not for
many more—& maybe me too.

Or him—this cousin Paddy—
69—a bachelor—the last of
"our Lallys" in County Galway where
I first went to see the famous bay
& was disappointed & excited all at
once—it was an August day but the
dampness & chill in the air made it
necessary for me to wear a coat, which
wasn't even enough when the wind
began to blow—dark clouds filled the sky—
rain fell sporadically—the water could
not have looked less inviting—darker
than any I've ever seen outside of dreams—
& choppy, like a major winter storm
was brewing, when everywhere else I
had just been—L.A., New York—my friends
& family were stewing in the end-of-summer
heat waves of our new world order
weather—but here, in Galway, sweaters
were the order of the day—& no way
would anybody be able to see through the
thick sky cover any moon going
down on any bay—

        & I had all I
could do to keep on my side of the
"highway," which meant any road big

enough for two cars to pass without
a heart attack, as I tried to get
away from the toy like streets of
Galway City, so narrow they were best
suited for donkey carts and the
proverbial wheelbarrow, not compact
cars like the one I'm having trouble
negotiating through this *faux* rush
hour when I accidentally bump a car
in front of me and out jumps a young
lady yelling things like "stupid" at
me & all I can do is roll down my
window & explain I'm not used to
driving on this side of the road
or car because I'm from America—
"Well, I'm not!" she shouts as she
shakes her head at I guess what
must be a rare occurrence, although
I can't see why since they all drive,
as McCarthy says, like Indians who
just got ahold of their first ponies.

& where are they all off to anyway
on an island not big enough to take
that long to reach the edges of—
nowhere, I discover, as they pass
me going 85 & I'm just trying not
to slide off into the hedges or
the stone walls that line these
country roads, because when I
come around the next bend, there
they are, backed up and waiting
patiently while someone drives
their cows on home, or stops to
chat up a neighbor—no honking
horns, no impatient scorn, no

guns drawn, just acceptance of
the situation—until it's time
to move again, & then they're
off, around blind curves with
little enough room for two cars
going opposite directions, let
alone a third trying to make
a move straight down the middle
at 85 or 90, & me still trying
to remember which side is mine.

& then there they are—the
"fields of Athenry" celebrated
in song and family legend—I
know my grandfather came from
nearby & wonder if these stone
walls and almost treeless views
were ones he knew, the rich
green meadows & pastures, the
sheep & cows & occasional bandy-
legged dog looking out on it all
as if it could care less about
the rest of the world, including
me passing by on my way to three
days of leads to "Lallys" who
are no relations—much gossip
of who married whom & church records,
only the wrong church, sending
me to suspicious farmers who
ignore the hand I extend until
they come to understand I don't
want anything more than the
lore of my family.

I get led on by one who comes off
like Richard Harris in *The Field*
the movie the folks I'm staying

with say is the one about their
country they found most real—
& so did I—that angry patriarch
so narrow-minded & mean & yet
somehow heroic, reminding me
of my grandfather & what I
remembered of a man who always
seemed to scowl & need a shave
& dress like a bum & have been
drinking, that stinking smell
of alcohol & old worn-for-years-
through-everything-that-mattered
clothes, still sturdy though,
like him the neighbors saw as the
local character, but to us he was
"Himself," the father of our clan.

And now here I am where he began,
following one false lead after another,
meeting available widows ten years
my senior, whose brothers point out
ruins of peasant huts they swear
is where my grandfather grew up,
the stones so tightly fitted, like
the walls all around this country,
"knitted" as they say, so that
even without mortar or cement they
can withstand water or contain
bulls, except the human ones—
the interlocking shapes & sizes
keeping out the wind & rain while
the thatched roofs equally as
intricate keep the water out too
& the warmth in—these places
fascinate me, each one could be
a place my grandfather knew.

I don't mind the dead ends
because they all lead to the
kitchens of farmhouses where
everyone seems ready to share
a bottle or some tea and an
anecdote about the ones now
gone across the sea, some never
known or long forgotten, their
children or grandchildren turning
up "back home" so many years later,
like me, here now, trying to uncover
what? the answer to my never being
able to identify with who I was
brought up with & wondering why—

But now I'm sharing some bread or
sandwiches or cakes when they
take me to the oldest living
memory in the neighborhood to ask
"Do you remember any Lallys
in these parts, ones who
went away?" & I say "In the
last century, late 1800s, he
died in 1956" and they reply
"That's not so long ago, someone
should know if he came back for
visits, as you say, now that'd
be something to remember then,
a Yank coming home in the '30s
or '40s would be an event, sure
it would"—& I could almost feel
myself relaxing, something old
& familiar in these scenes, not
just the fear I had of my Irish
grandparents but the closeness—
they were always there, right

down the street, waiting for me
to come & greet them as my mother
always made me do at least once a
week—I only wish I knew then
what I do now so I could have slowed
down those brief encounters &
maybe remember—what?—what
I think I'm feeling now—the
comfort & ease of being at peace
with who you are—I am.

When, through some unacknowledged
or too subtle for my eyes and ears
decision is reached and it's
time to go, no one remembering
my grandfather "Mike," someone
suggesting another little place with its
own name despite the fact that it isn't
on the map & all it means is a handful
of houses more or less close
by each other, and another
peat fire in the kitchen heating
stove, and the best chair, closest
to the heat, to be my place,
and there's no haste at all
to get on with their farmers day,
& I get the impression these
people would rather talk than
work anyway, & they'd rather
hear a poem recited than talk
& why recite a poem if someone
can sing a song all the way through—
they just know what they like best,
& it seems to be the articulation
of the human mind at rest & glad of it.

Finally I get in touch with "my
brother the priest" as we say,
who has lived in Japan these 30
years or more & who had once
come looking around here maybe
that long ago—he tells me
the place to look is called Bookeen,
another handful of houses where some
relatives lived but with a different
last name, having descended from one
of grandpa's sisters who stayed
behind, but there is no use
he says looking grandpa up in
the local church because our
Lallys had gone somewhere else,
the "Redemptorist monastery"
a few miles the other way—
& when I tell this to the man of the
house where I am staying, he says
"I know your man, I'm sure he's
related for his name is Lally &
he lives at Tallyho Cross—" (which
I later learn means crossroads)
"—not far from Bookeen but closer to
Esker"—the Redemptorist place—

& he takes me to see this Paddy
Lally in an old "two story" as
they call them when they are,
"too dilapidated" to invite me
in, he tells my host, so he comes
out to the car instead and gets
in the back and we shake hands
and I see something familiar in
the strength of his nose and
unshaven chin and the look in

his eye and even the way his old
clothes are worn & thick with
accumulated what can I call it
but life? It's hard to describe
without sounding the way "the
Americans" did when they talked of
my grandfather, only worse,
like a homeless person might
look now, not even that good
in a way, what can I say? he
wears a suit coat that has seen
better days a long long time ago—
obviously he works in it,
lives in it, maybe every day—
but he has a full head of hair
and as much on his upper cheeks
as if he had forgotten to shave
there—later I will discover
in a book that it was traditional
for the Irish men of the West to
let their face hair grow and only
shave it for special occasions
but never the hair in their nose
or low on their throat or upper
cheeks, a sign of their connection
to the past, their fathers and
theirs, but now he only looks
like he had missed the hairs
a long time ago—

                    Anyway, I
say my grandfather's name was
Michael, like mine, & my father's
name was James—he says his
father's name was Frank & I say
I had an uncle Frank, & he says

his grandfather's name was Pat
& I say my great grandfather's name
was that, and the other man points
out that my grandfather came back
for visits & wouldn't he remember
that and Paddy says "Ah, it was a
long time ago" and looks me in
the eye and with a sort of sigh
says, "There was a priest here
once from America, he lived in
Japan, but I never met him"—
"That'd be my brother" I say—
"You know you can go over to
Galway City and find a book on names
that'll tell you all you'd want to
know about the Lallys, not us though,
but about the name—ah, but
what's in a name" he goes on "a
rose by any other name would
smell as sweet, wasn't it Mister
Shakespeare said that—" he doesn't
really ask, a kind of glow in
his eye as though he's trying to
put one by me as I smile & reply
"That's so, Shakespeare said that,
and maybe you're right, I'm content
to just be here, near where I know
my grandfather came from—it's enough."

& then he looks at me again, as if
seeing something else & says real low,
as though throwing it away, "I remember
Mike" & the hairs on the back of
my neck stand up—"he used to take
Patsy Lally into Athenry to the pubs,
Patsy liked his drink, Mike was

alright . . ." and I am home again in
my heart, this is the start of
something bigger than I remembered
or expected, because it is so simple
& so every day, as we sit there in
my host's little car, Paddy in the back,
the two of them sharing a smoke, Paddy
quiet again, and looking at his big,
gnarly hands and not at us, as my host
begins to figure out the dates & how
it is we are or might be related,
Paddy & me, ". . . aye, then Paddy's
father is your grandfather's youngest
brother which would make Paddy here
you father's first cousin & your
first cousin once removed . . ."

We all mull over that, me looking out
at the incredible display of clouds
that jam up the Irish sky in ever
more complicated ways, creating that
just-before-a-storm-begins deep silvery
light I always loved when I was a kid
& still do & would always stop
whatever I was doing to sit and stare
as I'm doing now, this is me, doing
what I always loved to do, attracted
to this view as if I knew it & these
two men who seem to know it, & therefore,
maybe me, too—& finally our host says,
"You know, Michael lives out
in California near Hollywood
& works sometimes in the fill-im business"
& without missing a beat Paddy says "I
hear that business isn't doing so good
these days" & then goes on to say "Maybe

you'd remember who said, after shaking
hands on a deal, 'This contract isn't
worth the paper it's written on'" &
I smile & say "Sam Goldwyn," having read
maybe the same source he had,
& Paddy nods into his gnarled & cupped
hands & the cigarette smoke they
seem to embrace "Aye, that'd be Mister
Goldwyn said that—would you like to
see where your grandfather lived?"

The place is called "Tallyho Cross"
because it's where they once kept
the kennels for the hunting dogs
back when the landlords ruled
this land & my grandfather's clan
lived in the thatched-roof cottage
Paddy grew up in & takes us to now—
someone else lived there until four
years ago, and now it's on its way
to slow decay or what they call being
"knocked" for "knocked down" I guess,
like all the ruins that dot this
countryside, they don't mean knocked
down by human hands, that would be
"tumbled," an older term from harsher
times when that's what the landlord
and British would do to those whose
meager potato crops might fail &
the law of the land would prevail,
being he who owns it gets to eat &
he who doesn't gets to starve or
somehow get away to foreign lands—

But on this day I have returned from
one and as I stand before this ancient

peasant place where my grandfather
first faced the life he would live,
I remember a song my father would
sing as he shaved & gave himself his
morning "Jewish bath," meaning splashing
water on himself from the stopped-up
tiny bathroom sink while we all waited
our turn, dreading the puddles we would
find but kind of digging the lines of
the music lilting our way from behind the
bathroom door, which were more or less:
"Oh my name is" I always thought he next
sang "Paddy Lee" but maybe it was "Pat
Lally" and went on "I'm an Irishman you
see, I was born in County Galway, Tallyho—"

I always thought that last was some
sort of exclamation, not a place, but
here it is, the ancestral home, not
even a bone's throw from where the kennels
once stood & now I stand, & Paddy
explains how the old thatch roof cottage
won't last much longer because when
the fire goes out—a flame that
may have burned unrelentingly for
centuries, can you imagine?—
the moisture seeps in and begins to
make the place uninhabitable &
slowly it begins to rot and then
cave in, but not before I made it
here to see it & to stand before it
on the dark green grass fed by these
manic clouds and it all feels so
familiar in ways I would have dismissed
if you'd told me all this just days
before—& then there was more.

More time just being ourselves, alone,
together there, in that damp crisp
brilliantly pure of pollution air,
until Paddy says "Would you like to
see the house where John Huston
lived?" & of course I say sure—
It's nearby, one of the old "big
houses" that once was the landlords—
an Englishman lives there now but
that doesn't stop my host from driving
up the long driveway as if it was
his own, or parking right before the
front door so we can get a good long
look—& Paddy tells a story of
the way it was in the days of the
landlords, when my grandfather was a
boy, when two boys, much like he
must have been, decide to ambush the
landlord on his way home, so they
wait by the road for him to pass
as he does every day, only two hours
after he should have come the one
turns to the other & says "I hope
the poor man hasn't had an accident"
—& the humor in that, if you can't
see it is, that he meant it, & so
did his friend, as Paddy said "That's
the way they were then" & sometimes
still are, because they would shoot
the man just the same—oh what's in
a name—

For the next few days Paddy takes me
around to meet others who might remember
my grandfather or more lore about the family
than he seems to care about but thinks I do—

like the 92-year-old woman whose memory
would be the longest in that small
place—her name is Rose like my
grandmother's & she has a face that
glows with health & interest & a
sparkle in her eye that makes me think
she's being flirtatious—she's in
fine shape, as most of them seem to be,
despite the fatty ham they call bacon
& rashers & tons of bread & jam & quarts
of strong tea—in fact, she moves &
speaks & remembers local history like
the women back in L.A. who work out &
run & meditate half the day & are only
20- or 30-something—she lives alone
across the road from her daughter &
that daughter's schoolaged farmer sons
& schoolteacher daughter & another one
who is a "scholar" too, as they call
all students here—they all seem
caught up in the details of their
history & more, the international farm &
political sccnc & their place in all that—

I'm surprised & delighted at how well
read they all seem to be—especially
Paddy—who is quiet, & much like a
man who lives alone, in the kitchens
of these homes he takes me to where
he is nonetheless treated with great
respect—as a "good man" a "decent
man" who never did anyone harm, but
sometimes did them good—& it seems
to be understood that dress &
appearance mean nothing in this
neighborhood—although the kids

look hip enough when they get
dressed up to go dancing around 10—
that seems to be the style—
stay up late if you can & have a
good time & nobody will mind because
what else is life for but to sing
& dance & drink & eat & talk like
you didn't care where the next dollar
or pound is coming from, even if some
of the talk would make you think
they do—although my host, a man
my age but with four kids still at
home, the one where I'm staying, says
"Ah, the rich don't seem happy though,
now do they Michael?" & what can I say,
never really having been that way—
rich—myself, &—happy? I'm not
sure I even know what it means, though
it seems to be coming clearer as I sit
among these people maybe I can call my
own—

I could have stayed all night
in every country kitchen
Paddy took me to—or sat in the
car or waited out the rain in a
cow shed while he smoked & we
both lived in our heads & if I
spoke he would always reply with
a quote, not in any arrogant
show off way, but kind of shy,
as if to say, now what about
this, doesn't this apply? that
somebody else said—& it always
did—the man quoted Bhudda
& Montezuma to me when I mentioned

stuff that had to do with peace
or Mexico—how did he know?—
this man who lived alone in the
middle of nowhere with no car,
just an old well-used bike, the few
neighborhood boys helping him out
by mowing the land around his
house so he could get in and out
to the road & him helping
others with this & that down in
the fields & the bogs in his old
dark-stained suit coat & unshaven
face & big gnarly hands & manly
smile—I fell in love with his
way & his manner & the fact that
he obviously was as addicted as I
am to words on the page as they
express worlds in the minds & the
lives of others so far from us—

I never knew—my father with his
seventh-grade education tried so hard
to be American he withdrew from
all that had to do with books,
except the Catholic ones, & I
somehow got the impression the people
I came from were illiterate & I
was the anomaly & would feel
fucked up for wanting to read &
write poetry & be who I am instead
of what my father thought America
wanted him to be—but now I know,
Paddy told me, that his grandfather,
my grandfather's father Pat, loved
to read, & had a special fondness
for history, as so many here do,

not knowing who the latest "star"
in the USA might be, or caring,
but remembering some long gone
ancestral feat of only local renown
or the deeper nuances & subtleties of
the European story that never quite
reached this far, the very edge of
that world, facing the Atlantic that
I stick my hands into before I get
on the plane to go, the wind still
blowing & the rain coming & going,
and the water deep & dark with that
metallic hue, but it is unexpectedly
warm, as I am too despite the damp
& chill, I'm thinking of Paddy & the
moments spent alone, together, quiet,
or sharing some profound thought of his
he puts off on someone he has read—
& what he said when I asked if there
was anything I could send from "the
States" & he replied "what would I
need from there—" & I hesitatingly
suggest a book, and he lets me know,
as he already did a few days before,
that he's only studying "the one book
now, for my final exam—" with that
manly smile, unafraid of who he is
or who I might be or am—ah, it was
a grand visit, as they might say, &
now I want to run away before I stay
forever . . .

OF

(Quiet Lion Press 1999)

from OF

People say things in their enthusiasm, and you
hear them in your need.

People—snow—the cold—
I forgot how the cold could heal you—
how soothing the snow can be—
I just want to live with true humility—
which somehow the snow falling teaches me—
I used to want to make you see
everything that mattered to me—
now—I just want to
let it be—
a part of—

I was a good looking man
I lived the life of a good looking man
sometimes that meant things—
some things—came easy—
sometimes that meant I was underestimated—
my anger—my fear—my need—my worth—
& sometimes that meant
I thought I had to do more than you
always

yeah sometimes is sometimes *always*—
& you are sometimes me—
& let it be means letting go—
& humility means be real & go slow—
& once is enough when it's not even there
& sometimes *everybody* looks black
& *everybody* looks white—
& I've been a poet *all my life*
& it still means I have to
prove it—

People say things
from their enthusiasm
and I hear them
with my need

again & again
I miss the ones
I let go—*of*—
I wanted to be a man
with few regrets & no excuses
but but but but—

when I hear myself say
"my first wife"
it sounds like somebody
else's life—I never meant
to be that kind of man—
I was this handsome
smart guy with an
eye for *nothing* that
wasn't *true romance*
so how did I end up
alone with past lives
and ex-wives I never
intended to have—
& not even have any
good novels or plays
out of the whole deal—
yet—
yet—
I'm forty-fucking-seven
this ain't no game—
this is heaven—
yes—
because *the man* said
"the kingdom of heaven is within"

& what's coming out of there
is this so
this must be heaven or
the verbal expression
of

[. . .]

the other night
after our hike
in the new fallen snow
knee deep in places
across the pond
and up the hill to
the top and beyond
where she showed me
another of her special
places & we paused
to take in the
beauty & surrender to
the silence & the
snow laden trees so
majestic & living hip—
accepting it all—even
their fall which can
only lead to ours—
their meditative presence
one day-long breath
& nightly exhalation
that frees us to breathe
that frees our breath—
the memory of what
that means, of what
that meant, left me
on the verge of tears
when we got back but

only because I felt so
grateful for my kids
& the overwhelming love
I feel for them I *have*
for them I *am* for them
no way to compare that
experience with any other
just the reality of the
love saying to myself
I love my children—now
grown—so much—the
world is not enough in
all its awesome calm &
beauty when approached
on days like this in
settings like these to
compare—it goes beyond
the new walls of galaxies
they keep finding out there—
beyond that sense of
wonder & gratitude that
makes us stand & stare
at natural gifts like
trees in winter snow
and the way a movie
star can glow even
in her own home

[. . .]

I couldn't sleep til 3—
& when I woke I could see
the trees & hills we hiked in
out the window of the
room I'm in—& closer in
the biggest pines with

branches longer than this
room the lowest ones sweeping
the snow like edges of their
skirts reminding me of women
I never knew except in my head—
she calls them "the three sisters"
these majestic but sensual pines—
my heart climbs them like a
bird in love every time I look
at them in search of the word
to describe these ecstasies of—
"of"—

[. . .]

It's January & outside there's
still ten inches of snow but
in here there's a fly that
just won't go to sleep or
away—it keeps buzzing
& crashing into the lamp—
why?—why do I feel this
will be the year of more
death—in my family—the
one I grew up with at home
and in the home of my
heart—Barbara Stanwyck—
Ava Gardner—tough broads
who I should have known—
I thought I married one twice—
"tough broads"—but they weren't
so tough—and they weren't so
nice—sometimes—and neither
was I—and neither is she—
or you—of who—"whom"—
will too be in the tomb

of memory some day—
I remember thinking
I was just a sexier
Jesus—only it all
depended on my hair—
I'd look in the mirror
and say—hey you look
so good today you better
get out there and share
it—with who?—you—
only you couldn't bear
what you thought was
conceit and I couldn't
find that way that some
heroes have of being
full of themselves and
endearing about it—
so then I'd have to
shout it out & turn
into some kind of fool
—a tool of my own
confused emotions tearing
around inside me—up
and down the stairs from
my heart to my head
like a cat you almost
wish dead because you're
in bed trying to get
your last night of sleep
in the Berkshires and
it won't let you, so
full of— [. . .]

I just don't have the heart
for it anymore—sometimes
I can't find myself in any

of it—I don't mean not
fit I mean not there—as
if my shame & fear have the
power to make me disappear even
from my own memory—see—
I'm back in L.A. again—but
this time it's a *cold* wind that's
blowing the brown air away
today & there's no way my
life will stay mean to me—
It's St. Valentine's day anyway
& I got a date with a stranger
I want to break—for the
first time in my life—there's
no one I really want to take
out tonight—I'd like to
just spend it at home—
alone—writing this poem
and reading it—I hope that's
not a sign of—

[. . .]

& lo, he went into the
valley of death, the desert
of loneliness, where the people
were old & nurtured a deep
and cranky bitterness & hurt
like a child alone in the world
& he said things in his enthusiasm
& they heard him with their
need to be left alone & right—
& in the night it was cold
but in the day the light was old
& the tones were deep with the
memory of the world created

alone with itself & the tones
of creation that immortalized
death as if it was her child
but when she smiled it was
an old lady on her toes as
though she still could dance
& then she did and it enhanced
this valley with a meaning
no one could have thought of
except her & for 20 years
every Friday, Saturday &
Monday nights her aging
city high bred body took
flight on the stage *she*
had created & with all
her might she transformed
the thoughts inside their
graying heads to visions that
the lives they fled were
richer than they had remembered—
& he too felt transformed
as though his mistakes were
signs of an awkward grace
this place entranced & made
light of—

[. . .]

"of" is the barometer of
my trust in you in all
this—& I do trust you—
obviously—how else explain
me still playing this poetry
game—going on fifty—
with all expectation of fame
behind me—
sort of

[. . .]

night of the living airports—
Kennedy to LaGuardia for
another missed connection
that was 3 hours late but
once we were in the air in
this "flying crate" that
held only a handful of us
stuffed together like eggs in
a cardboard carton & I still
felt great sitting behind the
pilots watching their instruments
glow in the night especially
the altimeter on the far right
spinning as we climbed to the
right height for the bulk of
the flight & then spinning
wildly the other way as we
descended into Albany where
my "little girl" now 22 waited
with her "beau" as my sisters
still used to say when I was
a kid sort of kidding with
that term from another day
the way my mother & grand-
mother did with them when
they'd tease about it being
"Thursday" & how that was
"beau night" & they didn't
have a date & therefore would
grow up to be old maids who
everybody knew just sit
& wait for the "beau" who
never comes like in that Katherine
Anne Porter story my friend
directed once for PBS where

I didn't play the "beau" although
she told me I had eyes that
would glow through the screen &
make this character work in
ways no other man could—but—
we've all heard stuff like that
& wondered why we ended up
without the fate those compliments
led us to believe was our right,
like my sisters did when they
finally went out on "beau
night" & caught the guy of their
dream, or maybe someone else's
so they wouldn't end up old
maids like Dustin Hoffman
almost did in "Tootsie"—& me
here in the Ramada Inn in
Bennington Vermont not too
far from where I began this
"poem" in Monterey, Mass where
she & he are getting ready to drive
over tonight to hear my daughter
sing for us in ways that
have had her "depressed" for
days out of fear she won't
get the "feelings" right the
way her instructors have
taught her to & pointed
out to her when she
doesn't—& I'm here
trying to think of something
I can do to make it
easier for her besides laying
in bed writing down what's
going on in my head in
ways that tie it all

together with the theme
of—

[. . .]

she called to say she
was thinking about her
mother all day & really
sad she wasn't there to
see her "triumph"—well,
that's my word—she was
just sorry her mother
couldn't live to hear
her sing for an audience
that loved it—& I heard
the sadness of my own
heart—in my daughter's—
& I don't know what to
do or say to make it
go away—she says
she finally feels like an
"adult" now—& I guess
that means I must be
too—this way
we have of—

[. . .]

& then tonight there was a fight
between two women like the old days
on the street only this was a poet &
her one time friend while mine
stayed behind & I couldn't stop
thinking about *all* these beautiful
"Black" women & the ways they wake
me up to the full spectrum of

possibilities—oh shit I wish I
still played horn—I taught my
cousin after I taught myself—
a way to make 50 more cents a
week on top of the money from
my paper route—I already played
trumpet & piano & sang & I
knew I was gonna go down
as the best, the baddest,
the most def, the saint of
music that told the truth—
I see how it turned out
so far—no saint—but
now & then in touch with
an angel inside—not the
angel of truth—too elusive
& perfect for most of us—
but not the angel of fear
either—or of lust or of
hesitation or of bluff or
of anger or hype or of meanness
& pride & ego & judgment—
not even the angel of
love, as much as I try—
or of grief or relief or even
rhyme—no,—but maybe
in time the angel of—

"of"

"The whole struggle is to squeeze into that public record some tiny
essence of the perpetual inner melody."

—Henry Miller (*Plexus*)

some tiny essence
of

IT'S NOT NOSTALGIA

(Black Sparrow Press 1999)

IT'S NOT NOSTALGIA—IT'S ALWAYS THERE

for Harris Schiff

they're so good to
look at, standing
in the bath tub,
towel around the
hair, powder in
hand, making all
the soft stuff
softer—
      there's only
them & us & the
others, but the others
don't count, except
when they're always
getting in the way—

once outside of
Greenville, South Carolina,
in 1962, two black guys
picked me up hitchin
on the highway drunk
at 3AM & after some
jiving & juicehead
boasts & fantasies
they took me to some
old shack—woke up the
grumbling ancient black lady
who sold the "dog bite"
& watched me down a
big kitchen tumbler full
& then smile before I passed out

In Greenville I played

piano at "The Ghana"
—"the South's largest
colored resort" with
a troupe that did the
Southern Soul circuit
—Baby June & the
Swinging Shepherds—15
performers—musicians &
dancers—June played the
trumpet & sang & was a
tough dude but affectionate
& protective boss—I met
him when he got salty
at my white presence
& I, pretending to ignore it,
asked him what the
name of one of the foxy
dancers was cause I had
to meet her she was so
fine—eventually he
hired me to be the crazy
white boy piano player
running onto the stage with
the rest of them—screaming
in sequined "waiters jackets,"
cummerbunds, crazy colored
show clothes doing a crazy
colored show—with one crazy
white boy pounding
the ivories, standing up,
jumping, dancing while
I comped those chords
and felt the joy of
being my own love
affair with music as
the romance of my air—

the audiences loved it—
I would out sblib the
sblibs & stay in the
background to do it
cause in fact I couldn't
hold a musical candle to
those wonderful motherfuckers

I wish I had hung on to
that outfit—
                    Sidney
Bechet was corny to me
then—though like "Pops"
he was great anyway—
now I can fuck to the music of both,
digging how close they
came to turning it all
around with just their
sound—shit—aint
that what the ladies
do to me & you?—
turning us around too?—

Mayday means a lot to me
—processions with a
statue of Our Lady &
the girls in white dresses
scattering flowers all
the way—speeches by
the priests against the
Commies who were
having their own parades—
and theirs all started in
Chicago & the fight for
the 8-hour-day—ours in

the forests of Europe &
the worshipping of May
as the start of the good
times of Spring & Summer
—fucking in the woods
all day—

     dreaming—
like
you in the Southwest
where I'd be so scared
& was when the sheriff
& his boys stopped me
outside Needles in my
van looking for the
Manson family &
suspecting us!—my
hippie friends & wife
& baby—

     guns drawn—
"everybody out with
your hands up!"

—where's Alice & her
bigtime Needles father?

nobody here but us
& these hungry looking
special deputies—I'm
so cold I stick my hands
in my bell bottoms
& some nervous kid's
gun starts shaking
at me!
    "get'em
up!"—& I do—
holy shit—they mean

it—I'm the father—
the owner of the van—
the one who sensed the
trouble coming before
the guy driving—I
demand a fucking
explanation—
                    "we're
looking for some hippie
murderers—now get
back in this thing &
get the fuck outa
here"—
                    you fucker
—I'm a taxpayer &
one time I ran
for sheriff myself—
                    only I'm
also soft & sensitive
& tired of all the
rough stuff—I'm
going home—
                    only
that's been 24
places in the 18 years
since I left my first home
for good—
                    she's outa
                    the tub
                    & into
                    my life
                    again &
                    this is the
                    one I want
                    to stay in—

it's your book did it
Harris—
                 so distant
          from my life
                    but—
          goddamit I
            love *the truth*

as we see it

unfolding our moments alone

to share

just out of the Air Force
in 1966 walking down
the main street of a
midwest farm & college
town a bunch of local
boys drive up to where
me & my wife are
strolling & start calling
me names I thought
I'd left behind—"What!?"
I yell, half an ice
cream popsicle in my
hand, the wrapper in
my other hand, both
out a few inches from
my sides—unthreatening
alone with my bride
of two years—I'm 24
& glad to be free of
court martials & brown
shoe reactionaries riding
herd—or trying to—on

me—& now these cow
town boys are piling
out of their old Chevie
to my amazement
not believing they really
were cursing at me—
I dont even know them!
I think—nobody would
take this kind of chance
in a city—I might
be *packing a piece*!
ready to dust these
dudes off the earth—
only they been watchin
TV too & one big blond
boy punches me right
in the face—only I dont
go down, I just bounce
back a little on my
feet while he looks
surprised & I drop my
popsicle & paper &
go crazy—grab him
by the hair and
start banging his
head on the fender
of a nearby car—
another, older guy
jumps on my back
yelling "Leggo my
brother" & me screaming
back, not letting go,
"Whadda ya mean,
let go? He just *hit*
me!"—fraternity jocks
& their dates are out of

the local bars to see
the commotion & out
of the Chevie comes
the smallest & oldest
guy—older than me—
maybe as old as I am
now—35—& he coaxes
the boys back into the
car & I see there's four
of them—goddamn!—
I'm glad it's the main
street!—they pull
off and as they do
the one who hit me
leans out & curses me
again—just then a
cop walks up—my
wife, almost hysterical
starts screaming at him
to do something about
what just happened—
he listens then looks at
me & says "Well, with
hair like that, whadda ya
expect?"—& walks
away—Lee cursing *him*
all the way—

—at home I check the
mirror—it looks
worse—much worse
than it feels—it's
all swollen & cut
& a black & blue &
yellow eye for sure—
my first one—all

the fights & scuffles
& getting 86'd—proud
of my clean face even
if I'm skinny—now
I'm proud of this—
I was just letting my
hair grow cause I was
so happy to be free of
the A. F. regulations—
still in my pointy-toed
shoes & tight pants—
I didn't know I was
part of a movement—
but now I got my
badge—the next
meeting I went to
about Viet Nam I gave
a little rap on being
an ex-serviceman
getting beat up by
kids who hadn't even
voted or paid taxes or
been drafted yet—I
was a big hit—and
it was all true—
I meant it—my
face was fucked up
from it—my fellow
anti-war activists
were impressed—I needed
a way to remember
being fast with your
hands wasn't always
the answer—any more

I take her picture

with her hair still
wet & tangled &
it's sexy & different
& all about how we
see things—not in
the magazine ads
or latest fads—punk
or chic or Soho elite—
it's about how dis-
tracted she is & tense
—her father's dying
like the rest of us
only he knows when
or about when & is
fighting with nothing—
the words of strangers—
promises—treatments—
operations—only to
delay or maybe
not even that useful—maybe
only to offer the appearance
of stalling the effects of
what we know will get
some of us—the epidemic
of cancer—industrial
civilization's answer to
our polluting the rest
of life & the world's
natural forces—I don't
mean anymore with
that than my own
frustration & anger—

        shit—
it's like
Mayday—

             a call for
             help—
the Haymarket riot—
all the dead workers
(Mayday 1937 in Colorado
—the film of those
cops arriving at the
strikers picnic to open
fire on unarmed men,
and women, and
children—all that
death—deliberate &
against *us—our
kind*—
             continues—
and us
against   each other—
             your book again
                 Harris—
   "running for cover"
she covers her frustrations
with the rituals of covering
her body only to uncover
it soon enough to lose
it—or so I hope—
& believe—for a while
with mine—
                 Ted says his
                 "bye bye Jack"
                 telegram
aint the same
as Duchamp's to Picabia—
he's right of course—
it's never the same—
Winch is an orphan—
you're an orphan now—

me too—& this isn't
even her "real" father—
it's her "step-father"—
only the only one she
knows—& she loves
him—& he's dying—&
taking some time to do it
in—the changes making
him mad, depressed, dis-
tracted, determined, deadly—

shit—does all this "art"
really do anything to help
me outwit my fate?—I
wanna think I'm great—
& sometimes do—& some-
times you & others—
like her & not only for
me—but her father?—
what can he tell me?—
what can I do for
him?—what does it matter
to either of us?—with
her between us & death
so close—I don't
wanna die for a long
time & when I do I
want it to be gentle—
but I know there aint
shit I can do—my
grandmother would say
"If you're born to be
shot, you'll never be hung"
I wish we knew—
                    only
he knows & it must be

driving him crazy—it's
getting to her—& that's
getting to me—&
into this & therefore to
you—who knows what
I'm talking about that's
why I'm "talking"—not
"walking" like I sometimes
do—I mean in my work—

her work—it moves me like
the books I love—including
yours—never do—her
music especially—is that
enough?—to live with &
love & be loved by a
person who creates music
that few get to hear but
me & it moves me beyond
my greatest expectations
for any art?—is this
the Paradise they sing
about in *Saturday Night
Fever* or Reznikoff
wrote of in his Adam
& Eve in the contemporary
city—New York in the
'30s?—poem? I read in
the late '50s & recognized
(so have in me still as
I will yours & all I ex-
perience that shocks me
with its clarity—I *love*
to *see* the edges *and* the
blurs—I'd like to be in
Frank O'Hara's mind when

he's drunk & in love & the
city is out of focus but
gorgeous & his—when he
wrote those things—some
of them—I was drunk
too & in love & wandering
the same streets—a kid—
away from Jersey & home—
immersed in my romantic
self-pity & incredibly in-
telligent perceptions about
life & wages of concern &
sensitivity—it was the
'50s—you were in the
Bronx maybe?—or on
the same Manhattan
streets—I slept in the
park, walked in the
rain, was afraid of
anyone as graceful &
erudite as O'Hara or
I can be sometimes now—
& she—
she was getting to know
her new dad—jealous of
him & his son—she was
a little kid already
planning her escape—
while we were practicing
ours—
        this time three
        years ago I came
        back—to the
        city—for good—
(drove my Toyoto back to
D.C. to my ex-wife's

house—who hasn't driven
in 15 years—& gave her
the car keys & title—letting
my license expire—through
with my "ace" driving days—
& I loved driving in the
city—that's what I'd do
now—if it was then—
drive around for a few
hours, shifting gears hard
& fast, outflanking
traffic, judging tight
spaces like a cat, feeling
the limits with my
shoulders as if I were
the car—I loved driving
—making love to the
street with my body-
machine—but I love
so much else I had to
give it up—I was
coming out the other
end anyway brother
& dig it—we are too
often the ones who die
first or use it up fast
or never get to it—
not me—
I want to do it all
once as fast and intense as I can
& then move on—
                    but
I'm here now—back
where I started or
started starting—
& 3 moves later in 3 years

it's Mayday, the
anniversary of my
farewell to D.C. where
I "came out" not only
as a lover of men but
a lover of men who loves
women in all those ways
as well and did so
first and will always—
I dont know what that
means—it confuses me
too—but I know I feel
good about feeling good
about me & loving the
way she smells &
moves & feels & lets me
get close as I can—
I loved it sometimes with the men—
but not as easily—as
gracefully—as romantically
—that's it—there was too
much cynicism & con-
fusion there—& not just
dope—that's maybe
the thing I've clung to
most—turned on the
first time by a black
dude at the Figaro
Cafe—McDougal &
Bleecker—in 1959—I was
17—always in love—
romantically with
women—brotherly
with men—
        Charles Wicks
—"Charlie"—"Cochese"—

the football star of
my youth—Columbia
High—when I was in
grammar school—the
toughest spade in town—
maybe the toughest
period—no white guy
ever tried—he was
beautiful—from a
poor family, with a
wife like a picture &
all the women he
could do—& he did—
& told me how he did
& who & what I should
do & I was already doing
by the time we were
friends in 1957 or 58—
in 1972 I realized how
much I loved that dude—
& saw him again then—
a little paunchy &
pushing 40—me just
30 & newly into my
own beauty—so late—
but *in time* goddamnit
in time—
  Charles was so
sweet—but always noble
& generous & offhand in
his easy masculinity & pride
—I never knew a kinder
man—he helped me see
that kindness could be
more than rules & gestures—
& so did you—& I hardly

know you—& maybe it
isn't always true—but
it made me think of
all this & you in it—
it's the first Mayday in
12 years I haven't done
something to commemorate—
& now I have—thank you

NYC April 28-May 2 1978

PATTERNS

assembly line breaks—
the critic combing our cells as though on the
table's keys, wallet (worn)
coins, comb, did not
imply empty pockets or
empty (clean) ashtray non-
smoker or extra tidy guest—
the bad tasting, worse
smelling water (only
matched by the dogs here)—
empty case for eyeglasses—someone reading or watching
TV—or writing in a note-
book the choices of a career
in self-observational anti-
cipation—*life*—like that—

making a lamp out of a
milk can in Virginia—
out near the mountains—
kids at the swimming hole
of 1978 using the language

of the beatnik bar of 1958—
a hairbrush—a Christopher Isherwood book (early and
relatively obscure)—the
sudden burst of '60s "rock"
from outside competing with
the river ("born under a bad
sign")—dirty socks—crickets in gangs—the nastiness of
flying ants—the "pleasures" of the country life outweighed
by the inconveniences for
those addicted to the "pleasures"
of city life—open doorway
to adjoining bathroom that
serves the teenaged daughter's room as well—more
aged than teened—not old but
older—her yellow bathing-suit and big boned girlishness—
the remnant's of a doper's life—
the single wildflower in the cut
glass vase—the blues base of
most rock—tiresome "black"
derivation—unlike the real country origins of non-
blacks—sun supporting
somehow the haze that defuses its explosive
impact on everything here—
more trees than people in Manhattan—no more horizons
outside the stereo or TV and
those all inside now—the
end of a century before it
has ended—we look up once
before—

4.4.80

ex-wife in semi-coma
daughter moves in for good

joins brother and father
reluctant (she) to accept
her mother no longer able
to be her mother as she
has been, though, whatever
"brain damage" means
her father doesn't even
try to explain or use
these terms, instead
"won't get much better"
"why me?" asks son
then spends days making
"sick" jokes about death
and brain damage, though
no one mentioned either
in his presence, and
he's the younger though
raised in New York City
with father these years
where dreams keep father
going despite despair
and recognition confusion
(is he gay or what? no,
he's sensitive and at times
super-sensual to the point
of not caring what's
different or the same—
is he any good or what?
so much potential etc.)
38 going on 17, 10 going
on 50 (the son) 12 going
on 6 going on 80 going on,
whoever survives survives,
it doesn't seem to matter
how, only who, we all
make do, you'll never

understand who or how
though try, please try,
I got a why that won't
quit, though my ex-wife
didn't always like it
and now she's shit fucking
fighting for some fraction
of a life she used to have
and everything is different
even in my dreams, I
don't know shit & can't
compete even with myself
anymore, just let me do
it once the way I meant
to be remembered, she
seems to have, despite
whatever got between us
& I hardly knew, so
fucking scared & hungry.

LOST ANGELS

for Peggy Feury

We are the generation of lost
angels. We rarely feel these
days like we have anything new
to do or say & yet our lives
are totally changed, even from
what they were a year ago, three
months ago, yesterday, trying
to *finally* be honest about our
feelings about each other's fame
& glory, while still trying to
get or forget our own, as Billy

Idol sings and the expression
"thrillsville" is recycled in
some teenaged woman's bed, or
"oh my god" we did that too
the way rocknroll connects us
with the folks we never knew,
maybe spoiling us for joy &
hope & honest bullshit as we
once said to people who were
"naturals" like ourselves before
we disillusioned on the anti-
antis . . . like wanting to be a
movie star forever despite the
rocknroll & dope & beatniks
who still can't finesse the
necessary kind of classic
heroism we all continue to
love, like the idols of the
silver screen we injected
directly into the limelight
of our brains and hearts for
smarts the schoolrooms dis
possessed and all the rest;
we don't expect *too* much, just
freedom from the assholes we
suspect have been enthralled
by their own egos making money
off ours.

We don't wanna go crazy & die
in some nuthouse with no teeth
like Antonin Artuad, the world's
first poet movie star and father
of whatever wave obsesses us now
in the New York-L.A.-Berlin-Paris-
Tokyo-Melbourne-London scene that
is the unbraining of Hollywood's

being influenced by us! (the obvious
vice versa has been *feeling* our
brains since we mainlined Marilyn
& Marlon) & what about the "blues"
of John Wayne? That's how we
survived. And now it's all one,
the sum of our music and movie
influences spread across the
globe for anyone to use as in
"the new technology" which has
been in our cells since "action"
was a label for painting and
not just the order for the start
of our hearts' flicks . . .
We *love* being alive
and trying to share the craziness
of what it means to know it! I mean
did we really come too late for true greatness
or just on time? What is this new place
that defines L.A.-New York and all
the rest as just a state of mind?
Energy versus Peace? FUCK THAT SHIT!
The Peace of Energy that makes us
generate a void of minuscule delights
like we once relied on artificial
stimulants for, no more, maybe at last
we can reflect the serious sensuality
of the stars we talk to in our walk
through the sea we have become—

We are the masses who survived
the troubled times that rhymed
our lives the way old Hollywood
serials did, and understand our
laughter matters. Literally.
That's the secret of creation,

transforming *laughter into matter*.
We can finally *accept* and still
hope, like reality is the freedom
of knowing who we are and where
we're at and the ideal is sharing
that completely, without fear,
then letting go, not hanging on
but knowing anyway, because we're
smart at last and allow ourselves
to be. What are these humming
motors anyway but mammals of our
fantasies! Sure we talk to cars
and TVs and expect the music to
invade our brains, the motors
of our smarts that drive our
hearts to caring about it all.

Hey, what's L.A. but the
city of Lost Angels where
we all were born, even in
New Jersey cause what's
left of that is something
close to nothing, as the
categories fade and rede-
fining the specifics is
less thrilling. Like Elvis
isn't. I wish they'd fish
him over the rainbow of
telescopic infinitude so I
wouldn't have to bother with
the memory of his collar
turned up and hair that thick
I thought it was hereditary.
The Shirelles, now there's
some memories that never quit
changing, big women and still
growing. We made ourselves

in the images of images and
then got rid of it before we
came. Coming isn't the game
it once was. And neither is
going.

***

I only wanted to go far, be a star,
understand the way you all are.
Love, money, friends, family,
a stimulating environment, some good books,
records, art, photographs, furniture,
place to sleep and eat and work,
make love and shower, shit and entertain in,
maybe a good car,
some free time,
your name in the paper now and then,
or in a magazine,
or on TV,
your image too,
or in a movie, on a record, in a book,
or on the cover,
in the titles,
on the lips of strangers,
in the minds of a worldwide audience . . .

So you move to El Lay
to make money and become a star.
So you lived in New York City
to make art and smart sexy friends.
Which wasn't enough.
So you move to El Lay where
she has almost transparently blue eyes,
so intense they give the impression
that there has never been a person

they haven't seen through.
She has to be over fifty,
perhaps well over, like in her sixties.
It's so hard to tell these days;
or was it always?
Her eyes communicate such strength
when you look into her still beautiful face
you feel beyond time.
Her body gives it away a little.
Small, but not delicate,
there's something obviously
deteriorated about it
that seems in such contrast to her face,
unlike those strenuously physical
geriatric exercisers whose bodies
always seem to be made up of knots
and wires and strings and really ugly
imitations of some impossible youth.
Anyway,
I love her.
I fell in love with her the first time I
looked into her eyes. I can't resist a
woman who sees right through me and
is beautiful too. She's the real thing,
a total woman, smart, beautiful, and
old enough to be my lover, I mean mother,
maybe. Maybe not.
I'm not that young myself anymore, just
having walked through the door marked forty.
The best thing about which was
suddenly realizing why old guys can find old gals
sexy. When I was a kid I could never understand
the obvious attraction
my middleaged aunts could still retain for
my middleaged uncles and vice versa.
Now I know. There's a girlish glow

to most grown women that never disappears,
and if you went through the same or close-by years
with them, you can't help but see it,
and it makes you feel some kind of sympathy and
understanding for them, and then
on top of it they have this look
of having been through some things,
around the block as many times as you,
and that creates some crazy sexy feelings too.
It's all so new,
being old,
I mean older than I thought I'd ever live to be
and still be *me*.

These are some thoughts that moving from New York
to El Lay has provoked. There's so much space here
to panic in. The idea of "image" was crucified here
for everyone's sins and then resurrected to be
worshipped for as long as this place lasts
and influences the rest of the world.
Hollywood, one of the greatest sources of power
the world has known, and no real throne, no armies
or obvious superiority except occasionally
in technical, even artistic, ways.
But oh these fucking days of driving from
one crazy studio lot to another and feeling
as much at home as I ever did
in the apartments of my peers through all the years
of poetic ecstasy and self-destruction.
What other homes have we ever had, let's face it,
then Hollywood, the New York of bebop & jazz
& street scenes & energy highs (& its flip side:
galleries & Frank O'Hara, off & off-off and then
on Broadway again) or "on the road" or on TV
or radio or stereo or juke box.

Let's face it Charlie,
we coulda been real home lovers
instead of dream chasers which is what we are.
Only worse than the Romantics of old,
we can get real cold
and see right through that bullshit
as we watch the technology unfold
into a future of dreams & nightmares we never
forgot.

SIX YEARS IN ANOTHER TOWN

And I can't believe all that's gone down—
I'm talking to the trees again
and I haven't done that since
God knows when—because I guess
it's Him, or Her, or It I'm talking to
when I look up at a tree and say
you got any advice for me today?—
and they always respond the same way
Frank O'Hara did, when he appeared to me
in the back of a checkered cab
on my way back from cheating
on the then woman in my life
a Costa Rican beauty I still miss
as I miss you all, even if I don't
call you too often—or at all—
I was high—on boo and other stuff—
we'd met at a literary awards event
where John Ashbery, O'Hara's close friend
had just received the nation's highest
poetic honor—or close enough—
and then we all piled into this bus
that took us back to the Plaza Hotel,

where Eloise once romped when I was
just her age only now it was me
thinking about this Canadian Jewish
beauty, famous for her literary liaisons
and how it would feel to be inside her
and know her famous beau, who was a rich
kid still at fifty, wouldn't know,
but I would the next time he looked
down his nose at me and my much
tougher poetry, the way I saw it—
anyway, I was full of guilt by now—
having been inside her and her home
and done the jitterbug of life and
then got up to leave and though I
had never deceived her, had told
her of my life with Ana and my son
from a still undivorced ex-wife—
she got mad and threw books at me
calling me "you bastard you son of
a bitch" as I fled down the stairs
and out into the New York night and
the checker cab that sped downtown
with me mumbling in the back seat
about my guilt although I'd never
cheated on Ana before and wouldn't
again and she'd never know—and
when we broke up it was because she
couldn't stay away from some younger
version of myself who gave her the
baby and marriage she wanted and
followed her home to Costa Rica
and some position in her family's
mini-empire—but this night we
were still alright except for my
feelings of being a rat to everyone
concerned because I never seemed to

learn that the possibility of making
love was not an imperative—I
felt so bad I thought I was dying—
from the dope and loss of hope that
I would ever be the man I thought
I was—when all of a sudden there
beside me in the cab was Frank O'Hara
in white shirt, open at the collar,
sleeves rolled up, and khaki pants
and penny loafers—he put an arm
around my shoulder and in the voice
I'd only heard on tapes and records
told me it was alright, that if I
hadn't done what I'd done that night
I wouldn't be me—the Michael
my friends seemed to love and even
admire—and that I wasn't gonna
die—or even have to lie—because
nobody would know—and I was so
relieved I cried a little—something
I only do when watching TV or a movie
and when I got home Ana didn't seem
to notice anything, only Miles, my
little five-year-old locked eyes
with mine and asked "What's wrong?"
and when I told him nothing, he
kept looking to see if I was telling
the truth, so I added "I'm just
glad to be home" which he accepted
as true, because it was—

Wait a minute, that was so many years ago,
what does it have to do with being here
in Southern California with you, writing
about "six years in another town" for
the new friends I have now, who never

knew me when I jitterbugged through
life's opportunities, cutting a rug,
giving everyone a hug of true affection
because I knew, or thought I knew back
then that every person was a friend
because inside they wanted just what
I did, to be free to really dig what
life has given us, including each other—
Even the woman I moved here with in 1982,
even the files they keep on me and you
to see if we might get in the way of
Bush or J. Danforth Quayle or whoever
else the powers that be get to run the
show up front while they continue to
milk us all for what they need to keep
that power to themselves, and if that
sounds like another decade, well, it's
almost 1989, time for this one to end
and leave us, my friends, as Dukakis
always calls complete strangers—and
leave us with only memories of what
someone has accurately called "The Mean
Decade"—and enter the time of
saving ourselves and each other again—
it's the earth and the universe too
now—what an awesome responsibility—
and how we continue to fuck it up—but
hey, we're only human, doing our best
to muddle through until tomorrow when
somebody else gets the job we thought
we wanted—I remember after Ted Berrigan
died, who also knew Frank when he was
alive, like I didn't—two Irish-American
poets like me, haunted by Catholic guilt
and dreams of sainthood and sex—or
sexhood and saint—I always think of

O'Hara as Saint Frank—and Ted, the
last time I saw him was in heaven—
I guess it was a dream—but there he
was, newly arrived—looking better than
he ever did when he was alive, trim and
healthy and clean and sharp and totally
quiet—a big surprise for a man who
lived on speed and machine-gunned his
every thought into the faces and minds
of anyone who crossed his path and even
those who didn't—he didn't say a
word, and I walked over to him and sat
down beside him to tell him how good
he looked and how happy I was to see
him because I was, he was my friend,
who helped me out when I needed help—
he knew the same codes I did and lived
his life that way so he could say, when
he loaned me a few hundred bucks he didn't
really have and I promised to pay it back
right away—"Hey, Michael, it would be
an insult for you to give this back man,
it's a gift, it's nothing compared to
all the pleasure your poetry has given
me" and I could say, when I did the same
for him when he was down and out like me,
which we both were most of the time back
then, I could tell him "vice versa only
double"—he was my friend—and now
here he was, in heaven, and not saying a
word until he smiled at me, as handsome
as I ever saw him, when I asked how he
was doing (dead and in heaven) and he
said "Michael, you don't know how great
 it is not to have to talk anymore" and
it hit me, that must be heaven to a

guy like him, who never shut up and only
because he was so generous and smart and
had such a huge heart did we all put up
with the din when he let us in when we
went to pay him a visit—

Wait a minute! What has all this
got to do with living in L.A.?
Well, Ted passed away after I moved
here, and it pissed me off so much
I got in touch with my own need to
pass up speed and all the rest and
try to be the best I could be for
whatever time I had left—including
letting go of sex as the answer to
my disappointments in life—but
hey, it isn't always used that way—
sometimes it's just the most exciting
and convenient and fastest way to say
we're still alive today and glad of it—
Hey, you all say, wait a minute, he
calls this stuff poetry? I can do
that—which makes me feel real good
because the code of this boy's art
is the normal heart no matter how
surreal the circumstances—what
I mean is, the scene I dug the most,
came up through, and once was host to,
made it clear that if you're smart
you don't have to keep on proving it
in the work so that the person on
the receiving end goes: wow, I could
never do that, it's so difficult
and clever and precious and like a
machine I wasn't trained to run—
but we say, fuck that look-at-me-

I'm-educated-up-the-ass bullshit—
we say the work has got to be fun
even while it's taking on the Huns
of our existence, the bad guys in
the house of lies who disguise it
all as in our best interest—
these guys hypnotize with banality
as mean as genocide—while they
hide their true intent behind the
sense of expertise and techniques
we can only compromise—forget it—
art that makes you go, hey, I can
do that too is what moves me to see
life through to the end and still
be friends with myself—forget
the "off the shelf" operations that
the experts think we're better off
not knowing about—NO WAY! we
gotta shout our way back into history
because it's ours, just like these
six years here were mine—a time
when I got clean and sober unlike
any film by that name, but not so
different I couldn't recognize the
games we all play with denial in
those phony smiles Keaton threw around
playing the clown for death instead
of life where we all live whether we
like it or not—hey, wait a minute!
I wanted to tell you about my first
Oscar party at Spago—where I
threw some tuxedoed guy against
the wall when he tried to tell me I
couldn't cut in front of him on the line
to the mens room—I thought I blew
my whole career as a star when I'd

realized what I'd done—but later
he told my then wife that it was
the most exciting thing that had
happened to him all year—
I thought, wow, I'm glad I'm here
where coked up craziness gets
rewarded—only really I was full
of fear when I moved here a few
weeks later in '82 and met a lot of you,
fear I'd never be able to expose
myself as honestly as I had to friends
that went back so much further—
fear that I wasn't good enough
because I didn't have the money—
was like the honey the health nuts
pretend is better for you than all
that sugar we consumed when we were
kids—wait, I really want to stay
on track and get back to the art
I came out here to practice—and
did—that's what's gone down
in these six years too—I did get
to see myself on TV in a way I used
to dream I would—and even when it
wasn't very good—or I wasn't—
hey—goddamnit it was fun!—after
all it isn't like the war on AIDS or
the creeps who think this government
is theirs to run is gonna be lost or
won by what I do as a bad guy on a
nighttime soap—no, what it's gonna
do is give hope to the people I came
up with who think, or thought, that
guys like us didn't get this far and
if we did we were stars then and forgot
what it was like to not take any of it

too seriously—oh six years in another
town without the renown I thought would
be mine has left me so much more humble
which is something I guess I need
to be—but it has also left me
with all of you—and the chance to
make a new dance beyond the jitterbug
I flew through the bedrooms and back
seats and closets of my past with—
I mean hey, in '86 the dirty tricks
of Nixon were dismissed and suddenly
he's an "elder statesman" and if that
doesn't make us wake up and laugh
out loud at all those who would make
us proud of our worst qualities what
will? We still got some time left—
for some of us to get tough with the
stuff of life that turns us on and hold
a light to it for the rest of us to get some—
I mean I gave a reading where I read
for the first time only work written
here in this town, and it not only
went okay, an old old friend did
say—"Now that's a real poetry
reading"—and I thought they all
were—and they were—only now—
it's not to stir your juices only
and have you remember me as the star
of poetry that sounds the way we
sometimes think and talk and share
what we're afraid others might find
trite or at least not as mighty as
the real art stuff—no—I meant
to share a vision that has driven me
since my first memory—of a world
where love is not just an advertiser's

cliché but a way of life that isn't
serious like lying, but hopeful and
funny and important and honest and
significant and something that effects
all of us, the entire community, the
community of the universe, like dying
does—okay, that's not heavy, just
take a second look, what I'm saying is
there is no book of love without death
and there is no death without love—
unless it's a death that is lying—
and I know that truth is something
so illusive we can never really reach
it, but hey, we can approach it if
we try, and there's nothing saying we
can't dance as we do, and even dance
til we die, even if our dance is only
in the eye of those who love us—
that's what's really gone down these
six years, my heart, to the depths of
despair and fear and regret and sorrow
only to rise again for the miracle of
today that was only yesterday's tomorrow.

ON NOVEMBER SECOND NINETEEN NINETY THREE

I spent four hours and more
on a strip of the Pacific Coast Highway
traveling between Rambla Vista and Sunset Boulevard
which would normally take ten to fifteen minutes.
It had been the brightest, clearest day
of my eleven years so far living on the Santa Monica Bay.
But it grew dark from clouds of smoke
billowing up from the ridges lining the road

and blowing over the backed up panicked
and yet patient traffic and on out over the Pacific.
We—my girlfriend and roommate Kristal and me—
had driven to Malibu when we walked out of
the laundromat on Montana Avenue and saw the
piercing blue sky encroached upon by a thick and
sinewy cloud of smoke that seemed to be coming
from Santa Monica Canyon. But once there,
where we drove, on Kristal's instigation, we saw
it was further up the coast and without any
hesitation kept driving until we reached my
daughter Caitlin's street, which winds up from
the coast and bends back down, and with
her boyfriend Nels Brown she lived until that
day on which the house, the apartment they
shared was in, burnt down to the ground
of the hillside from which she had been
admiring the clarity of that day's view in
which the ocean met the sky in the kind
of sharply drawn line we thought would
always be there when I was a boy a continent
and ocean away. I mean it was a perfectly
clear day, the kind that once was normal
and expected before smog and haze and all
kinds of pollution and distortions of God's
beauty was accepted. My daughter didn't want
to leave at first. It was still early in
the fire's growth and no warnings had
preceded ours. We talked about it for an hour.
We even discussed what she might take were
a disaster truly imminent, and joked about
her dragging a foot locker full of things
from her baby years and childhood I kept for her
until she grew and moved away. But
not that day. She didn't want to make
a fuss. Every item we'd discuss and I'd

suggest might be best to take she'd get
upset and insist it would be too difficult
to try and differentiate. "It would be like
moving," she said, and instead just finally
took a couple of things, some photo albums,
address and check books, a change of clothes
for her and her boyfriend. She, and even
Kristal, had made fun of my persistent
insistence that we should go before we got
stuck up there and PCH got closed down.
But when we finally got her cat and
few possessions that she took into her car
and mine and drove down to the highway
it was already a parking lot. And the
wind had grown so strong and hot it
seemed the fire was already in the air
if not yet visible in flame and smoke
where we were. But it soon was and
thank God by then we had been creeping
forward inch by inch, it seemed, enough
to just stay forward of the smoke and
rushing flames. At one point Kristal got
out and took a walk and Caitlin opened
her door and I did mine and she said:
"Thanks—you're a pain sometimes but
thank you." And I wanted to cry and
go back and get that foot locker and
her paintings and her boyfriend's keyboards
and music and all the rest. And I wish
I had the power to make it all right.
But I don't—and never will. The rightness
is in knowing that and going on with it
still as though I didn't know. I do.

MY LIFE 2

When I was 10,
I thought I was "Irish,"
even though I was
born in the USA.

When I was 20,
I thought I was "Black,"
even though my skin
is pink & freckled,
my hair is straight,
and I have no
African ancestry.

When I was 30,
I thought I was "queer,"
even though I was
married and had
two children, and
all my fantasies
& obsessions & com-
pulsions & attractions
were and had always
been about women.

When I was 40,
I thought I was a
"movie star," even
though the movies
were terrible, and
I was terrible in
them, and almost
no one knew them,
or who I might
have been in them.

When I was 50,
I thought I was
"enlightened," even
though I wasn't.

But of course I was
and am—enlightened,
as I was and still am
—an Irish-Black-
Queer-Movie-Star.

IT TAKES ONE
TO KNOW ONE

(Black Sparrow Press 2001)

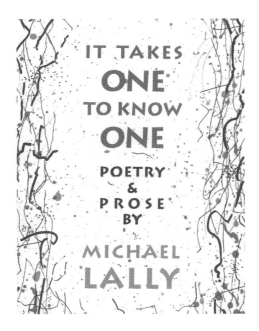

WHAT?

Who won? I feel like
I'm almost there—what
were we competing for?
"the store" "the farm"
 the barn where it all
began—the can of spice—
the nice lips on her face—
the place where we fell
asleep at last in peace &
woke up to the air we
remembered that isn't
there anymore—the emp-
eror has no lungs left—
he's only pretending to
breathe—& as for us—
who won—what?

HEAVEN & HELL

1. HELL

Hell is
       no escape.
              And no acceptance.

2. HEAVEN

Ah, heaven.
       Heaven is
              more complicated.

WHO ARE WE NOW

We are too tired to figure this one out—
We want someone else to do it for us—
We want to be told what it's all about
and not have to pay any attention—
We want to have sex with everyone we meet
almost, but not risk death by having sex
with anyone—We want a relationship
that will last forever if only the one
we're in will come to an end so we can
find the right one—again—We want
to be poets and actors and songwriters
and directors and politicians and saviors
and gods—but while we're waiting for
all that to happen let's just see how
much fun we can make of all those other
poets and actors and songwriters and
directors and politicians and saviors
and gods—We want it all but it's
just too much—We want each other but
we feel like we're being suffocated so
we just want to be alone so we can spend
all our time on the computer or phone
with someone else who is also alone—
We want our own homes if somebody else
will clean them and care for them and
maybe even pay the bills—We can take
care of ourselves as long as we really don't
have to because then we're so tired of
doing just that we have to get a cat or
a dog or several of each and birds and
pigs and take up smoking the cigs again
until we're so crowded with plants and
electronic devices we have to find some
one to share all this bliss but none of

them seem to know how to kiss anymore
and we're not so enlightened that we
want to be bored with the lovers we're
prepared to change a few things for
as long as their willing to change
everything for us—not because we
want to control them, we just want
to make sure they really love us,
because now we're not so sure we
really love them but it's too much
trouble and time and energy and risk
to start this shit all over again with
someone new—so we will be whoever
they want us to for awhile until we
can get them to be who we wish we
really were back when we knew who
we wanted to be by now—ourselves,
only better.

IS AS

It's time for beauty
to make its return—
not anorexic girls in
post-heroin mode—not
middle-class children of
divorce pretending to be
death until they are—
not aging babies crying
for their milk & honey—
not "not"—any of it—
just sit & wonder, awed—
owed the comfort of an
eye in sight of itself—

this is a fact, beauty
doesn't ache, it reverberates
inside our consciousness of
bliss—I can't believe I just
said that—"Rip don't!"—
"Nardo—Nar—*doe*"—"Aghhh!"—
What I mean here is De-
liverance—from all that is
so boringly appalling about
fate—a turning on to all that
is inspiringly appealing about
hate for the nondescript of—
make a list—your own—of
what you'd want to hear on
the phone—see in the mirror
out the window of your car—
another world—the one we're
in—kiss me—touch my hair—
anywhere—show me the cover
of a book that is as beautiful
as we all once were—be.

from HARDWORK

[. . .]

"Frank O'Hara is the
Fred Astaire of American Poetry"
whispers Bruce Andrews during
That's Entertainment, Part II

I wanted to be the Frank Sinatra

*

I thought the Garden of Eden a
metaphor for pubic hair—I meant
the garden I wanted to give
—I couldn't help what it was
there—at 34 I don't think too much
about death but it's there as a
comfort to the living—
—despite the fun—and
joy!—in the twist of the torso
perfecting its fall—o my god how
I thank you for all the bodies—
the gardens—
what's there—

[. . .]

shit
I could always predict
but couldn't *make* anything on it!

lacked—still do—more so—
a certain kind of "wit" I so admire
and covet and am entertained by—

the difference between Gene Kelly
and Fred Astaire—
Tom Raworth and Edmund White—

I appreciate and hear them all
the "decongealment" of the
imaginative
function

the ideology of *mass*
they call it "spreading it thin"
two "it"s contradicting *the* mass

in our home the communion of
"art" in "the masses" of my father
(now dead) saying "work, work, work"
in my head and the rest in *theirs*
the Clint Eastwoods of

"competence"

imagine the chance again—
nice summer day—1958
at the kitchen sink
getting a drink of water—
sun pouring in through the windows—
two views and the air through
the open "sashes" and the sound
of the traffic—occasional and
distant till a horn honks in
front and you know *it's for you*—
something to do!
(here too—August 1976 New York City—
   the sky is an historical blue
   through the windows and the air
   through the open "casements"—)
shit—*that chance*—"gone"—
and the wit to grasp it with it—

October 24, 1951

. . . Oh my goodness I almost
forgot to tell you. Michael got a
regular report card for the first time
and his average was 97.2. We were
all very excited about it. His marks
were Religion 95, Arith. 96, English 97,
History 98, Reading 99, Geog. 100, Spelling
96, Penmanship (like all the rest of you
kids) 85.

. . . Michael has a teacher this year (it is
her first year teaching) and she told
Joan that he is a brilliant child (?).
We shall see by the end of the year if
she knows what she is talking about.
I doubt it.
[. . .]

from THE RAIN TRILOGY

[. . .]

7—my son—with me
missing his mother & sister

his sister with his mother
missing him & me—

me missing his sister, having
missed him before he was
with me—everyone sad—

                    *

9 years old—my daughter
I wanted to take her with us
I am conciliatory or resigned

[. . .]

"boom"   my son
                    asleep
crouched at the end
of a narrow bed
"the way he likes it"

& me
       working hard at

"the job"—

like "dues"—
   endless & pointless

call from *her*—
   job no longer "pointless"
   now necessary to make
   money to live "the life"
   (dinner, dance, date,
   "darling" . . .)—

[. . .]

                              shit—
I *need* her
and a month ago
I didn't even *know* her—

[. . .]

I just flash all day
on her smile and touch
and all the good things
I love so much—

everything—oh oh oh—

[. . .]

meanwhile Miles
cried after *West
Side Story* (on TV)

"not because I'm
sad—but because
it was *so good*"
said it was his
favorite movie—even
better than *Star
Wars*

       —later
said he'd wear his
levis, a plain tee
shirt ("no writing
on it") and his
reversible jacket
with the beige side
out—as an extension
of *West Side Story* style—
7 years old!—a "genius"

[. . .]

still not only "good"
but getting *better*!

made love 4 times after
waking up—3 times before
going to sleep!—and
could've kept going

[. . .]

the sunsets from
the Chrysler building & beyond

    & *love*

[. . .]

have so much to do
& I'm not doing
any of it
etc.

        *

(reading Laura Riding
& Gerald Burns)
(talking with Miles—football,
school, food, the past, etc. & reading to him
from William Saroyan story collection)

[. . .]

my son—   & me—
          our *love*—
      what I had long wanted—

more than etc.

        *

        raining

        I love it

    dark days in the city

     somehow
      so many in the '50s
        early '60s—when I was
      here—considering it *home*
    no matter where I was

"stationed" or coming from—

    alone on the wet streets
        cold, but not freezing—
      reading the
            atmosphere
      the sound of the car tires
      on the slick dark
        the ways the water
          falling makes *everyone*
        eccentric
             and alone—

    I always loved rainy days like today
so much more than etc.

[. . .]

BROTHER CAN YOU SPARE A RHYME?

Once upon a time
I could rhyme
anything, but
thought it was
a cheap trick,
like being born
with a big dick
and using it
to get ahead
in Hollywood.

I would never do that.

Or like those old

cowboy movies
where the hero
always wore a white hat,
and the bad guys black.
That seemed to be
a California perception
of what looked good
on a handsome man.

Back East white was
the color for dairy queens
and guys so rich they
were terminally passive.
Black was the color
for the kind of men
who wouldn't have
known what a den
is for, or ever bore
us with their lack
of passion.
The hottest women
wore black, and
the classiest,
the saddest,
the smartest.

White and black,
now and then,
me and you,
what'll we do
about all we know
to be no longer true,
and yet still be truthful
so we can survive
these new dark ages, huh?

Maybe, you can go
home again
if you're willing to
take responsibility for
what you find there.

Even the air
is tired from what we've
all been through,
the scare
we've all been talking to
when we talk to each other
and discover
we're all a lot more
careful in the ways
we own our lives.
Some people say
there's an art to that—
yeah, the art of compromise.

KNOW

Gertrude Stein
wine
I don't know
I think they've lost their glow
for me.
See, I haven't been able to
drink either one for years now.
How did I know?
I mean, what to keep and
what had to go—
Like all those William Saroyan and
William C. Williams tomes—

those little homes I grew up in
even if I was already grown
when I first started reading them.
J.W. Dant bourbon was the thing
I liked the most.
Toasting is what Blacks called
rapping back in the old days
before it became a part of the music biz.
"The Wiz" was an underrated movie,
says D. M., as he produces another
amazing TV show, buys and sells horses,
makes his BMW go with me in it
and I still owe him several big ones.
The man's a genius, says his agent,
after he tells me "your eyes glow,"
and all I know is my heart has broken
like those horses they send out too soon
to compete in races they can't win yet.
Only I ain't no horse,
and I been out there for years,
they didn't just send me out too early.
Although—
Hey, what do I know?

WALK ON THE WILD SIDE

I'm so dependent on what other people think about me.
That's not the way I want to be.
I don't want to be like Lawrence Harvey in
Walk on the Wild Side either. I only saw it
because it was the first time Jane Fonda played a whore.
That was long before the Viet Nam war—
or not, that wasn't a war, I forgot, Congress never
declared war on anybody in that one, that was—

what? What was that one? Not a "police action"—
that was the Korean War—it's funny isn't it,
how we're allowed to call them wars after they're over—
well, they're never really over, anyway—
I can't remember anything about that movie—
except Jane Fonda was almost as young as I was then,
and she was beautiful in this fragile sexy
teenage woman kind of way that she isn't today—
somewhere in there she turned from fragile to brittle,
the kind of distinctions real poets love to play with
but not before they throw out a lot of obviously
intelligent and imaginatively deep images so that
everyone will know it's poetry—and smart poetry
which is why I stopped doing that a long time ago
except now and then just to slow down the pace
of the ideas that always race through my mind
when it's time to write a poem which for me is
any and all the time because you see I'm a poet
and I can always make it rhyme just like the
rappers do, only middle-aged white poets ain't
supposed to, they're supposed to write about
how the rocks are talking to them tonight in
the muffled tones of their ex-wife which
implies a marriage to the earth that has been
broken up, only, when the rocks talk to me they
say stuff like what up honky homey? or whoa,
you see that stone, check her out, or, hey man,
it's okay, you're gonna make it through today
and come tonight you'll be alright no matter
what they say, you are just as much who you
were meant to be as we are brother, and the
earth is our mother too, hey someday you
might be a rock yourself like you
thought you were in 1956—
when the colored girls *did* go
"doo, da doo, da doo"—

THE HEALING POEM

When I wrote this poem
      I thought there was a healing going on—
            a profound healing. I thought it was
no accident that movies like
      Field of Dreams and *Rain Man*
            (no matter how we feel about
their politics or art) were proving
      the lie in all the cynical projections
            of what people want. What they want
is a healing to take place.

      Gorbachov became a hero
            around the world not because
he knew how to manipulate
      the media—remember his speeches?
            It wasn't *him*, it was what he represented,
the healing of a wound almost
      a century old. Wasn't it obvious
            by the response of the world to him,
or to the Chinese students in
      Tieneman Square, or the release
            of Nelson Mandela, or the fall of the
Berlin Wall, or the Russian people
      standing up to the tanks & the old ideas—
            it's a healing we all want?

& hey, I knew all about "wilding"
      and gang rape and gang violence
            and gang stupidity and cowardice
and all the rest. I was in a couple
      of gangs when I was a kid. I also
            know the cops can be a gang too sometimes.
I come from a family of cops, &
      if you don't think it's tough being
            stopped by the police & hearing

"What's your brother gonna say?"
     —just think about a cop asking—
          "What's this gonna do to Ma?"

But I think we know and so do
     those kids what's good for the soul,
          the spirit, the heart. Yet when that good
has been torn apart by public figures
     who act as if they have no responsibility
          toward this world—whose world is it anyway?
Or rocknrollers or movie stars
     or TV celebrities who speak out
          about pollution and then personalize it in
their own lives by polluting hearts
     and souls and minds with messages
          they take no responsibility for.

And I'm not talking about sexual
     jokes and innuendoes. I'm talking
          about violence that is presented as power
and reward and even inspirational.
     I'm talking about accepting and even
          celebrating the cynical attitudes that everyone
seemed to acquiesce to in the '80s—
     the "Reagan Years"—for which we are
          all now paying the price. I'm talking about
adding to the confusion and fear
     and hatred and rage by accepting
          the unacceptable, by ignoring the unignorable,
by pretending reality is worse than
     it is and then giving in to that pretension
          until it becomes reality. I WANT THE HEALING.

And I believe with everything that's in me
     that even those who will write parodies,
          or speak them, as soon as they finish reading this,
of what they can easily dismiss

and turn into a self-defensive joke
        about my own hypocrisy or pretensions—
even the wits who can turn misery
        into charisma, and though I know I'm
                no wit I also know I sometimes can do it too—
even us poor victims of our own
        delusions of sincerity, no matter how hip,
                WANT A HEALING TO OCCUR and want it now.

The whole world is longing and
        has been longing for just that.
                Why else is Jesus so popular? Or Buddha?
Or the Mohammed of the real Koran?
        What is it that repulses us in the struggle
                of the Arabs and the Jews, or Bosnians and
Serbs or Blacks and Whites in
        South Africa or here not so long ago,
                but the lack of a healing between two cultures
that generate all our own fears
        about differences and the rage
                that fear of the different and unknown
can create in total strangers
        when they see us tearing down
                the walls that make those differences.

I've said it before and I'm not
        gonna stop—I don't care if
                you're from *Time* because you think
some "star" is reading poetry
        somewhere, or from the academy
                because you think one of your own is there—
or look down your nose at those
        whose poetry is accessible and
                even vital to people who don't care—
that's not what people come out to hear—
        I believe they come for the healing, for in

          hearing the troubles and longings and truth
of other lives, no matter how famous or rich
          or unknown or Jewish or young or frail or
                    perfect or a wreck, they see the common thread,
that it isn't about women and men
          and young and old and black and white
                    and rich and poor and famous and unknown,
it's about this deep and abiding and
          relentless yearning for a healing to
                    take place in all of us and between all of us.

It's not even about humans and animals
          and nature and commerce and all that either.
                    Because even there, even businesses and trees
and cars and the very air and sea
          and earth itself are making that
                    longing known. You can hear it in the wind
and smell it on the flower. All creation
          is crying out for a healing to take place.
                    It is time. It is beyond time, it is timeless.
And yes of course it begins with me
          and you, who else? And yes I have
                    felt it since we met and held each other in a way
that offered no defenses no obeisance
          to the differences that we know so well
                    and so truly are just the flowering of the creative
imagination of the universe and not
          a reason to run or quit or give up in
                    frustration and anger and cynicism. No,
the differences only help us to see
          how much we are the same in our souls—
                    soulmates for sure. How else explain that two
such unlikely people can feel
          so comfortable in each other's arms,
                    can ignore all the warnings from past experiences
and cynical friends that something

is unreal if there is no doubt, no struggle.
             The only struggle is with acceptance—acceptance
of the truth. And the truth is
             we all need a healing. And you
                          and I can feel it happening for us, in ways that
go beyond our simple male and
             femaleness, our white and blackness,
                          our age differences, our family and career and
neighborhood and all the other
             differences, beyond our humanness—
                          a healing that like Selby says heals those issues
for all time, in all eternity, for all
             the years we've spent on earth so far
                          and all we will continue to spend. And if that
can happen for us, in the simple act
             of *trust*—what more can it do for
                          the rest of the world.

I never believed people who said
             you can't make movies or music or
                          books that don't have violence or superficial values
or all the bullshit negativity
             this town and every town and
                          every business tries to lay on those of us
who refuse to relinquish our
             innocence and hope because
                          we have not succumbed to the dope of
giving up. Hey I know this sounds
             like preaching, so hold me accountable.
                          I'm talking about a healing here, that I needed
desperately all my life and still do,
             and that I finally feel has truly begun
                          with you. And not just you, but others too.
Oh people people let us start anew
             and pledge right now to each other
                          that we will no longer take part in any project
whether business or art or any affair

356

of the heart or collaboration or conversation
or celebration or even thought that isn't true.
So let's start, right here, with me
& you—& you & you & you & you
& you . . .

FORBIDDEN FRUIT

all the forbidden fruit I ever
dreamt of—or was taught to
resist and fear—ripens and
blossoms under the palms of my
hands as they uncover and explore
you—and in the most secret
corners of my heart as it discovers
and adores you—the forbidden fruit
of forgiveness—the forbidden fruit
of finally feeling the happiness
you were afraid you didn't deserve—
the forbidden fruit of my life's labor
—the just payment I have avoided
since my father taught me how—
the forbidden fruit of the secret
language of our survivors' souls as
they unfold each other's secret
ballots—the ones where we voted
for our first secret desires to come
true—there's so much more
I want to say to you—but for
the first time in my life I'm at
a loss for words—because
(I understand at last)
I don't need them
to be heard by you.

BAD BOYS AND WOMEN WHO WANT IT ALL

I wasn't bad,
I was just misunderstood.

I wasn't trying to burn down my grammar school.
I was just experimenting out of boredom,
to see how much oxygen it took to keep the
matches going before I slammed my desk shut
on the flames—and one time I waited too long.

But hey, that's how you learn, right?

I was just bored—weren't you?
Isn't that why you wanted it all,
while I got suspended, expelled,
kicked out, arrested, tried, court
martialed, exiled, 86ed, asked to leave,
fired, let go, walked out on, divorced,
broke, hurt, kicked in the ass, the
heart, the brain, again and again,
knowing all along it was only because
I was misunderstood—but I understood
you, and you understood me, I was
the bad boy and you were the woman
who wanted it all, wanted the flowers
and the poems, the soft caress and
the sweet sweet acceptance of your
getting it all wrong every time you
tried to dress the part or break my
heart because I was too bad when all
you wanted was just bad enough to
make you feel the love was tough
enough to last and still be passionate.
But bad boys don't last, that's
what makes them bad—you can't

depend on them for anything but
not being there when it gets too
square and you want square too
because you are the woman who
wants it all—the lawyer and
the biker bum, the guy who never
leaves and the guy who only knows
how to run. And you think you might
see that in me because I'm slowing
down, I'm learning how to clown
around with the bad boy image
before it gets sad 'cause a guy
ain't a boy no more. I mean bad boys
are one thing but bad old men—
that's something else again,
even when you're the woman
who wants it all.

ATTITUDE, GRATITUDE, AND BEATITUDE

The news all seems bad—
just like it all seemed good only a year or so ago—
the money isn't where we thought it was—
neither are we—
How does it work?
Does anybody know?
Where did the music go?
Did you see Michael Jackson's video?
I did this thing I do—I saw this woman and
felt the need to give her all my power—then
I couldn't think of anything but her & getting
her to be my mate because I needed her because
she had the power.

"So what," they say, "that's nothing new."
They think I did the same with you.

I know, it's true that
recessions come & go, like wars, conspiracies,
& music you can really listen to.
What's permanent is—what?
That's what we all would like to know.
It isn't attitude—thank God that changes
as we grow.   It isn't gratitude—sometimes
it comes too slow or not at all—& what
the hell is "beatitude" anyway?—another
fancy word for feeling good at nobody's
expense? I call that "love"—the only
guarantee of happiness, & not for me
coming from you but coming from me
for whatever, if I can let the fear of
loving go—you know—like how you feel
when you just love that song or pet or
painting or book or person or job or joke
or all that stuff you loved so long ago—
or not so long ago.   Do it again—let
the fear of loving go—no matter what you
know—because you know this too—that
it is the only way to go to go.

MORE THAN ENOUGH

there's more than more than more than
more than enough so why isn't enough enough and where is it
written that enough will never be enough except
in the amazing arrogance of societies and
institutions and governing bodies of immune deficiency
allowances of tabloid mentalities that breeed breeeed

breeeeed breeeeeeed breeeeeeeeeeeeeeeeeeeed infinity when
all we are asking for is food.

all we are asking for is enough space to live a life of
enough space to enough space to live a life of gratitude

when all we are asking for is no more hope no more dope no
more ways of being anything less than the stewards of all
that god has created including each other which means
caretakers which means taking care of which means caring for
each other and every other living thing and everything *is*
living from that star that is supposed to have died so many
thousands of years ago and yet still shines in your eyes to
that grain of sand in the shoe of the man sleeping on the rock
of all our past discouragement—

I'm talking about the reason we are here today
to look at each other and say what can I do for you
to help you get through whatever lack is causing you pain or
sadness or fear or anger or feelings of victimization—

there is only one nation, and it is the nation of
love, we weren't wrong in the '60s we were just too
self-righteous about it thinking whatever made us shout
also gave us the clout to have it all our way so I ask
today for the humility of the saints and the bodhisattvas,
the courage of the martyrs and the *Kama Sutra* the love of
every god who ever gave solace to any lonely soul like
mine and yours, I am reassured by that love no matter how
many tanks and guns and chemical weapons our collective
greed has ignited in the hearts of even lonelier souls who
have no recourse but belligerence and death to satisfy the
myth of their invulnerability—

we are all vulnerable, today's success stories, tomorrow's
homeless, let us all be warriors for love as if we were

sent from above to heal these wounds of neglect, because,
hey, guess what—we were.

IT TAKES ONE TO KNOW ONE

One what?—

Nigger, kike, wop, honky, paddy, redneck, frog,
cocksucker, bastard, bitch, motherfucker, dog—
punk, nerd, dweeb, sissy, jerkoff, creep,
queen, faggot, bulldyke, Republican sheep,
right-wing, leftist, Trotskyite, capitalist pig,
facelifted faketitted phony-in-a-wig,
impotent, premature ejaculator,
stand-up comic, poet, actor,
waiter, chauffeur, screenwriter, masturbator,
sibling, in-law, spouse, kid, victim, manipulator,
codependent, alcoholic, addict, abuser,
liar, cheater, thief, quitter, loser,
photographer, reporter, lawyer, dealer,
doctor, chef, model, hair-stylist, healer,
quack, booshie, commie, jock, gambler, gangster,
fuck-up, greedhead, homie, rambler, prankster,
hippie, yuppie, beatnik, artist, freak,
monster, asskisser, cartoonist, geek,
hoser, dickhead, wanker, slant-eyed dwarf,
fatso, pasty-face, nothin-but-soft,
sexist, racist, ageist, whore,
Buddhist, born-again, sober bore,
white, brown, yellow, red, black and blue,
he, she, them, us, it, me, you,
rocks, mountains, clouds, trees,
rivers, valleys, inlets, seas,
birds, horses, whales, kittens, bees . . .

Hey!—
This could go on forever,
when all we really gotta say is:
Everything and us—

Us
            and
                        everything—

from the smallest quark
to the biggest galaxy—
it's all the same,
and it only takes one
to know one.

One what?

MARCH 18, 2003

(Libellum 2004)

from MARCH 18, 2003

I don't have any answers,
just some questions:
Who's gonna win the Oscar for best actor?
Was Bush sedated at that press conference?
When innocent people die is it worse
than when the guilty do?
Guilty of what?
Can you define dry drunk?
Are you as tired as I am
of these right-wing fundamentalists
trying to reverse what little progress
we've managed to make in our attempts
to create, as Che once said, a world
where love is more possible?
Are some kids more precious than others?

[. . .]

Do my relatives in uniform support Bush
because the right-wing fundamentalists
are really that good at manipulating the media,
a media mostly owned by them
but which they continue to attack as liberal
in order to debunk any questioning of their tactics
and actions by the small percentage
of media outlets that are halfway independent of them?
You call this a poem?
Are the Arabs to blame for their problems?
Are Native Americans?
Are Irish Catholics in Northern Ireland?
Are the Tutus? The North Koreans?
Patty Hearst? Muhammad Ali?
Chris Reeves? The Jews? The Tibetans?
Southern Baptists? Hollywood?

Wall Street? Enron? Ford? Mariah Carey?
Crispin Glover? The Catholic priesthood
The Chechens? The Colombians?
The troops in Kuwait and Iraq?
Are we?
What makes me think I can wait till the last minute
to write a poem about how humbled
I am by the idea
that poetry can do anything to stop
the carnage anywhere—except in our hearts
however briefly?
Wasn't I the only veteran on the stage,
the night in 1966 when I took part in my first
anti-war poetry reading?
If Bush wins in Iraq and Osama is caught and
the economy rebounds enough to give people
some hope is his reelection inevitable?
Is it inevitable anyway?
Should those who voted for Nader be forced
to apologize to the innocent victims of Bush's policies?
Or for his renewed attack on the environment
in the hypocritical but seemingly successful guise
of a man who actually cares about clean air?
Why are Democrats who are smart enough and
tough enough and good enough politicians to play hard ball
with the right-wing pricks so rare?
Do we only care about war
and the innocent lives it takes
when Americans are at risk?
Isn't it obvious that wars never end,
they just move?
What good did our pointing out that Malcolm X
and Martin Luther King were only assassinated
after they stopped talking about race and began
talking about class and the rights of poor people do?
Isn't it obvious these right-wing fundamentalists

are still pissed off about what FDR did for working folk
with social security and tried to do with health care
and other programs that they've since managed to
dismantle or are still attempting to? Isn't it ironic
how much they hate Carter for being a true Christian
and showing them up for the hypocrites they are?
Do these right-wing fundamentalists really believe
that the founding fathers were born-again Christians
who believe, like Bush, that only they'll go to heaven
when "the rapture" comes,
when the framers of the constitution
barely believed in organized religion
and none took the Bible literally?
If the right-wing fundamentalists
really believe we should all follow the Bible's
directions, why wasn't Newt Gingrich
buried in sand up to his neck and stoned to death
when he cheated on his first wife with his second
and then on his second with his third?
Can you get more hypocritical than to try and impeach
a president for adulterous sex with an intern
when you are doing the same exact thing
at the same exact time?
Is it true even Newt thinks this attack on Iraq is ill conceived?

[. . .]

In the past, wasn't the vast right-wing conspiracy
always on the wrong side of history—
for the king, *against* the revolution,
for slavery, *against* the eight-hour day,
for child labor and Jim Crow segregation,
against votes for women,
for legal discrimination, *against* immigrants
and Catholics, Hispanics and African Americans,
for treating corporations like privileged

individuals, and individuals like
corporate privileges?
Or is history still on their
side with that one, as corporate power
grows and equality slows, at least the kind
based on the chance to make a living?
Isn't it true that during the fabulous
fucked-up fifties they pretend to be
so nostalgic for, they ignore the part
about how ordinary citizens won the war
and came home to a nation tired of
depression and built unions strong enough
to give a working man a chance to
own a home and keep up with the Joneses
if not the Walkers and Bushes?
Wasn't the difference between liberal capitalists
and conservative capitalists summed up best
by JFK's old man during the Depression—
when he said he was willing to give up half of what he had
to keep the other half while
the conservatives aren't
willing to give up anything?
Wasn't the first thing they protected after 9/11
offshore banking and headquarters for corporations
and wealthy individuals to avoid paying the taxes
the rest of us do even if that's how and where
the terrorists and drug barons hide their money too?
Wasn't the next thing they bailed out the airlines
because of all the fuel they use and anything that
helps make unconscionable profits for oil companies
is their first priority?
[. . .]
Didn't the CIA overthrow
the democratically elected leader of Iran in 1953
with the help of a Nazi collaborator
who immediately set up 25-year leases

on Iran's oil for three U.S. firms including Gulf Oil?
Didn't Kermit Roosevelt, the CIA head of that region,
retire shortly thereafter to a
vice presidency of—Gulf Oil?
Didn't the CIA back the coup
that overthrew the democratically elected
president of 1950s Guatemala because of his proposal
to nationalize some of United Fruit's vast holdings?
Didn't Walter Bedell Smith,
the CIA man in charge, within a year
become a member of the board of directors
of—you guessed it—The United Fruit Company?
Does anyone see echoes of that today
in Cheney's connections to Halliburton
or Bush's to Enron?
Isn't it true that this shit has been going on forever?
Isn't it also true that our government,
which usually means one of the secret agencies
with secret funding for which the Constitution
never allowed,
trained and paid the leaders of Al Qaeda
in the Afghan proxy war with the Soviets
as well as supplied the necessary
ingredients for Saddam's weapons
of mass destruction including the gas he used
against the Kurds and the helicopters to transport it
and that Bush and his cohorts including his wife
never mentioned the ways the Taliban oppressed women
or Saddam killed his own people until it was convenient politically
and still don't talk about how daddy's cohorts and business
partners in Saudi Arabia have links to Osama and his movement
and oppress women and all the other atrocities
dictatorships and oligarchies have been committing
with our government's blessings
throughout our history?
You call this poetry?

[. . .]

Aren't we all gonna die?
Are we obsessed with the denial of that reality?
As a kid did you, like I, feel
you owned death, like a furry little pet
sitting on your shoulder, and any time you wanted
you could turn your head and see it, or kiss it,
or pet it, or remind yourself how close it was,
but in truth, you thought of it rarely,
more frequently of everyone else's,
because theirs seemed more imminent
even though back then you felt it
breathing on your neck in reassurance?
Or is that just me because I've seen
a lot of people pass, or die, as you might say,
from one thing or another, including my mother
in a way that seemed unfair and certainly
unnecessary and arbitrary and cruel?
But what death isn't?
Those I remember that were no surprise,
though devastating anyway in their
now-you-see-me
now-you-never-will-again
finality?
Is that why now it's life I'm obsessed with?
Or is that because when I watched
the second plane crash into the second tower on TV
a thin blue tube hung from my urethra,
attached to a clear plastic bag, the remnant of a
cancer operation the week before,
unaware an old friend was on that flight,
at that moment incinerated,
a woman who was kind to me when
she didn't need to be?
How many people have died

before you got the chance to tell them what you meant to?
Does it seem there's
not enough
sometimes because it is
too much?
Haven't I said and written more than once
that poetry saved my life?
Did it for you?

[. . .]

Isn't it true the world hasn't been easy for a long time?
Wasn't it once?
Weren't there kids—little
girls in dresses with
skinny legs and bare arms—
and boys too shy to make
as much noise as the others—
under street lamps—out
late, because it's too warm
to go to bed yet—and
nothing good for kids on
the radio anyway—
and nobody really afraid of
anything too strange and
disturbing to threaten their
hopes for more evenings like
this?
Wasn't
the world easy
once?
Wasn't that because we didn't know
and maybe didn't want to
like my nephews and nieces don't
today, as they sail away to foreign ports
called up in the reserves or on the active duty

they see as a way out of the confusion
of a working class that thinks it isn't,
or that class doesn't matter, at least not on
the talk radio they listen to?
Is there no other way for them to go?
Isn't that all they know
despite my talks and books and e-mails?
Don't they say it worked for me,
it's how I first got out into the world?
When I try to tell them why they're wrong
to believe their leaders and the right-wing
corporate radio pimps, isn't it difficult for them to
see, as it was for me, when I used the GI Bill
to attend a university that filled my head with information
that made me dizzy, made me feel crazy,
made me feel alienated from all I'd known
and grown to love the further away
I got from it?

[. . .]

Am I saying
the gang who tried to permanently eliminate Jews
and Gypsies and queers and the retarded and
deformed and more is what our troops and
their commanders replicate in our name?
Or am I saying war brings out the best and
worst of—but haven't you heard all that before?
Aren't your souls and hearts as sore as mine
from all the confusion and obfuscation and distortion
and repulsion of what others do to others
in the name of having been done to us?
Didn't our government use the same tactics it
deplores Saddam for?
Didn't we try to be honest?
But didn't the truth keep changing on us?

When I was a kid, didn't they teach us that
"Uncle Joe Stalin" helped us win the war?
When I was a man, didn't
Ronald Reagan remember scenes from
war movies as if they really happened
and he was there though he was in Hollywood
the entire time making movies he remembered
as reality?
In the light of his later disease
don't we understand that?
Don't we understand everything, sometimes—
or once?
Is this the way we count the time to go
to get to where we know it will be all right for us again?
Or have we walked through the door to the future
and found ourselves on fire before we can see
the flames and what remains and what must go
is all these fools are fighting over when they pose
as people-in-the-know on where we all have been
and might be going?
Does it matter where we are or the color
of our skin or religion of our ancestors or is that
incidental because what's fundamental about these times
is the way the long hot Summer starts in Winter
one unexpected day and then, say, turns up in Spring
for more than a week, or peaks in Fall
when all we want is a breath of fresh crisp air,
the kind we find some mornings in the mountains
or the North but not as many as before,
before the earth became a living/dying litmus test
of our deceit in dealing with these tired times
when even trees are gasping to survive
and they're the ones who keep *us* alive?
How much do the changing weather patterns
over Afghanistan that caused the years of drought
that impoverished the country that embraced a Taliban

solution to their problems have to do with lives lost
and the other costs of 9/11?
What legacy do we end with?
Too many CDs and DVDs and not enough
of what it takes to keep us all from baking in the long
hot Summer of a race's demise despite the seemingly
old fashioned winter we've just survived?
Is it a surprise, that the fate we share is in the air
not in the eyes of some tenacious politician
who pretends he's one of us?
Was Duchamp correct when he said, only in French,
"Tools that are no good require more skill"?
Isn't it too noisy these days?
Can you hear yourself think
with all these hard surfaces
reflecting the clatter
of all the shit that doesn't
even matter anymore?
Can't we just close the door?
Does it help?
To lock it, bolt it,
reinforce it with armed
guards and VCRs and lipo-
suction and cost reduction
and all the seduction your
memory can muster?
Is it
still too noisy in here?
Out there, is that the smell
of blood and fire in the air?
Has the star that
led us here disappeared
over the horizon, while we're
still waiting for some-
thing else to happen, as if
we hadn't had enough already?

Haven't I too felt like beating or bombing someone
who frightened me or pissed me off because of the way
they looked or acted or seem to be?
Can't we all just get along?
Don't you want to believe we can?
But when your friends are turning up with lies
and alibis for all their sadness and depression
and the recession is supposed to be ending
just when your money's running out,
and they keep smoking and slamming
and jabbing themselves with ways to deform
what they can't even accept yet,
what are we doing here anyway?
Am I wrong?
Was I always?
Is it not about healing, but about tearing
each other's eyes out because we don't
see things the same way?
Is it all about blame?
We're all alive and depend on the ocean and trees,
and the air they give us to breathe—so what are we doing?
Going to any lengths to rip each other off
and tear each other down?
Has the smoke gone away, or not,
because it isn't from the flames
but from the fire that only burns
our lungs like marshmallows at the camps
we never went to, too busy getting here,
where there is no air we can't see,
and the fee for being cynical, like I'm feeling tonight,
is to get up tomorrow and fight my way into a breath
I can remember before this war on all our simple
dreams of harmony got started?
Aren't you feeling brokenhearted too these days?
But not like you lost a lover,
like you're losing the sustainers of your soul and very breath?

Can't we do something about it?
Can't we all just get along—
as in people and trees and animals and seas
and the breeze that will someday stop if we
don't start letting it all go—or never stop—
the hurt and the hate and the need to forget it
with stuff that just adds to the noise and pollution?
Isn't there only one life and one problem and one solution
from the streets to the elite?
Don't we all have a seat
in this universe we share?
Is ours now at the feet
of the oil oligarchy running
what once was our home?
You call this a poem?
Didn't they
used to say
"the best things in life are free"
when they meant
the air and the trees and the sea?
But we know
better now, don't we?
When death is no longer imaginary,
doesn't it all seem like poetry?
Or—is that just me?

SWING THEORY

(Hanging Loose Press 2015)

BEFORE YOU WERE BORN

I could memorize my poems
and declaim them from stages
in avant-garde spaces and
coffee house traces of
somebody else's ideas
and call it performance art,
but I already did that
before you were born.

I could put them on stages as a one-man show
or in the mouths of pros and blow you away
with the passion story of my life
and call it avant-garde post-modern
deconstructivist language theater,
but I did that too, when you
were still in grade school.

I could live on the streets
sleep in abandoned buildings
drink cheap rotgut
take whatever drugs are offered
and tell you to go fuck yourself
when you tell me to give up
the life of a poet and get a job,
but I already did that
before you were a gob of spit
hanging from the lip of
Charles Bukowski who had a
nice secure job at the post office back then.

I paid so many dues for the life of
the poet I lived, I once nailed all my shoes
to a board and called it art and then
tore it apart so I could wear them again.

I suffered, I starved, and so did my kids,
I did what I did for poetry I thought
and I never sold out, and even when I did
nobody bought.

I could memorize my poems
and declaim them from stages in
avant-garde spaces and coffee house
traces of somebody else's ideas
and call it performance art,

but I already did that
before you were born.

c. 1980

BIRTH/REBIRTH

Here he is,
             emerging
from
     his mother,
               head first,
face down,
        neck
strangled by
        umbilical cord,
her holding him
         there, his body still
part of hers,
       in her,
            head and neck free
of natal confinement,
         out now,

in the world,
            as the midwife
struggles to remove the cord:

       "Just hold him there, don't push,
       hold him hold him"
                  and damn
his eyes open,
          wide.

             He lifts his
head, takes
         a look around,
             cranes his enwrapped
neck to see
         further to the sides,
              lifts it
to see
       more of the ceiling and lights
and then
       directly
         into your own eyes
with
       a profound
          and deep
              meaning
you understand instantly
          and completely
but could never
       articulate.

           And then
the cord is free and

       "Okay, push"

and she emits a mashup of

                  grunt
and growl
       and yowl—

       and whoosh
he's one of us,
       his eyes still open,
just looking,
       seeing what there is
to see,
     a miracle embodied.

Our seats in the universe
           shift,
to make room
       for him
         at its
center,
     rather than us,
        or you,
or anyone other than
        him,
for now,
     and possibly
        always,
or
     the always we're allowed.

Look at that river,
        those trees,
this way of
       moving information
and ideas
      around,
        between,
         among—

How will it effect him?

How does it?

Can he drink that water,
swim in that
stream,
climb that tree
or cut it down?

Where is it all going?

Or are we?

He's with us now,
and so is she,
and them and
all of us and
how
can we include that in
our choices,
our ways of
moving forward,
or not,
staying put,
going back
to where it all begins,
or doesn't.

How big a spirit
does the universe
embody?

Embrace?

Project?

Be?

And we?

     What are the
connections?

         Interpretations?

Resolutions?

         Mysteries?

Our eyes open,
         or not,
            hearts
and minds
     more importantly,
as we
     stand up
         for what is possible,
the infinite,
         the finite,
               the real
and surreal,
         the answers posing
as questions,
         as they always do.

More births,
         more universes,
more shifting
         perspectives,
more undenying,
            more unlying,
more retrospective

understanding.

Oh,
        this is tomorrow,
                now,
                        and
he is among us
        until he isn't,
as are we,
        and she
                and all who
accept
        the eternal delight
                        of
inevitable change,
                        inevitable
containment of every
                        opposite,
of compliance with
                        the universal
laws of creation
                and destruction,
up and down,
                good and bad,
old and new,
                the future and
the past,
        all stranded,
                        with us,
and him,
        and her
                        and them,
here,
        in the eternally
                        unfolding
now.

THE GOD POEMS

1.

Isn't that God
I see in you? The sycamores
on my street? The sweetness
in the angel food cake I eat
every single day in my com-
pulsive God-like way? The
explanations in books that try
to teach us something we might
not know? The slowness I some-
times mistake for profundity?
The sea that is the mother of
us all? The dying I recall from
childhood that stood my world
on scarred terrain I couldn't
wait to vacate?

2.

Isn't that God in you?
When you are true to
the darkness that
excites you—entices
you to abandon
all caution—all
fear—for what is nearest
your heart's delight
is gratitude for the
night you despise
when she is in it
without you—
But isn't God there too?

In her desperation
and passion for thrills
of unmeasurable joy
that never last because
God is the sun that dispels
the shadows of guiltlessness
—is the sleep that overtakes
her—the sleep she
subsides in when
all else fails—
Isn't God the
failure too?
The broken line?
The useless thought?
The way upstairs that
causes hesitation in
the air she breathes
with you no longer?

3.

She's gone—
He's not—
Their little boy bounces between
Is seen by God as God's own
Heart—a little boy—hurt
and trying not to be—See!
says God—my
        Heart!

4.

You are my heart, God.
You are my blood.

You are the nerve endings
in my tongue,
my scalp, the soles
of my feet, my
penis, my thighs—
You are my eyes.

You corrupt me
with your love
as I have my
sons and daughter.
You are the water
in which I choose
to drown—you
pull me down—
I can't resist.

SWING THEORY: 1

He could be pushed he could go faster
he could stay still. After he could pump
himself up I'd get scared when he'd go
so high the chains would go slack and
I'd expect the seat to plummet straight
down to the ground and I'd yell but
he'd be laughing too loud to hear me
as the seat would jolt back into place
coming back the other way and then
when he reached the apogee of swing-
ing he'd let go and jump and land fur-
ther away than the bigger kids could,
who were the only ones who'd even try
that maneuver, and I'd be proud of him.

THE GEESE DON'T FLY SOUTH

The geese don't fly South
in Winter any more.
Only Latvia is worse than the U. S.
in rates of infant mortality
among the so-called industrial nations.
Where have all the
protestors gone?
I've tried to be a
birder but
they never conform
to the photos and
drawings in the guides
I've bought, including
Sibley's. That
hasn't stopped me
from loving them.
I have often fallen
hardest in love
with those whose
names I never knew.
My Jersey Irish relatives
all live in the South now,
where homes are cheaper
and taxes almost nonexistent.
The red state is where all
our tax money goes,
to prop up cheaper lifestyles.
It's where all the divorces
seem to be too, liberal
Massachusetts having
the lowest rate of divorce.
Or did I mean blue?
I always get confused about
who's who. I don't

mean the book, I've
been in that for years.
But so has Bush.
All the Bushes I suppose.
Let's face it, you can
get away with murder
if you're family always
has. Has yours?
No, I didn't think so.
Or maybe I mean if
your family always
has because of its
position, power and
money, and maybe
couldn't anymore if
those things were removed.
There's cranes and egrets,
swans and mallards, as well
as the various blackbirds
sprinkled all through the
Jersey meadowlands that
once stunk so strongly
my father swore breathing
the air there was a known cure
for asthma, of which
there is so much more now
than when I was a boy and
he was still around. The ground
on which we stand is shifting,
as perhaps it always was, but
now we can't deny it.
The South did rise again.
Trees are more common
in the Northeast now than
they were when I was a boy,
despite the blights and infectious

insects invading from the South.
The tundra is melting so drastically,
houses in Alaska have begun to tilt
like mini-towers of Pisa.
Pizza was an American invention
I heard. Although when I was a boy
there was a kind of loaf of bread
you could buy from the local
Italian immigrants, round and
flatter than most loaves of bread,
that the Italians called Pisa bread.
Two guys who grew up across
the street from me were nicknamed
Loaf and Half-a-Loaf.
When I returned to live in Jersey
after forty years away,
before the last of my siblings still here,
Robert, an ex-cop, moved to Georgia,
he asked me after we left the local A&P
if I'd noticed the rotund old Italian man
who nodded to him at the checkout line,
and when I said I had, he said,
"Know who that was?"
I didn't, so he told me: "Half-a-Loaf."
Bluebirds have come back to New England.
I wonder about the white cliffs of Dover.
Thank God for Turner Classic Movies.
Where have all the heroes gone?
I know the servicemen and women
and firemen and women and other
public servants have done heroic deeds,
I meant in the movies. And politics.
The Bogies and the Robert Kennedys,
the Jimmy Cagneys and the Roosevelts,
the Waynes and the Washingtons,
despite their politics,

and Coopers, Jeffersons Stewarts and
Doctor Kings—Rosa Parks,
Barbara Stanwyks and Joans of Arc,
Queen Maeves and Jean Arthurs
and Mother Joneses.
The Bush family tree, the Walker and
Bush ancestry, have always been
expert at exploiting the systems
of American politics and business
to their advantage and especially
the disadvantage of others,
coming out ahead even when
the rest of us are begging
for a scrap of bread from
the tables they control.
How whole can you be
when you can't see anything
other than your own perspective?
How wrong were we as kids
to think our romantic nostalgia
for revolutions past could
pass the test of our time.
Will it matter when the climate
changes so severely, everyone
we know might end up
destitute like those Katrina
victims who missed the boat,
literally. And what has
literature wrought? Remember
the heroes of Sir Walter Scott?
But that was boyhood heroics.
As a young man it was the
heroes and heroines of
Joyce or Toomer or Rhys.
Certainly no heroes
or heroines in the conventional

sense. Like my
current taste for
the war journalism of
Martha Gellhorn. What
could be more courageous
than her writing? Her life,
I'd say. With all her war
reporting from the front
or near enough to bear
the brunt of bombs and
manmade disaster. And
all her exes,
yet alone in the end.
Or Lee Miller's
commitment to *her* life as
her true masterpiece. Or
should that be *mistresspiece*?
The language fails us now. Orwell
was right, about some things.
"Oh well" is what they wrote
under my high school yearbook
photo as my favorite expression.
*Oh well in*fucking*deed.*

GIVE ME FIVE MINUTES MORE

To sell this thing
To tell my story
To straighten it out
To see her again
To calm him down
To explain to them
To fix that thing
To turn it off

To answer the question
To find the solution
To look it up
To explain myself
To win or lose
To get it right
To let it go
To say goodbye
To say hello
To tell him why
To ask for permission
To show them the way
To pick it up
To put it down
To make them laugh
To calm them down
To shift to neutral
To put it in park
To stand on my head
To remain in the dark
To split the infinitive
To reunite the movement
To fight for the right
To make the improvement
To settle for less
To look for proof
To expose the lies
To check the roof
To fill the cracks
To seal our fate
To kiss the girl
To close the gate
To master the technique
To plug the leak
To acknowledge the geek
To protect the weak

To discover their worth
To inherit the earth
To explode in mirth
To quench this thirst
To quiet that moan
To dig up the bone
To get off the phone
To find a home
To rewrite this poem

DEAR BIRDS

Thank you for your example.

And for eating pesky insects,

and making incessant music

everywhere, like the crow

that woke me my first morning

in Tokyo, with a caw that

sounded strange, as though

in another language than

the ones I knew back home.

I mean the ducks of you, how

do you float on wet feathers?!

The genius of your oily ducts

and webbed feet! And geese,

despite the mess you make

especially now that flying South

is no longer necessary,

you still appear majestic

in your realm, and cranes

and egrets and swans in

dirty polluted pools of

Jersey wasteland. The miracle

of you, and pigeons, so

despised, I still admire

for your tenacity and survival

skills and unique beauty,

the ways you snap your heads

from side to side as if by

some other rhythm than the

ones I know, but most of all you

little ones, sparrows and

finches and wrens and the rest,

and those big among the

small, you Robin Red Breasts,

so proud and independent,

and astonishing Cardinals

and admonishing Blue Jays.

(I just learned from my fourth-

grade son's science project

hummingbirds are actually

aggressive too, like you!) You

constantly amaze and surprise

me with new facts, oh birds,

which never contradict the in-

spiration of your ability to float

on breezes and make the wind

your world. Ah birds, don't

let us diminish your variety

with our greed and lack of

a united will. Keep using the

sky for your canvas, making

art that never ceases to

engage the child in us.

from THE 2008 SONNETS

MARCH

John Adams is still missed by some—
others miss Thomas Jefferson. Jon-
athan Williams, endless campaigns,
how debased the word has become.

The loss of my brother Robert, the
quirks of our clan, the culture we
come from, or what I haven't
figured out yet and maybe never will.

I'm grateful my adolescent dis-
appointment and anger over their
foibles and mistakes, even wrongs,
has given way to an acceptance

that transcends expectations of a
perfection we're all incapable of.

APRIL

I don't know about you but beauty
still thrills me—as I pass a small tree
with low hanging branches filled
with extraordinarily bright, white,
blossoms, I have the urge to kiss
one, or all of them, in gratitude.
My day feels more satisfying, my life
more vital, my heart more light and
light filled than before I spied them.
Jason Shinder suffered his illness for
so long, yet, in his presence, you got
the impression his only concern was
your well being despite, given the
odds, his presence being—miraculous.

MAY—THE INFINITE POSSIBILITIES OF ART

Robert Rauschenberg—who is Rachel
Schutz? Can these frightened people who
think their religion's being suppressed in
this country name one atheist in government
in any prominent position? What is it with
the women in Asian martial arts movies
that makes them so lovely? The lighting?
The make up? Their natural good looks? Like
the young Elizabeth Taylor or Ava Gardner
or Halle Berry. There's all kinds of beauty,
and beauty in all kinds, but the kind that
lights up movie screens through the star
of a face—Johnny Depp's, Keri Russell's,
Takechi Kaneshiro's—its own delight.

JULY

The food was delicious and ridiculously
cheap. I thanked her for it, and she thanked
me, genuinely, almost teary-eyed grateful
for my patronage. I asked if the new police
station was helping her business. She shrugged
and said, "little bit" and then "no good now,
everything" then threw up her hands and
ended with "this country broken"—the air
we breathe, generation kill, the terrorist bump,
The New Yorker diversion, Thomas M. Disch,
the gist he killed himself, the book about the
toaster, new wave sci-fi, but I knew him as
a poet, a mischievous glint in his eye, more
deaths of troops in Afghanistan forgotten.

AUGUST

The oil companies that control the Republican
hierarchy, or are it. She's big into drilling
everywhere and anywhere and making our
economy, like Alaska's, completely dependent
on oil and oil companies, the governor of
a population one quarter that of Brooklyn.
They care more about Smith Barney than
Barney Smith. Obama's family members
crowded the stage, this wonderful array of
supposed categories of us, from what's called
"white" to "black" to Asian to Latino, but
is just the face of this country not as it
should be but as it is sweet moment.
Biden a single father of two—like I once was.

SEPTEMBER

Paul Newman carried his beauty lightly, with
grace and generosity the older he got and the
softer yet more striking his looks became. His
life exemplary to me. Not just the charity but
the clarity of knowing how lucky he was. I can't
think of another poet outside of Emily Dickinson
as cryptic and yet totally revealing of her inner
life as Joanne Kyger. Obama calmer, taller,
younger, made his points clearly and connected
them more logically, McCain, whiter, more smart
ass, simpler, more repetitive, and meaner, which,
obviously, some like. Think Obama would
even get this far? Why not just loan them the
money at high interest rates like they do to us?

OCTOBER—DESTROY OUR COUNTRY FIRST!

Doggone it, she sure is a regular joe sixpack hockey
mom kinda gal next door who's gonna get that darn
fed'ral government to help out folks at Saturday's
soccer game and'll just have to not be too specific how
(wink wink) 'cause doggone it who wants to hear about
her ol' end times beliefs (what the heck, the world's comin'
to an end soon anyway an' Alaska, according to her pastor,
is gonna be the refuge state for all those believers in the
lower 48 who'll need a place to run to when the anti-Christ
shows up—and we know who that might be (wink wink)
—and the Rapture sends all the Jews and Catholics and
atheists to hell and even some of those darn Protestants
who just don't get it that there's only one way to be saved)
with a gotcha satisfied smile behind every rehearsed lie.

NOVEMBER

It should be a no brainer, voting in the church
around the corner, walked to from my apartment
over sidewalks covered in such amazing
colors from the fallen leaves I feel incapable
of describing this scene, so vividly Autumnal,
such a range of hues, like us, thrilled and
overwhelmed with gratitude, there's nothing
to compare it to, and yes, I did cry—"think
of the children" they constantly cried back
when I wanted a "black girl" for my bride,
now it looks like that argument was as
backward as I labeled it as a kid, 'cause here
that theoretical child is—proving yes we can
—create a new world again. Knock on wood.

TEA PARTY SUMMER

Can you
believe
this shit?

I know
it's all
mostly
contrived
but man
alive.

Or not
if the
"socialist"
"facist"
 "foreign-

born"
"terrorist"
gets his
way with
us old
white
men.

And women.

Like that one
collapsing in
tears sobbing
"I want my
America back . . ."

And yes some
of us see the
implied racism
in all that. But

it's so
much
more.

A door
is closing
in their
universe
and they're
afraid they'll
be locked
inside forever.

They, and
even some
of us, can't

see there's
a window
still wide
open on the
other side.

The window
that's letting
all that fresh
air in. Let
the future
begin.

SWING THEORY 2

The mood swings unpredictable but
reliable, from affectionate to hostile,
from I want you to I hope you have
a heart attack and drop dead now.
From get the fuck out of my house
to please please don't go, from don't
ever talk to me again to unable to stop
talking, from let's play to don't touch
me, from you retard lazy liar to you're
so handsome stylish and cool. From
cruel to caring. Then react to insulting
jokes with anything but total accept-
ance or dare joke back in a similar
vein and: You'll never see me again.

POEM ON THE THEME: ARTHRITIS
for John Godfrey

My Irish peasant
               immigrant grandfather
the first policeman
               ever in our Jersey town
—badge number one
               —carried an old,
shriveled up, petrified
               potato in his pants
pocket to ward off
               the pain of arthritis and
claimed it worked.
               Though it may have
been the booze—
               the beer and ale and
fermented dandelion
               juice he'd make in
his bathtub from
               the yellow blossoms he
picked in the high
               school playing field
across the street
               from his little house.
Sometimes, when
               he was even more drunk
than usual, we kids
               would see him bent over
the grass with his
               old, dark stained fedora
on his silver haired head,
               a collarless shirt
no longer quite
               white drooping down
over what we'd

all be giggling at but
secretly embarrassed
                by, his underpants,
having forgotten to
                put on the slacks in
the pocket of which
                would be the old,
shriveled up, petrified
                potato to ward off
the pain of his arthritis,
                which obviously
he didn't need on
                these days, so intent
on harvesting the
                dandelions, his square
unshaven silver speckled
                jaw jutting forward
displaying the resolve
                and fortitude necessary
for the only job he
                seemed to have once
he retired from the force.
                I never heard him
complain of any kind
                of pain. Maybe that's
why they called
                him "Iron Mike."

His seventh-grade
                drop out son, my father
one of eight kids who
                lived a while, though
one sister died in the
                influenza pandemic of
1918, and one brother
                in what my father always

felt was a phony
                    suicide attempt that went awry,
didn't believe in
                    the old superstitions (though
his wife, my mother,
                    the high school graduate
of the family certainly
                    did, as she seemed
to also believe in
                    "the little people" she blamed
for household mishaps
                    that couldn't be laid
at the feet of her six
                    children who lived
beyond infancy out
                    of the seven she had
that I was the youngest
                    of) so dad didn't
carry an old petrified
                    potato around in his pants
pocket, but wore a
                    copper bracelet instead,
insisting it worked wonders
                    for his arthritic joints,
and maybe it did. I never
                    heard him complain
about any pain either,
                    except the kind he felt
I caused to his
                    heart and head.

Ma died from heart
                    failure after an operation
to remove cancerous
                    growths from her colon
and more, so my

father moved in with my
oldest sister who
was always ailing from
surviving childhood
diabetes, suffering much
pain from various
disorders as a result of it,
or the medications
used to fight it, and when
that war seemed finally
lost, daddy took to
his bed to beat her
to the other side, and did,
though she eventually
joined him there,
from her kidneys
giving out, after several
bouts with her own
cancers and heart failures
and enough pain to
go around for our whole
clan, if it was needed.

The last of my brothers
to join them passed
last year just as Spring
was about to arrive
and miss him, the only
cop among our siblings
and the only one to have
a bout of arthritis himself,
or so the awful pain in his
wrists was diagnosed
as for a while, after Lyme
Disease and several
other guesses. He kept them

wrapped in those

    soft casts for several months,

doctors orders,

    while they fed him various

medicines including

    the antibiotics we're all too

familiar with,

    and then one day the pain

was gone, not that

    he ever complained when

it was still there.

    I remember one time visiting

him in a childless

    old people's enclave outside

of Atlanta, Georgia,

    where he and his wife had

moved to be closer

    to their grown children and

their families who'd

    left New Jersey for the newer

and bigger yet somehow

    cheaper houses there with

one tenth the taxes they

    faced here. When he bragged

about these facts,

    I said, "Yeah, but you live in

Georgia" as he and I

    took a walk around the complex

he seemed to be

    the unelected mayor of, greeting

fellow retirees

    with the same gruff brevity

he addressed the

    rest of us with, until I had

to stop to catch

    my breath and let the pain

in my chest that
                      still plagued me then subside,
as we paused
                      in our stroll around his domain
I asked him
                      if he ever had pain that kept
him from doing things
                      like mine was now, and his
abrupt reply I
                      should have foreseen after
a lifetime of
                      similar responses "And if I did,
what would be
                      the point of talking about it?"
which made me
                      smile at how reliable he'd
always been. He died
                      of a rare cancer they only
discovered when it
                      caused him to erupt in spots
and sores all over
                      his freckled Irish skin,
"stage four" they said
                      having missed the first
three and ordered up
                      heavy chemo sessions that
turned him from a
                      vital seventy-nine-year old
who could throw
                      heavy furniture into the back
of a truck by
                      himself that would take you
and me both to
                      lift a few inches off the ground,
he went from
                      that kind of older brother

(remember the scene
                in *Godfather Two* where
the mob informant
                is about to squeal to a
platform full of Senators
                until he sees his aging
older brother, just
                flown in from Italy,
sitting silently in the gallery
                and clams up, accepting
prison or even death
                before exposing himself
to his big brother's
                approbation, that's the way
I felt about my brother
                the ex-cop) who'd just driven
from Georgia to Jersey
                and back again like a teenager
on a lark, but
                after only two sessions of
this chemo supposed
                solution, he was transformed
into a frail, old man
                who couldn't stand on his
own, or walk without
                a cane at first, then walker,
then one of those
                electric carts. He resisted
the final passage for
                my sister-in-law's sake,
not complaining of
                the obvious pain let alone
discomfort, but
                looking more sour with
every hour until
                I told her to let him go,

bring him home
                from the hospital for hospice
care and tell him
                she'd fare okay on her own,
that he could go
                home to where our sister
and other brothers
                and parents had gone, and
as soon as she said it,
                he did.

The only encounters
                I've had with arthritis,
outside the above,
                were when I made my first
movie with a Holly
                wood star, whose hands
were so gnarled they
                looked like mushrooms grew
wild under his pale skin.
                John Carradine played
my character's grand
                father and still had the force
of all the roles I'd
                seen him play since I was a boy,
as he stared at me from
                behind the camera while
I prepared for my close up
                at his supposed deathbed
and the director leaned in
                to whisper in my ear
he'd like to see some tears
                on my face then yelled
"Action!" and I panicked
                thinking I'm not good enough
to cry on cue but John

Carradine stared into my eyes
with the intensity of his
                and as I looked away in
search of an alternative
                I saw his hands, those
knuckles erupting under
                his skin with fierce
independence like an
                alternative artwork of
organic confusion
                blossoming into fingers that
extended in every direction,
                uncontrollably bent and
stiffened and askew and
                the tears flew from my eyes,
much to my surprise and
                the rest of the cast and crew
who after "Cut!" was
                shouted erupted in spontaneous
applause but none from
                John Carradine who couldn't
have clapped if he'd
                wanted to, he just kept looking
into my eyes as he
                nodded his head in approval
and smiled slyly.

As for me, knock
                on wood, so far so good
when it comes to
                the arthritis of my male
progenitors, though
                not so good for other
ailments, like heart
                problems I take more
medication for than

they even had back then,
or the cancer that
                    rendered me useless in
some departments
                    for awhile and kept me in
a hospital bed and
                    pain I didn't mind complaining
of, though not as
                    much as I'd have liked to. It
gave me insight
                    into what these men and women
in my family en
                    dured so silently, an intensity
that only those who
                    have gone through it can
describe but so few
                    ever do. The best I could
come up with in
                    response to the priest who
stopped by my room
                    to ask how I was doing
one day, and as he
                    spoke I suffered a wave of
"discomfort" (in
                    quotes) as close to a ten on
the pain scale they
                    were always asking me to rate
as you can get, I
                    told him that before this experience
I always thought
                    God was Love, but now I
understood that
                    God is Pain, and he nodded as
though he under
                    stood as I do now, they are
the same.

SWING THEORY: 3

On Halloween afternoon the town
closed off the main street in the village
center plus part of the street the old
house our apartment was in was on
so the kids in their costumes could
wander the streets on their way to
getting candy from store owners. My
boy and some of his friends took a
break to throw a football around and
one kid left in a huff over something,
coming back with his parents, a gor-
geous young "black" woman and her
Waspy-styled "white," though now
red-faced, husband looking angry.

Earlier sitting on the top step of the
stoop, noticing her in the street I felt
flattered that she looked at me with
seeming interest, but now she glared
behind her husband who was accusing
my little boy of harming his, because
of the color of his child's skin! I was
calm at first pointing out I'd been there
all along and no one deliberately hurt
anyone, but that made him madder.
He was in my face, taller and heftier
than my skinny frame. I felt my own
rage start, then my heart screaming
with the angina I take medication for.

I tried to reason with this man calling
me and my boy prejudiced against his
because we were so-called "white"
Irish-looking males. I pointed out the

417

two best friends my son was standing
watching this with were brown, both
mixed race, one Asian and "white" the
other "black" and "white" like this man's
son, but he didn't seem to hear. I didn't
want my son and his friends to see me
"chicken out" but as the chest pain in-
creased I thought what's worse, to see
me back down or drop dead on the spot?
So I stopped arguing and stepped back.

The man, almost spitting by now let his
wife pull him away, and as they backed
down the street he kept yelling for every-
one to hear that I was racist scum and so
on, me wanting, and maybe even trying
to yell back that I walked these streets
fifty years ago with my black love and
got beat up and spit on and run out of
town for it and now smiled every time I
saw a racially mixed couple stroll by as
though without a care because now they
could in this town, and I felt I'd been
a part of what caused that change but
now was being blamed for the opposite.

STRING THEORY

I wasn't good at a lot of it—
but there were things—
strings connecting me to
music—jazz & r&b mostly—
I could play piano—I had a feel—
soul some said—(like poet

Ralph Dickey who had more
keyboard technique but lacked a
certain swinging intuitive
rhythm)—and words—mine—
not maybe most original—
but originally mine in ways
that favored reverence for
a truth I never found any-
where else—and movies—
or those serial movies that
are TV—in my time I
made a contribution—whether
anyone noticed or not—
I tried to step back, like
Lao Tsu says, but found it
complicated—more complicated
than I knew how—simplicity
being my mission—my love
for the boy I couldn't protect
in me back then but vowed
to stay connected to—do you
hear those one-syllable words?—
they're the ones that trip me
up since they removed that
foreign object from my brain
that explains my poetry now—
though it always did—

from SO AND

jasmine—Tunisia
—how evocative
like '40s films
black & white

yet fragrant &
bursting with life—
vital in a way
that's filled with
the more subtle
colors light
and shadow
provide through
skills no longer
needed or applied
—extent—is that
what I meant?

[. . .]
I know I haven't done
enough—oh sure I've
stood by my core beliefs,
thank God, most of the time,
haven't you? and often
paid the price for telling
the truth, even if it was
inconvenient or impolitic
at times, or made myself
look not so good—even
genuine heroics I've had
my part in, as I'm sure
we all have at least once
more or less—but I confess
I didn't fly to Liberty
Square in Cairo to take
my place among the heroes
of this season, like I hitched
to places all across this
nation in the 'sixties &
beyond to stand up for
the truth of our common

humanity in the face of
racism and war—more
bullying confronted and
sometimes the victim of
—love, I thought then
was the answer—as so
many of us did and I
still do—not just like
anyone who wakes up
in an operating room or
just before they go in
feels all that matters is
their loved ones—but
too the love of all our
commonality even when
wired differently so that
simplified slogans can
sway one wiring this way,
the other that, to see the
spirit of love in all things
not just creatures like us
and those apes over there
staring into our eyes
with a look that is so
tired of the lies about
our differences, their
"inferiority" they
know intuitively isn't
real beyond the deal we've
made to behave like it is—

I still talk to rocks, let alone
trees, and they always talk back,
mountains and clouds and
meadows and shadows
and the glories winged

cousins bring to any view—
the choice we always
have to get as close as
we ever will to the truth
in the heart of all things,
even the despicable bullies
holding Weiwei hostage
as we meet here tonight
to celebrate our love of
all creative attempts
to fulfill our humanity . . .

I wanted to write
a special poem for
this night like I
sometimes have before
to tell what I know
as well as I know
my heart's scars

but my brain's scarred
now too and it doesn't
work as well as it once
did, nor do the connections
between my thoughts
and the fingers typing this
(I know I should move to
voice activated programs
so I don't have to go through
the hassle of retyping
and retyping and retyping
until the word I meant
to write is finally on the
screen—but I've been
using my fingers to
express myself in so

many ways, on the
keys of the old portable
typewrites of my tough
(I meant to write "type-
writers" of my "youth"
and would normally
make the correction
but both words make sense
for that period of my life:
"typewrites" and "tough")
and electric typewriters
of my thirties and early
forties and computer key-
boards ever since, or
the keys of pianos, upright,
grand, electric and acoustic,
or organs or Rolands or
Rhodes or whatever was
available, but I can no
longer do with the same
facility I once had—I know
a lot of folks have the same
problems who didn't have
brain surgery—but the way
it happened for me was sudden—
before the growth affected me
I typed and played piano as
fast and as accurately as always
—and then one day I didn't
anymore, and that's still the
way it is tonight—I can never
get it right the first time, but
have to try and try again until
I do, like a child just learning,
again, but now who understands
so much he never did before

because too much came too easily,
and what didn't I usually ignored—
but that door—the "easily"—is
closed, if I want to enjoy the
pleasures writing and playing
piano always gifted me—
I know musicians much younger
whose injured wrists or elbows or
arms or vocal chords or other
physical restraints have caused
them to face the same crisis of
inability, I'm not comparing
myself or complaining, even
if it may sound that way to
you, I'm explaining because
that's what I do, I say "this
is the way I'm experiencing the
truth of my life right now and
what I see around me, and you?"

the bright bursts of yellow
announce a spring still
struggling to arrive—forsythia
and daffodils followed by
the eye-opening white blossoms
of the dogwood tree in our yard
or neon pinks of the cherry
blossoms in the nearby park—

the more exotic blossoms on
the screen or page when I
try to write, here's some
uncorrected typing:
and oc cour se it's all\si
fucking meningliess oh
what thrtwa thy asportiaons

ame upont this whatever
\

yes, we all noticed how
the force of "fucking"
somehow survived intact—

but that's not all
that's moved on

[. . .]

what happened
was I went
but I came back
I did it but
then I stopped
I knew but
then I forgot
I was but
now I'm not

now it's old news
the blues I play
never come out
right 'cause
that connection
between the keys and
fingers and brain
ain't, like I said,
the same anymore,
but when a door closes
for now or ever as always
a window opens and
new synapses replace
the old flashes with

bold distinctions—

like how I always found
Meryl Streep and Anette Beining
unattractive, no matter how much
I admired their talent, or
Mitzi Gaynor's girl-next-door looks
so abrasive—

I liked the darker
beauties and
their darker arts—
then they removed
that part of my brain that
wasn't supposed to be there
and where once having been
born in the Swing Era
made it always about
rhythm & tone, now those
old ideas were gone and
whenever Meryl or Annette
or Mitzi's image shines
from old movies on TV
I feel actual glee at
their presence in my
living room, overflowing
with desires I never knew
I had because I hadn't
until now & this rewiring—
the Meryl-Annette-Mitzi-
attraction and affection
connection—so that when
they aren't beaming from
the small screen I swear
I feel no attraction or
affection for them at all

but when they are—the
mysteries of what I always
believed was me
but now know as merely
electric impulses in
the thought battery
that's the hybrid
of my brain . . .

the smell of
rain here—
or the way
here smells
when it rains

don't fight
the goodness
in you or
anyone else—
Hubert Selby Jr.
taught me that

you know how
long it took me
to type
and retype
and retype and re-
type until all
the words were
actually the
ones I intended?

of course a lot
of what comes out
is more "poetic"
in some sense—

like "tough" for "youth"
or "angels" for "angles"
and "tripe" for "type"
"sea age" for "message"
"meadow" for "Meryl"
and line break for
apostrophe and
frustration for
accuracy and bottomless
self-pity for stamina and
perseverance—timidity
was never an option
although it ruled
so much of what
appeared as bravado
—am I making sense
and why do I feel I
should—do I repeat
myself and in so less
exiting ways than
Weiwei does—man
I admire that guy,
his presence even
just in photographs,
and then in films,
you can see his spirit
and its generosity and
acceptance of what is,
then using it for what
can be—

I've never been
humble enough—
I wasn't tough
or noble or good
enough to shine

at sports—but
I was smarter
about most
stuff than anyone
I grew up around—
and I had a pro-
found respect
for originality,
of which I thought
I had my share—
when it didn't
seem to get me
where I thought
I should be—I
made it known
in ways that put
the onus on you
for not doing
enough to bring
justice to my
cause—my due—
my getting through
the obstacles I
knew were there—
where others
seemed spared
from the reper-
cussions I drew
fire from—come,
let's kiss and
make up, like
Nina Simone
always wanted
then refused
to do—original?
she was—as is

Ai Weiwei
who surprisingly
looks up to
Andy Warhol
who risked so
little, although
maybe not—
he got shot
by a woman I
knew, that's right,
Valerie Salinas,
when she got out of
the hospital for the
criminally insane
someone dropped her
on the steps of my
"commune" as we
called them in those
days—the women who
till then had been big
admirers became afraid
once she moved in—
they feared her constant
pacing and muttering and
rage at those she thought
had taken advantage of
her—like the time I came
home to find the upstairs
toilet plugged because
she'd ripped up the house
copy of her *S.C.U.M.*
Manifesto and tried to
flush it—then left it,
as they all did, for me
to plunge until the
pages all came out

and the toilet worked
again and my kids could
use it and when I went
away for a reading in
Boston with some friends—
Ed Cox, Tim Dlugos,
Terence Winch—the
women in this radical
lesbian-feminist "commune"
—don't ask—told Valerie
I didn't want her there
so she moved out and
when I got back and they
told me I was dismayed—
I got along fine with her
and kind of enjoyed the
way she made all visitors
so nervous with her smoke
filled pacing and muttering
in our communal living room—
I liked a lot of her ideas too—
she was the first person I knew
to explain the differences between
men and women by the nerve
endings in their genitals and
taste buds on their tongues
and olfactory absorbers in
their sense of smell, and color
recognition facets of their eyes—
men are simpler, she'd explain,
they have so much less of all
of that they just miss a lot—
it was one of the reasons she
said she didn't mind having sex
with them for money (she
became a hooker for a living

after she left the house we all
rented and I moved out of not
long after this) because they
were so easy to satisfy, so
simpleminded and biologically
formed, but she only loved
women and preferred their
bodies and complexities,
though she found the ones
in our supposedly revolutionary
commune chickenshit—

you don't know
what you're missing,
people I love
get ignored or
forgotten, poets
artists, actors
musicians
I don't always
know what *I'm*
missing

the trees *always*
talk back—

Valerie thought the solution
was electricity, to somehow
make men more sensitive,
like the women she loved,
they needed to be wired
with more electricity—

I understood in those first few months
after the operation, when I couldn't
read and then only out loud and then

finally could, well enough to pass—
what it felt like to be a child with
learning disabilities or an adult with
rightwing simplicities or—and this
was maybe the most difficult to
accept—blissfully contented with
only the capacity to eat and drink
and hold conversations with one
person at a time, sublime satisfaction

sometimes I'm still overwhelmed
by too much stimuli, a crowd, a TV
on and phone ringing and someone
talking, at first I couldn't see the way
things are parts of a bigger picture,
as a single blossom blends into
a landscape, not anymore, as
each item popped out, individualized
and so distinct it was like a nightmare—
no grasping of the whole picture
just its individual parts shouting
at me through my eyes to realize
each tiny aspect of the scene as
equally important and demanding
of attention, oh it hurt my head
just to open my eyes, and hearing
was even more of a surprise because
I couldn't close my ears but had
to hear each note distinctly in
even the most complicated music
so that this horn and that one were
distinct and each voice in harmony
to others was isolated in my ear
overwhelmed with all the disso-
nance no one else could hear . . .

my children know what
they mean to me, because
I always tell them and
hope my actions do too—

forgive me friends
for being so untrue—
I always mean to tell you
how much *you* mean to me,
the prominence you have
in my heart, but things
happen, I never start
that sentence until
you're gone or
I am, so let me
be clear and
say it here—
I love you all
in my own way
which is to say
I think of you often
and it always invites
a smile to the ongoing
project of time's
that is this face . . .

as George Oppen wrote
in that collection of authors'
self-portraits Burt Britton
once collected, under
Opppen's curved line of
an old man's back
he wrote: "which is
a very odd thing to happen
to a child" and it is—

jasmine—Tunisia
—how evocative
[. . .]

Fall 2011

THE JIMMY SCHUYLER SONNETS

1. THE KISS

At a party for Lawrence Ferlinghetti at
Barbara Guest's New York apartment in
1975, Jimmy approached me and asked:
Are you Michael Lally? I confessed I
was. Then he asked: May I kiss you?
Not something I particularly wanted,
but because he was James Schuyler I
said: Sure. So he did. I wasn't into it,
but he was. It was brief. He seemed
pleased. I figured he asked for the kiss
because he was attracted to me, so I
wanted to know why he first asked if
I was me. He said: To make sure you
were the man who writes those poems.

2. ELEGANT

As he was leaving the party a man asked
Jimmy if he would write down his address
for him. He had a book he wanted to send
him. Jimmy took the pen and paper the
man provided and wrote in an elegant
cursive style: James Schuyler. Then under-
neath that in the same old-style cursive,

but smaller, he wrote: James Schuyler.
Underneath that he wrote in even smaller
script: James Schuyler. I no longer recall
how many times he did this, but the last
had diminished to unreadable size. He gave
the paper and pen back to the man and
left him to read it and look up, mystified.

3. IN THEIR COMPANY

Over dinner at Darragh Park's 22nd Street
home with Darragh, Jimmy and Ana, the
Costa Rican woman I lived with at the
time, Jimmy was mostly silent. So she and
Darragh did a lot of the talking. I loved all
of them and was content to just be in their
company. Jimmy felt the same way about
us, as he revealed later to Darragh. He
especially liked that Ana and I looked him
in the eye and talked to him the way we
would anyone. Not everyone did that with
Jimmy when he was having a bad day,
unable or unwilling to talk, the meds taking
their toll on his capacity for communicating.

4. BEAUTY AND LOVE

In his room at The Chelsea Hotel, Jimmy
was telling me of his love for Tom Carey
as Helena reentered, back from an errand.
Jimmy loved them both, as did many of us.
Helena not just for the help she was to him
daily but for her delightful beauty and dis-
arming honesty and insight, and Tom for

his beauty as well, and sardonic wit despite
his serious troubles then. I was often arro-
gantly self important around my peers in
those years, and even some of my elders,
but never around Jimmy because of his
poems I loved so much and aspects of the
strategies in them I felt we had in common.

5. FORGIVEN

Jimmy's peers at times expressed frustration
with the childlike aspect of his need to be
cared for, not believing it was entirely
from his mental health struggles. I might
have some small insight into that now.
Not because I suffer as Jimmy did, but
because I worry some of my peers may
be exasperated with my childish need to
be forgiven or excused or tolerated or
indulged when I forget to respond or seem
to ignore or avoid so much and blame it
on the brain operation some may think I
use as a license to only do what I want, the
way some thought Jimmy sometimes did.

6. WHAT MATTERED

I've been copying lines from books
I read into a bound journal since 1962.
A few here and there, not a lot, but
several from James Schuyler poems.
Here are two: "Californians need to
do a thing to enjoy it./A smile in the
street may be loads! you don't have

to undress everybody." And the other:
"Did Beowulf call the sea 'the penis-
shrinker'?" I can pick up any book of
his and read any random lines and find
gems. I just did: "From the next room
the friendly clatter of an electric type-
writer." Jimmy knew what mattered.

NOVEMBER SONNET

On a perfectly clear Fall day, heading back to
Fort Monmouth, I watched as other cars on
The Garden State Parkway veered onto the
shoulder and stopped, the drivers not getting
out, just sitting there. At the toll booth the man
said The president's been shot. As I drove on,
more cars pulled off the road. I could see their
drivers weeping. Back in the barracks we stayed
in the rec room watching the black and white
TV, tension in the room like static. When they
named Lee Harvey Oswald, I watched the
black guys hold their breath, hoping that meant
redneck, not spade, and every muscle in their
faces relax when he turned out to be white.

THE SAN FRANCISCO SONNETS (1962)

1.

In a San Francisco Chinatown hotel, Bucks
slept off all his driving alone while I roamed
North Beach in my slept-in skinny suit with

action back jacket and pipe cleaner pants plus
my junkie sky piece and pointy-toed boots.
In Jimmy Valentine's Hot Dog Palace where
Columbus and Broadway met, with only a
quarter left I eyed the jazz-filled box and a
slice of chocolate cake in a glass case, chose
the box, dropped my coin in the slot and put-
ting my ear to the speaker felt a hand on my
left shoulder. Turning to my right as I rose
to avoid getting suckered I saw Andre, who
said Got a car? There's a party in Berkeley.

2.

I woke Bucks to drive us to BOP CITY a funky jazz
joint where Andre scored, then to a small druggie
party in Berkley in a little white bungalow where
another Michael, a crazy Jewish jazz sax player,
lived with a heartbreakingly crazy young blonde
who loved books we deeply discussed after we all
moved in. When he discovered Bucks was from
Darien, Andre spoke of rich families he knew there.
Bucks turned whiter than he already was. Andre
had been the only spade at a private school, he said,
his English becoming as polished as an old-style
movie star's, making mine sound like a spade Bowery
Boy's. Bucks sold his car for a motorcycle to split
for Colorado and the first commune I ever heard of.

3.

Crazy Michael got jealous of me and the blonde
so Andre took me back to North Beach to hang
at Mister Otis, a jazz club that let me sit in for

439

free drinks and Andre's lady, a French illegal,
hook wealthy johns. She said if I read Herman
Hesse's *Steppenwolf* it would change my life. But
it didn't. Later Andre snuck the three of us into a
hotel across from Valentine's thanks to the night
clerk he knew, then left to get me a pint to stop
my constant cough from my four or more packs
of Pall Malls a day, but we knew it was to score.
She tried to soothe me with sex but I said my
preference was darker chicks. I missed Bambi.
When Andre returned with the pint I emptied it.

4.

In the morning, the floor littered with sleepers,
an old lady burst in yelling Out! Out! Everyone
split except me and Andre. He spoke to the lady
like a prince to a peon and she left us alone to get
dressed. First he took a piss in the sink, did a few
ballet turns, then bought me another pint and got
me to call Dolores to propose. By then I didn't know
what I was doing. She said Yes. Andre disappeared.
I slept after that in a half constructed high rise with
other vagabonds like Gaylord, a large white cat I
knew from The Village who wore a blanket with
a hole for his head, looking like Jesus or an apostle.
He was the first person I knew who gave the V
sign palm out and said Peace when greeting you.

5.

I ran into Eileen Kaufman panhandling North
Beach tourists with Parker. Like Irish peasant
mothers of my Irish grandmother's time wand'-
ring the streets of Galway begging with their kids.

Paddy O'Sullivan tramped the streets of North
Beach dressed like Puss'n'Boots, wide brimmed
hat with feathery plume, cape and high fancy
boots, declaiming his poems to strangers. We
shared bottles while sitting against the wall of
Vesuvio in the alley next to City Lights Books.
After a few weeks I had my oldest sister, Joan,
wire me fifty dollars to fly back to base to face
a court martial where I was fined, busted to
no rank and given thirty days in the stockade.

SWING THEORY: 4

Every time I moved as a young man and
my now middle-aged older kids were
little, when we took the art and posters
from the walls there'd be fist-size holes
behind them made by me. Now it's the
same in his room and beyond as he re-
sponds to others' mood swings by taking
a swing at whatever's in front of him.
He wasn't around when I was doing the
same, so I wonder how that expression
of frustration came to him, if it's in the
angry genes inherited from my side and
—when coupled with the mood swings
from the other side—might be irresistible.

HOW THE DARK GETS OUT

Thelonious Monk said It's
always night or we wouldn't
need light. Saint John of The

Cross wrote *The Dark Night Of The Soul* which I always used to justify my research into darkness with the idea that the deeper I got into it the higher I would climb to the light when I came out of it. *If* I came out of it. Now I know how big that *if* was and how lucky I am to have found the light before it was too late—the light of love, the unconditional kind that we usually only find in kids and dogs and saints. What a quaint concept the latter is, and yet I bet you've known a few. I have too, and have aspired to be my own kind of one. Only what's done is done and can't be taken back. Though it can be taken *with*, as a reminder of all I have to make up for. But the easiest way is just to open that door and walk through it to the light, even when, like Monk says, it's always night.

TO THE LIGHT

There was a time
When I was a boy,
Eight or nine, and
Afraid of the dark.

Even in a tiny house
With tons of people
So small it took only
A few steps to walk

From one side to the
Other, and not too
Many more to walk
From front to back.

In a kitchen with my
Grandmother's room
Right next to it and
On the other side our

Little combination
Dining/living room
With people listen-
Ing to the radio or

Watching the black
And white thirteen-
Inch TV, siblings, or
The boarder, upstairs

Getting ready for
Bed, light and sound
Everywhere, even
Then, if the light was

Off in the kitchen
I'd refuse to go in to
Get something out
Of the refrigerator

Without a sister or
Brother or someone

Coming with me.
When I got older

So many women
Would get upset
That I left lights on
When we went out

At night. Every light
In the house they
Would say and
Almost be right.

But even though
There were times
In my life when I
Loved the dark,

Relished the dark,
Immersed myself
In the dark, I was
Always so happy

To come home
To the light.

LOVE NEVER DIES

Lots of shit dies
Love doesn't

Parts of me are
Already dead

But love isn't . . .
My appendix

Dead and buried
My prostate and

A disc from my back
Dead and gone too

And parts of my brain
Cut out with the

Dime size foreign body
That got in there somehow

To cause so much trouble . . .
The twin towers died

And all those lost with them
Like a woman who was

Kind to me when
She didn't have to be

Gone on one of those
Two planes, but

My love for her isn't . . .
Five of my siblings and

Our old man and ma
Passed on now for awhile

But not the love we shared
When we were honest . . .

The mother
Of my oldest kids, my

First wife, gone, but the love
She and I shared never

Died, though maybe the
Like did . . . my first true

Love, too, the love of my
Life, gone now for almost

A decade, but my love for
Her, and hers for me,

Never died even thru
All of our husbands and

Wives and lovers over
The years when we

Were out of touch with
Each other, none

Of that stopped the
Love we both felt

And affirmed whenever
We spoke again like

The week before she
Passed still working

To help troubled kids
Find families, those

Kids still grateful for
The love she showed them

That's still alive even if
She's with the ancestors now . . .

Or other women I've lived
With who have passed on

Or lovers long gone
Like Joan B or Joe B

Her face so sweet and tough
Voice still admonishing me to

Just be myself and not
Worry what others think

His voice so quiet and
Stuttering in my ear as I

Write this, his image on
My bookshelves with his books

His art on my walls, I only wish
He'd lived long enough

To see it didn't matter
How famous he did or

Didn't become, his work
Living on among us

Who love it, exhibited
Often since he passed

Or Tony gone so recently
A young man who went from

Ripping doors off their
Hinges when he was

Upset with his wife and
Kids to the gentlest giant

Of many I've known
His ex-skinhead rages

Transformed as he turned
The pages of his life from

Anger to compassion
His punk Buddhist

Practice enabling him
To live with the rare

Brain disease that
Took his physical

Presence from us
But not the love we

Who knew him shared . . .
I think of him every day

As I do a lot who live
Now only in our hearts

. . . oh
Lots of shit dies, like

Almost everything that was
New when I was a boy

Including the people . . .
If you live long enough

So much passes it feels
Like another world . . .

But it's the same one
Where love never dies . . .

FIGHTING WORDS

Poetry saved my life.
There is no life without poetry.
What life isn't a poem?
Open my brain, poems fly out.

How do I get the poems back?
That's not a poem, that's my life.
"My Life" was my most famous poem.
What life isn't a poem?

Poetry literally saved my life.
It made me feel not so alone.
It's not so easy now to write a poem
since the operation on my brain.

But I'd do it again, and again,
because in the end, what isn't a poem?

SWING THEORY: 5

When I first read about *string* theory I thought
What about *swing* theory? The ways the uni-
verse is secretly governed by the same laws
that sparked The Big Band Swing Era, park
swings and taking a swing at something or
someone. I thought of "Swinging On a Star"
or *Swing Time* I mean the ways reality swings
not just in the Hegelian sense but in the re-
galing sense and sensitivity to the ego swings
and mood swings of The Creator or whatever
force initiated this swinging cosmic vibe we
call Being Here Now, always, where every
sound's a note in the song of everything, ev-
ery moment a scene in the movie of our lives.

THE VILLAGE SONNETS

(Word Palace Press 2016)

from THE VILLAGE SONNETS (1959-1962)

I

When Nina Simone played THE VILLAGE
GATE I sat on the sidewalk leaning against
the grate above the basement stage, sharing
a bottle of Gallo half-and-half in a brown
paper bag with Destiny and writing poems
to send backstage. She never responded. I
spied James Baldwin once in OBIES. Cliff
said he'd introduce me, but I declined,
having heard he was queer. How would I
handle a pass if he made one? While Bald-
win held court among his admirers, Cliff
told me stories about the people in Harlem
he sold insurance to, as good as Langston
Hughes' *SIMPLE STORIES* only more real.

2

I took my ex-nun sister to see Nina Simone
who came onstage in a floor-length dress so
tight around her ankles she could take only
tiny steps to get to the piano, a Geisha girl
walking on ice. I heard rumors about her
love life. She was a lesbian, or married to a
cop, or having an affair with the guitarist the
only white man in her band. I championed
the cause of contrast, fixing that sister up
on a date with my drummer friend Sblibby.
It didn't work out. Maureen was an artist
and the coolest white Jersey girl I knew. I
fixed her up with Ralphie, my junkie street
friend. That turned out to be a mistake too.

3

Princess was a street fixture from the islands.
I never knew which one. I was with her at
OBIES when I first met Cliff, with Mel and
DeWitt. The only empty chairs were at their
table. When we sat down, they started riffing
about how they'd seen Malcolm speak at
the Harlem mosque earlier that week and
he'd asked Have you kicked a white devil
today? And how little white boys were
polluting the race. When I'd had enough
I stood up and said Which one of you
motherfuckers wants to step outside with
me? They laughed and said Sit down,
we're just fooling with you kid. And I did.

4

Curtis Powell introduced me to my first
Greenwich Village pad. I was seventeen,
already into the Village scene but as a
Jersey interloper digging it from the street.
He took me to the crib of an old white cat
in his thirties and his dark-haired wife in
her twenties, living with a blonde nineteen-
year-old not only pretty but nice. A pie-
slice studio on Cornelia and Sixth Avenue
with a big bed and little else to sit on and
nowhere else to sleep. It was obvious even
before Curtis hipped me to it, they all slept
together. I thought I preferred black chicks
but if this was beatnik living I wanted some.

5

Curtis was from South Orange, renowned
for French kissing a white girl in the public
pool in 1957 and smart enough to later earn
a scholarship to college and a PhD. Once he
took me to a rundown little flat on East 2nd
in the building where Ginsberg lived. Bob
Kaufman's crib. He wasn't in, just his dark-
haired Irish-looking wife Eileen and baby
Parker. I read Kaufman's *SECOND APRIL*
for free at Figaro's and smoked my first
joint after a young black dude invited me
to join him for a stroll around the block,
continuing our deep discussion begun inside
reentering with a whole new perspective.

6

Cliff, Mel and DeWitt lived on West Third near
the strip joints. Mel reminded me of Jackie
Robinson but with a deeper voice and more
eloquent. He spoke German from when they all
met there in the Army after the war. DeWitt was
the Army's first Negro heavyweight champ. Mel
held the yards gained record for college fullbacks.
Cliff, smaller, thinner and lighter skinned, had
a face freckled like mine. He did so well in the
black market he married the first post-war Miss
Berlin and flew her to the states and a house
on Long Island he paid cash for. When she saw
how race played here, she divorced him and
went on to be the blonde in WHITE RAIN ads.

7

Destiny was one of the gentlest humans I
knew and the first one with no home at all.
One day he jumped out from a doorway to
pull my coat and when I turned around said
Princess is a dyke, she's only using you.
And I said Using me? Someone has found
a use for me? Princess wore men's clothes
that hid a lovely little hourglass figure I
discovered in the bathroom at Mel, Dewitt
and Cliff's fifth floor walkup where we first
made love. It was one of those tiny ones
with only a toilet and water box overhead
you pulled a chain to flush. They took
baths in the kitchen sink, the deep side.

8

I crashed a Village party with street bros where
Red Mitchell was playing with a small combo.
When they took a break I stood his bass up and
played the melody to *MOANIN'*. Red made it
clear he didn't dig strangers playing his ax. I
laid it down but drunkenly tripped, putting a
tiny crack in it with my pointy-toed boot and
was thrown out. For a long time hip Villagers
knew me as the little J.D. who kicked a hole in
Red Mitchell's bass. At a Brooklyn party Lex
Humphries loaned me a rubber when I asked,
cause Princess insisted. We went up to the
roof, but it was tilted and covered in pebbles
that dug into our backs as we almost rolled off.

9

Met Bob Dylan at THE FAT BLACK PUSSY
CAT before he recorded or I heard him live,
thought he was jive. Passed e. e. cummings in
Washington Square only months before he died.
He looked like an old man, yet bohemian still
in a black beret, a cliché, but not on one from
the generation that created it. Diane di Prima
and Joel Oppenheimer were friendly. Gregory
Corso and LeRoi Jones not. Ginsberg came
across like a pushy hustler at times. Kerouac
drank way too much, like me. We both got 86'd
from THE KETTLE OF FISH. Bob Kaufman,
they said, was part European, African, Asian
and more, which seemed like the future to me.

10

When Sonny Clark's Trio took a break at THE
WHITE WHALE I sauntered to the piano. Pall
Mall between fingers still able to play, head
drooped toward the keys, a la one of the piano
trinity of my iconic history, Bill Evans, I was
the only white teenage cat with a black soul I
knew. I didn't notice the drummer return till I
heard the shhh shhhh shhhhh of his brushes on
the snare. Now I really felt solid in my groove.
Shit, the cat dug my sound so much he couldn't
resist. Then I grinned as the bass joined in. I
was the featured act now, the cats backing Clark
backing me, making music for all the world to
see, especially my new heart's delight: Bambi.

11

The song came to an end. The bassist whispered
HONEYSUCKLE ROSE, holding up some fingers
to indicate the key. But it was beyond me, and the
tempo they set was like climbing Mount Everest
in shorts and making it to the top before lunch.
After a few bars I felt a body sit down beside me
on the piano bench. Sonny Clark. He gave me a
pathetic look and swung his hip into mine as
though knocking me out of the way. Which he
was. The band wailed, the audience transfixed as
the white kid took a shaky walk back to his table.
I always wore shades except when in bed so the
tears in my eyes didn't shine in the lights just my
obvious flight from the jazz Olympus in my mind.

14

They called her Bambi cause of her big dark
cartoon-deer eyes that lit up the space around
her. We met in OBIES, the bar on Sixth Ave
across from West Third where I felt most at
home in the world, thanks to a mix of black
and white, old and young, straight and queer,
beat and hip, junkie and boozer, sophisticated
and not, like me who had no idea OBIES was
the name for the off-Broadway theater awards
despite the framed posters of winners on the
walls like *RED EYE OF LOVE*. I thought
Obie was the owner's name. One night there
I spied Bambi at a table with other teenagers
called colored or Negro. Or spade on the street.

15

After her eyes it was her skin, dark and smooth
like coffee without cream, her full lips, nose
wide and strong, Indian my spade friends said.
Thin as me, a year younger and just graduated
from a Catholic girls high school in Atlantic
City I learned, after we stop-motion stared at
each other before I pulled up a chair. A strange
sight to her in my Paul Sargent suit, thin tie and
Ray Charles wide-sided shades, a skinny white
boy talking bebop Harlem jive. She and her
roommate lived on Tompkins Square, the first
black chicks there. We made a date. I arrived
with Spanish Harry, who wasn't Spanish, and
Mamie, the contrast date I'd talked him into.

16

Already drunk I got aggressive, Bambi later
said, as we sat on her bed. She was scared till
I fell off onto the floor and she couldn't stop
laughing. Next night I came back to see her
again but an old friend from school had shown
up. She was spending the evening with him,
so gave me a rain check. But I never showed,
exposing her I hoped to how much I was hurt,
then felt like a jerk and called to apologize.
She said she waited for hours. Next time we
met at OBIES where we learned we had even
more in common. Like our fathers: self-made,
grammar-school dropouts with high-school
educated wives. Soon we were a Village item.

17

I was known among friends and family for
falling in love at the drop of an eyelash. But
this time was different. Even Mel, Cliff and
DeWitt got the intensity of it. We spent every
second we could with each other, getting close
to making love completely then backing off
to save her virginity for the night of our wed-
ding we needed our parents permission for,
too young to marry in Jersey or New York.
In states where we weren't, our so-called
races made it against the law. My father said
Men and women are different, so you start
with one strike against you. If the woman's
not Irish, that's two. Not Catholic, you're out.

18

When my music-man brother Buddy wanted
to marry my Italian sister-in-law, there were
whispered admonitions behind closed doors
about what would be in store for them and
their kids. That sense of forbidden fruit fueled
my boyhood crush on her dark Italian beauty.
My father couldn't argue that we had three
strikes against us: Bambi was Catholic. But
he argued anyway, that our kids would have
it too hard. Out of his hearing, ma said in
tears I don't care who you marry if you love
each other but I have to back your father,
he's my husband. Bambi's father hated
white people for what they'd done to him.

19

The night we gave up any hope of marrying
before she turned twenty-one, three long
years away, I decided Fuck them all. Fuck our
families fuck society fuck the stupid racial laws.
Then we finally made love all the way as she
whispered I'm sorry. I asked What for? That I
couldn't wait till we were married. But I swore
before God we were husband and wife. She
always said I was her first lover. Though I had
others, like Princess and Dolores, I felt she was
my first too. Later lying in each other's arms
she said I love you, in a way so surrendered, so
deeply sincere, so much an echo of the feelings
in my heart toward her, I knew it was true.

20

Bambi's roommate didn't dig me so we
hung at Mel, Cliff and Dewitt's talking and
making love when they were out. They gave
us a key. This was before Cliff got his own
place after walking in on Mel having sex
with Cliff's lady, the Harlem beauty Theresa.
Cliff and Mel were back being friends
before long, but Theresa was gone. Cliff's
new pad on Thompson had two bedrooms.
He rented one to Bull, a married man who
used it with just a mattress on the floor for
his rendezvous. Bambi and I used it too.
There were no examples of happy and
accepted mixed-race marriages we knew.

21

Mixed couples were rare, and outside The
Village found only in black neighborhoods,
where it was always black men with white
women. My Jersey friends Teddy and Lynn
seemed truly happy, but Lyn worked in an
office in Newark where her coworkers were
not even aware she was married to a Negro.
Her Italian relatives were. And her mother
lived with them. My brother-in-law Joe the
cop and me were working on the rectory
roof one day when Teddy rode by on his
Harley. Joe couldn't stop talking about The
flying jig on a motorcycle. Teddy treated Joe
as he did everyone, with kind acceptance.

22

White people in our parish were upset when
Teddy and Lynn got married in our church,
the first mixed-race wedding there. Except
for parties at their East Orange pad they didn't
socialize much. Just going to the store, people
stared or pointed or made nasty remarks. There
were no movies or books with happy stories
of mixed-race romance, let alone marriage.
Kerouac's short novel about his affair with a
black lady, *THE SUBTERRANEANS*, didn't
end happily. In the movie version she's played
by Leslie Caron. The closest Hollywood
would come to a mixed-race romance was to
turn the black chick into a white French one.

23

THE NEW YORK TIMES ran an article on
teens who copied the Beat or hip style but
came from Jersey or Long Island to The
Village on weekends. DOWNSTAIRS AT
THE DUPLEX had a piano I played when
no one else did. Like the day someone said
There's a reporter at MARIES CRISIS CAFÉ
looking for teenagers who aren't Village
natives. We knew it was us in the story,
the only mixed teenage couple then. The
original Marie was a Gypsy, but now was
a big black lady who played piano and sang.
Her most popular song's refrain was *No-
body cans cans like the garbage man can.*

24

Ted Joans was known as a Beat poet who ex-
ploited the tourist trade, a reputedly hip spade
usually wearing a black beret when I saw him.
In a photo in *THE BEAT SCENE* he sat on the
grass in Washington Square Park with a white
woman and four mixed kids and talked about
Loving every swinging soul. But he gave Bambi
a hard time cause I was white. She was so darkly
beautiful older black men wanted to protect her
or make her their own. Everyone noticed her
lovely face and lithe figure as she danced bare
foot on the grass in the park in flowery summer
dresses, a darker apparition and prediction of
what hippies would be like several years later.

Big Brown was a giant of a man, six-
feet-a-lot, with a fierce expression on
his dark face and a way of intimidating
everyone. One day in OBIES he told
Bambi she was wasting her foxy female
self on a skinny little nothing of a sheet,
a gray, a Mister Charlie, just as Cliff
walked in. Before I jumped salty, Cliff
said in his laconic way that if Brown dug
being black so much how come his hair
was gassed? A withering comment about
Brown's conk, a wavy almost Marcel
curl. Brown seemed to cringe, then huffed
and puffed some before disappearing.

27

The first time we slept with other street kids
in the empty fountain in Washington Square
we woke at dawn and went to the small
water fountain for a drink. I splashed some
on Bambi in fun, but she got all tight-jawed.
When she calmed down, she explained if
her hair, already misshapen from sleeping
on concrete, got wet, it would tighten up
and look even worse. I made sure I never
did that to any black woman again. I wrote
a story about it, adding it to some of the
ones I sent to magazines every week to
always keep some in the mail no matter how
many came back. Like that one kept doing.

28

When the bulls drove through the Washington
Square arch, like buses did to turn around till
they made Fifth Avenue one way, they'd roust
street kids sleeping in the fountain when dry.
I'd act all innocent and square when they asked
for my I.D. and saw I was from Jersey. Like
I was just a teenage tourist looking for Green-
wich Village kicks and got caught up with
the runaways, the teenage vipers and juvenile
delinquents, as I was called across the Hudson
and by some Villagers who knew me. Others
would say I was a little Jersey jitterbug or teen-
age version of what Norman Mailer wrote his
famous essay about: *THE WHITE NEGRO.*

29

Cal was Mel's twin but opposite. A high school
drop out with a wife and four kids in Penn-
sylvania, he talked fast with a distinct private
accent difficult to understand. Mel enunciated
every word like a 19th-century orator. Cal was
thinner and darker, with a nose so long and
sharply hooked he could pass in profile for an
ancient Egyptian. He'd been a paratrooper at
fifteen, lying about his age, in post-war Japan
then Korea. Mel wore impeccable suits. Cal
funky sweatshirts and jeans. Once, walking
up the Bowery, on that island where it turns
into Third Ave, Cal shouted out to the rainy
night: New York, you don't owe me a thing!

30

Sblibby named himself after the black street
term for what Southern racists called niggery,
pushing it in everyone's face. Ebony toned,
my height and weight, but more sinewy and
tight and a few years older, like me he wore
shades indoors and out every waking hour.
I never knew his real name. We met one
rainy afternoon when we were the only ones
at the bar in OBIES. Me at one end, him at
the other with drum sticks and a rubber
practice pad. Yaya let him play along with
the box since we were the only ones there.
When Eric Dolphy blew a phrase that made
us both laugh, we recognized each other.

31

Sblibby came into OBIES one afternoon with
a short dark man wearing thick eyeglasses
on his intense angry face. It was Cecil Taylor,
the piano-playing composer innovator changing
jazz. When I extended my hand to slip him
some skin he curled his lip in distaste. Sblib
didn't notice as he raved about me, suggesting
Taylor come to THE WHITE WHALE where
I could display my chops. Surprisingly he did.
There I started in on my version of Ahmad
Jamal's take on *SURREY WITH THE FRINGE
ON TOP*, only even more up-tempo so even
more difficult. But after only a few bars Taylor
got up and walked out without saying a word.

32

In the West Fourth Street station I ran into
Angela and told her about Bambi. She got
upset and wrote me later *You were meant
to marry me, if you marry a colored girl
neither race will accept your kids.* Bambi
quit her job under the influence of Villagers
who promoted free love and life, strangers
to me. Like Chico, light-brown skinned with
thick black hair, usually taken for a Puerto
Rican. He was skinny like Bambi and me,
but quieter than I could be. She wanted us
to hang together. But he had neither a job
nor home so was free to roam the Village
streets with her while I was busy working.

33

When Bambi said Chico was so broke he ate dog
food out of a can cause it was cheaper than Spam,
I ordered her not to see him anymore. She laughed
and went on doing what she wanted. I wanted a
darker version of Dostoevsky's Anna, not a free
spirit. I got so jealous, uptight and tired of her new
friends and life, when Chico came into OBIES
looking for her, I shoved him against a wall and
spit: I'll rip your lungs out through your throat if
you hurt her. Then drunkenly decided to join the
Army to show them both. My crippled grandma
who lived with us since Grandpa Dempsey died
always accused me of cutting off my nose to spite
my face. I never understood what she meant by it.

34

In my usual jazzman's outfit, shades and all,
I went to enlist at the Orange Post Office near
Orange Memorial Hospital where I was born.
An Air Force recruiter leaning against a wall
said What's happenin' man? A hip greeting for
any white man then, let alone one in uniform.
He stuck out his hand, and when I reflexively
did too, slapped mine, an even rarer thing for
a gray dude to do. He said the Army's no place
for a hip cat like you, but the Air Force is full
of hip mixed couples. He swore once they saw
me in uniform, Bambi would come running,
our fathers would give in, and I'd be playing
piano in an officer's club in The Big Apple.

35

I signed up for the four-year enlistment. Told
to report to New York the next day I made my
Jersey goodbyes, then met Mel at DOWN-
STAIRS AT THE DUPLEX. Arriving first I
went to the unoccupied piano. After I played
a few tunes the owner said his piano player
split and offered me the job at a hundred a
month. Cliff paid thirty for his two bedroom
pad. I could support the city life I'd always
fantasized. But too late. When Mel arrived I
told him. He laughed, seeing the humor in it.
I didn't. At OBIES, Cal, Cliff and DeWitt sent
me off with many toasts, Cliff calling me Me-
shell, as he always did, adding Bon voyage.

36

For unexplained reasons we were given three
more days of freedom. I spent it getting drunk
and high with street friends like Andre, a tall
dark junkie who knew where to crash. But the
last night I ended up alone in a bar unable to
stand. When they 86'd me, this square looking
Irish chick helped me walk to her crib on East
11th where to my surprise she lived with Pauline
a light-skinned mixed teen from Long Island
City who ran away at fifteen to arrive in the
Village pregnant. Before she began showing,
she had a body men fought over. But she was
too tough for me. Maybe she had to be. She
hooked to get by. Turned out Irish did too.

37

Stumbling in, we woke Pauline up. She threw
a clock at us but gave me one twin bed to sleep
in and they took the other. I woke at dawn to
stare at these two women an arm's length away,
Pauline on the outside, Irish against the wall.
The covers had slid down and one of Pauline's
legs dangled off the side, her slip up past her
thighs so everything was showing. I had my
horrible hangover, able to focus on nothing but
Pauline's everything, feeling oppressed by it,
as though it was all I was running from. The
power that blossom of female flesh had over me.
The Irish Catholic pain and shame and guilt
it represented. I split without saying goodbye.

NEW POEMS

(2004–2017)

from **NEW YORK NOTES (2004)**

[. . .]

The backs of women's
Knees still intrigue
Me, especially in
Winter when they seem
To wink at you from
Between the tops of
Boots and hems of
Skirts or dresses, I
Want to bless them
With gratitude and kisses—

[. . .]

The dusty slants of early
Morning light coming
Through the East window
Of what I still think of
As "the newly renovated"
Grand Central Station
Even though it's been
Years, as I cut through
From the Southwest corner
At 42nd to the Northeast
At Lexington and 43rd—

[. . .]

In Penn Station, the
Older deaf businessman
Speaking too loudly on
His earpiece cell phone—

Sounding like my deaf
Cousins I grew up with

[. . .]

The white woman with
Dark hair climbing the
Stairs in her heels, one
Shoulder of her coat falling
Off, wobbling from
The effort of keeping
Her balance as she
Climbs, hands full
Of purse and shopping
Bags, me watching
From below as I pass—

The amber skinned
Latina woman, thirty-
Something, auburn hair—
She reminds me of Easter candy
Not chocolate, not anything
Specific, just the sweet
Satisfaction of the feast—
The warmth of the day's
Pagan spring rite roots!—

[. . .]

The stunningly beautiful
Young woman, Latina
Her eyes surprise me
With their depth, their
Absolute acknowledgment
Of mine, oh hearts sublime

The two guys with their
Baseball caps turned backward
Walk by me in the rain,
With no umbrella, wiping
Rain drops from their faces as
If unaware that's what
The bills of their caps are
For and protection from the
Sun, baggy pants too—

[. . .]

The Asian woman in the
Subway car—as old as me,
Maybe—eyes me warily,
As if my gray haired phys-
Iognomy portends some
Memories of other times,
As if I may be one of those
Veterans of Viet Nam still
Searching for the solace
Once found in brown skin
They used to call yellow—

[. . .]

The many mixed couples
On streets and subway trains
These days—young ones,
Old ones, Arab looking with
Irish looking, African
Descent with Scandinavian—
Puerto Rican and Asian—
The mix of life's re-
Surgence, completion—

[. . .]

You can't cut through
Penn Station anymore
Like you still can Grand
Central—some doors and
Entrances are barricaded
And a new announcement
Over the New Jersey Transit
Loudspeakers warns
Passengers to look
Out for suspicious
Packages or people—

[. . .]

The bookstore on Tenth
Avenue I never noticed
Before—the quirky
Choice of poetry titles—
Of biographies and art
Books—the comforting
Smallness of the space—

[. . .]

The "soap" actress
In the restaurant who
Isn't even pretty in
Person—the old couple
In their seventies,
At least, more likely
Eighties, on the
Subway, the woman
Stunningly and
Naturally beautiful—

[. . .]

The black woman in
Her thirties, maybe
Forties, round dark
Face with bright red
Lipstick and brighter
Smile for me, maybe
Everyone, maybe not—

Then the tall young
Asian woman, no
Smile but sustained
Eye contact as we
Pass—the young WASPy
Woman, also, catching
My eye, not me hers—
Lingering, is that some
Kind of longing I see?

Sixty-two next month,
And a day like today,
Inexplicable to me as
Females of all types and
Ages seem genuinely
Interested in drawing
My attention and sus-
Taining it—smiles—
Nods—romances of
The eyes—the brief city
Street affairs poet James
Schuyler said are
Enough—and they are—

[. . .]

It's supposed to be Spring
But cutting across Bryant
Park on the Monday
Of Easter week there's
Only two people there,
One on a bench on the
South side, one on a chair
On the North—I sit for
A moment on another bench
With some sunlight on
It but the bitter, icy
Wind makes me get up
And go to the recently
Moved Coliseum Book
Store, now on Forty-
Second, to warm myself

Cutting across Bryant
Park on the following
Wednesday there's
No benches free as the
Fifty-eight degree sunny
Weather finally brings
The city-Spring I love,
People hanging outside,
Some with their coats
Off, the first blossoms
Of bare flesh—

The gray haired black
Lady, tall, in jeans and
Sweater, looking cool
And earthy and fine—

What is it about some
Asian women, especially

Older ones, that reminds
Me of my Irish aunts?
Something in the eyes
And round cheeks—

[. . .]

The cleaning woman
In Penn Station—in
Her dark blue workers
Outfit—as lovely a face
As any movie star's
I've seen this close—

The once, homeless
Man, who owns a
Building in Harlem,
Skin so black it's
Hard to see much
Definition in his
Face outside his eyes,
His wife a wealthy
White French woman,
Their little boy and girl
Both stunningly new and
Promisingly beautiful—

The "Jersey girls" so
Unpretentious and even
Humble in the thrill
They're obviously ex-
Periencing on their
Trip to Manhattan
To celebrate the
Fortieth birthday
Of one of them—

The Mongolian look of
The young woman
On the subway train—
like she might get
Off and mount a
Horse and ride off
Across the endless
Plains Genghis Kahn
Once roamed and
Called his own

[. . .]

Oh the variety, es-
Pecially on a day like
Today that started
Out cold and cloudy
And is now sunny
And bright, half
The people I pass in
Winter coats the
Other half in shirt
Sleeves and tees or
Low riding jeans
That show their bellies—

The beauty I remark
On is never conventional,
Nothing that can be
Bought, but character
And gene driven, de-
Riven, given—history
Alive in the eyes
And thighs and even
Oversize pants the
Two young men are wearing

Looking like little boys
With a load in their
Drawers and obviously
Unaware of that as
They swear in joy
And lechery at a
Passing beauty who
Totally ignores their
Crude adolescent show—

[…]

On Sixth Avenue
The black man
With beautiful eyes,
Perfectly groomed […]

The thing about the
Handsome sharply
Dressed black man
Is the confidence
And power he exudes
Although he can't
Be even five feet
Tall, as small as
A little boy, but
Perfectly proportioned
And totally handsome
And obviously comfortable
In his skin—

Only minutes later on
Forty-second street an
Equally small but
Homely white man
In sports regalia

Claps his hands
As he spies
The store he must
Have been looking
For and veers across
The sidewalk to
Enter one of those
Shops that specializes
In team clothes—
With local team
Logos, Rangers, Jets,
Yankees, Mets, Knicks,
And Nets and Metro Stars—

Later downtown on
The Lower East Side
The tall young black guy
Who waits on me
[. . .] keeps asking
About me, flashing his
Warm smile, plying me
With not just samples
Of men's products but
Full sized bottles, "gifts"
He says continuing to
Hold my eye and smile
Until I can see and
Register how handsome
He is in his way
And how he wants me
To acknowledge that
Connection and I do—

The pulse of life is
So strong on these
Streets, I remember

How just living here
When I was in my
Thirties made me feel
I'd not only survived
But somehow won—

As summer approaches—
The older black man
In the tan suede
Matching short sleeve
Shirt and slacks—
Not a wrinkle in either—

The pleasant odors
Of perfumes and
Colognes as people
Pass—like the African
Man in pressed slacks
And dress shoes and
Lacey, patterned,
White shirt
That falls to his knees
And through which
You can see his
White sleeveless undershirt—

Or the perfume on the
Asian woman in her
Forties in jeans and
Tight shirt—

The ages I guess at, could
Really be anything,
My eye for age always
Mediocre at best,
Seeing everyone's age as

Alive—I notice the eyes
And the mouths first,
Like that man in
The elevator with
A barely hidden
Smirk and condescending
Sparkle in his eyes[. . .]

Meet a TV writer friend at
PJ Clarke's on 3rd Avenue
And 55th Street—later we bump
Into a movie star I wrote
Some words for once and
When I'm introduced
He mentions
The movie and an old
Girlfriend of mine who
Married a friend of his[. . .]
Six degrees, or three,
Or two, among the
People we know—

Later, alone, walking down
Second Avenue from
55th to St. Mark's
Church on 10th, I
Pass so many varieties
Of human beauty
I want to shout in
Gratitude for their
Creator's ingenuity—

At one point, passing
All those high rises in
The twenties, teenagers
From the neighborhood

Imitate the gangster
Styles of the times,
Their black and Hispanic
Faces seeming older
Than their suburban
Counterparts—

As I pass, one says to
An older woman, maybe
Her mother—"She lives in
Santa Monica, on Princeton,
It's just North of . . . "—

[. . .]

At St. Mark's for
Poet and lyricist
Kenward Elmslie's
Seventy-fifth birthday
Celebration—a man
Who was so generous
To me [. . .] I took it for a
Sign of my success
Rather than his
Largesse, for which
I thank him,
I hope humbly, now—

I see old friends,
Old men
Like I've become or
Am becoming,
Others, my age who
Still retain a boyish
Spirit in aging bodies
And faces, all so

Fulfilling to my
Heart, just to know
They're still around
And seem happy to be—

On the way out I run
Into the painter Alex
Katz and his wife and
Favorite model Ada—who
I always admired—
Their son, poet and
Translator Vincent,
In the process of pub-
Lishing a long poem
I wrote on the eve
Of our latest war—
Alex is doing the cover
For it and when I
Thank him he declares
"It's an honor! That poem's
better than *Howl*!"!

I look around to see
If there's anyone else
On the street
But us, there isn't,
My heart the only witness—

[. . .]

In Lenox Hill[. . .]
To see another doctor,
Remembering stories of
York Avenue's old days
When little
German and Irish

Immigrant kids filled
The streets, like Jimmy
Cagney—now it's mostly
Generic looking, though Asian
And Caribbean cooking
Fills the gaps
In bland architecture—

Walking uptown from 40th
I passed four black
Men by a table
Display of black
Themed books, paper
And hardback,
Novels mostly, at
43rd and 6th, arguing
Passionately about
Politics, one saying
"Giuliani called my man
A nigger, and my man
Kicked Giuliani's ass!"

I wonder who his man is—

On 47th I stop at the Gotham
Book Mart, still there, the
Old sign "WISE MEN
FISH HERE" outside,
Almost lost among
The diamond stores—
And throngs of diamond
Merchants, messengers,
Traders, and customers—

The varieties of Jewish
Garb, from yarmulkes

On men in jeans and
Sneakers to old men
In black suits with
Black fedoras of mid
20th-century design, to
Men in long black over
Coats on what's becoming
A very warm day, with
Long curly locks for side-
Burns and hats of 19th
Century style, tassels
Hanging from beneath
Their shirts, I have to
Step into the street
To make any progress—

Back in Bryant Park—
The junkie's slouch,
The look of bad boy
Street sharpie gone to seed—

[. . .]

The apartment building
On the Northwest corner
Of 35th and 3rd with
The big USA flag
And three pink
Flamingos on the
Northern most
First floor balcony—

The black woman,
On 7th Avenue in
The "fashion district"
Overweight, low cut jeans,

Too tight, her love
Handles flopping
Out beneath her
Neon orange tee
Shirt calling
Attention to them—

The Asian woman
In what look like
Platform combat
Boots, making her
Several inches taller—
Stepping awkwardly—

Both of them
Beautiful to me
Especially considering
Death's domain—

The Chinese-American
Doctor says "I'll
Knock you out if
You argue with me Mike"
If he discovers excessive
Blockage
And wants to operate—

Or do some procedure—

The white haired
Man emerging from
The office building
In suit and tie his
Face neon bright
Pink as though
About to explode[. . .]

The beautiful black
Girl's face—her
Full lips and smooth
Dark skin and
Perfect dark eyes
That make me
Wish I was on the
Receiving end of the cell
Phone call she's in the
Midst of as she passes
Saying—"I paid it—it
Was twenty dollars"—not
Even noticing me,
This older gray haired
White—well, pink—man—

The young blonde
Crossing Sixth Avenue
At Thirty-First Street
Heading West as I head
East, bringing to mind
Old descriptive clichés
From the '50s when
I first began writing
Seriously, or with the
Intent of publishing—
Like "peroxide blonde"
With a "cigarette dangling
From her lips" and
"Porcelain skin" looking
"Sullen" and "like trouble"
—Troubled more like it—
Young and more vulnerable
Than she even knows I
Would guess from her dis-
Tracted, inward directed
"Filmy" gaze—

[. . .]

The waitress where
I eat at Chelsea
Market so solicitous
—The Green Table—
Organic fresh daily
Exotic salads and
"Protein" combinations
I imbibe while trying
To write about the
Wonder of mixes
That make up this
World now—the
Older "white" woman
Pushing the "black"
Baby—her nanny?
Grandmother? Mother?
"The infinite possibilities"—

[. . .]

Saying the Saint
Francis prayer—over
And over—as they
Wiggle and maneuver
The catheter through
The artery—my heart
Aches—literally—and
Not so unlike the
Ways it always has—

Lying on the slab
In this freezing room—
Heart stuck—listening
To them discuss my
Reaction to the new

Blood thinner—"Have
You ever seen this
Before?"—"Me
Neither"—"Let's
Stop and resume tomorrow"

[. . .]

I'm on my back and
Immobile for six
More hours—or four—
Depending on the
Nurse—their origins
So varied—Manhattan
Sidewalk symphony
Of accents in this
Hospital room with
A view of the East
River and the Fifty-
Ninth Street Bridge
That my "room
Mate" cannot share—
A seventy-two-year
Old Puerto Rican lady
On the other side of
The curtain dividing
Our not so private
Spaces here—she's
In for open heart
Surgery—my doctor
Reminds me I'm so
Lucky to not need—
For now—

More pain when they
Go back in, no

Drugs, "it's a ten"
I tell them—on the
Pain scale—they
Say now I'll know
What a heart attack
Feels like—later
When they take
The catheter out
I tell the two
Nurses working on me
That I'm feeling nauseous
And sweating—"I think I'm
Going into shock"—they
Look up from my groin
And suddenly seem panicked—
Start feeding syringes
Into the two i.v.s they
Have in both my arms—

 "If you never assume importance
You never lose it."
From Witter Bynner's
1944 translation of
LaoTzu's Tao Te Ching
Which he translates as
"The Way of Life" a
Pacifist interpretation
I've had with me
Since I was a teenager
And think of often—
Especially now as my
Life insists on teaching
Me a wisdom I have
Always resisted—even
As I sought it—

Three days, three pro-
Cedures, where there was
Supposed to be one—
The stories of others—
In and out of the hospital
In a day, instead of the
Four and more I spend
There—others knocked
Out, not even aware of
What was going on, me
Awake, alert, so the doctor
Can consult me about the
Stent, show me as it goes
In on the big screen over
The gurney I lie on—
[. . .]

Summer rain—
For days—lady
Walking under an
Umbrella the size
Of the one that
Protected our whole
Family at the beach
When I was a kid—

Duck into a restaurant
On Madison with
"Heaven" in the
Name though the
Food is anything
But celestial—
And I can't see
The mini-TV that
Hovers over the
Table like its

Clones dispersed
Throughout the
Place—the waitresses
All in neat WASPy
Uniforms of khaki pants
And striped button
Down shirts are all
Latin American—
The couple at the
Next table, an over-
Weight youngish
White man in a suit
And middle aged Asian
Woman in business
Lady clothes, discuss
Corporate strategy
At SONY and their
Positions as lawyers—
[. . .]

Writing this at an
Outdoor table in
Bryant Park next
To the carousel
Which is busy today—
The first dry day in
Almost a week—

Earlier lunch at
Victoria's on W.
38th in the fashion
District—a cafeteria
Style long narrow
Lunch only joint
The artist Don Mc
Laughlin took me to—

A couple of black
Women at the next
Table respond to my
Tray with woops of
Interest as they pause
In their intake of
Carbs to admire
My salad and grilled
Chicken plate—I
Should eat like them
Since I'm the one
With the coronary heart
Disease despite my
Sensibly healthy diet
For the last three
Decades—one has
That almost shaved
Hair style black women
Have worn for decades
That takes away nothing
From her feminine
Energy and seductiveness—
Thank God—

Then the George Schneeman/
Rudy Burkhardt show
At Tibor de Nagy—
Walking up Fifth Avenue
Passing all the tourists
And local business folks
The flock of teenage
Girls passing, noisy
And lovely in their
Self-centered-consciousness—
The Asian woman, lovely
Too, in fact model

Beautiful, I remember
Miles Davis' weird take
On Asian women, that
You had to catch them
Out of the corner of
Your eye, no direct eye
Contact—I try it
And it works! We pass
And she smiles and I
Smile as I catch
Her catching me back—

[. . .]

The young black
Woman, maybe
Not more than twenty,
Cupping the tip
Of her cigarette to a
Lit match as she steps
Off the curb on Sixth
Avenue—taller than
Me, six feet at least—
Darker than my hair
Used to be, exquisitely alone—

[. . .]

Hell's Kitchen where
My friend and fellow
Irish-American actor
John Michael Bolger
Resides[. . .] but
I can't rouse him on the
Phone so I go alone to
52nd Street near 11th

Avenue to a tiny theater
"The Magic Show" to
Hear poets Simon Pettet
And Jack Collum read their
Work—and run into
Cecilia Vicuna after
All these years—decades—
Of digging her poetry from
Afar, our friendship still
Intact in our hearts
As we catch up—and the
Pain of life silences
Me for a moment—

[. . .]on the street today
More rain—flooded
Intersection at Second
Avenue and Fourth Street—
Sunday in summer—
Back to the Bowery
Remembering Burroughs
And his bunker—
My grown children
Coming through the
Door of poet Bob
Holman's Bowery Poetry
Club across from
CBGBs—a block
From Second Avenue
Where Joe LeSeuer
Once lived, the poet
Frank O'Hara's early
Love, who always
Spoke to me
As if we shared
Something like

Beauty—or attractiveness
That was an entre to a
World we might not other-
Wise have been welcomed
In—[. . .] Francesco
Clemente with a young
Black woman whose
Skin is so perfectly
Smooth and unmarked
It is art—Don Mc
Laughlin and Paul Harryn—
Artists also—here
To listcn to a long
Poem of mine in
Book form as of today
—A way to celebrate it—

Poets Vincent Katz
—And his own little
Boys depicted on
The cover of what
We're here to celebrate—
And Cecilia Vicuna,
John Godfrey, and
Ted Greenwald—
Elaine Equi and
Jerome Sala too—
Make my day so
Full I want to cry—
And do after they've
All gone and I'm alone[. . .]

The black woman
With the crazy hair
And smile—[. . .]—the
Gypsy looking girl in her

Sunday best—the Asian
Man who looks so fierce
—The piercing eyes of
The white woman with
Dark brown hair, the
Way she stares at me
In the mirror of the
Little dessert café on
Second Avenue—as
If to say "you know
It's you"—I look away—

[. . .]

At the Chinese restaurant
In what looks like
The chandelier district—
Giant globs of illumination
Filling the store front
Windows, the only
Appetizer is a kind
Of porridge, but the
Added ingredients list
Is long and includes
"Pigs intestines" or "snails
Plus pigs liver" but
Poets Pettet and Vicuna
And me—we opt for
The vegetarian version—

Vicuna leans over
To me after we eat
And says "You have
Saved the honor of
American poets with
This poem Michael"

Meaning: "March 18,
2003"—she goes on
To explain some of
The technical achieve-
Ments of the poem as
Well, in terms that
Are so precise, yet
Lyrical, and gratifying,
I weep later to think
Of it—someone getting
It—what I intended—

What is all this crying
About?—from a man
Who never did for
Decades, and now at
The drop of a hat or
Compliment or sappy
Commercial on TV—

Today bright and
Summery, hot but
Breezy, the leftover
Puddles now looking
Like oil deposits—the
People like blossoms
Of pink and brown flesh—

I pass a lovely Asian
Woman and try the
Miles Davis technique
Again—look straight
Ahead until the last
Moment and then turn
My gaze toward her,
But only out of the

Corner of my eye,
My face still forward,
And sure enough I
Catch her checking
Me out and our eyes
Lock for the split
Second city sidewalk
Connection that promises
Nothing but fulfills
Almost everything a
Split second can—

[. . .]

The five police academy
Cadets—four "white"
One "black"—like the
Old days when "blacks"
Had to take careers
Beneath their brains
And talents and still
Be better at the basics
Than their "white"
Counterparts, the "black"
Cadet is the tallest,
Most self-contained,
Most handsome and
His clothes are sharp—
Pressed, perfectly
Fitted—his shoes
Shined better than
New, he looks like
A hero already—
A movie hero—

On the subway,
Seated in a row,

A muscle bound,
Tan, blonde, sleeveless
Tee shirted "white" man
In shorts, like an ad for a
Gay men's magazine, next
To a short overweight man
Next to a stunning blonde
Woman, next to an even
More stunning Asian teen-
Ager, next to a middle-aged
Couple holding hands in
A way that seems like
Clutching for their lives
As they look around in
Amused bewilderment—

The twin brothers in
The Long Island Railroad
Station at 34th Street
Playing twin guitars—
One chording, one
Improvising a melody—
Exquisite music, fast
And wildly rhythmic
And joyful, I can't help
Applauding when they
Finish with a run up the
Strings to so high pitched
It's barely audible—
But no one else applauds—
A rush hour crowd but
Still enough people standing,
Not moving, listening, how
Could they not applaud?

A lot of impatience on
The street today, people

Barking into cell phones,
At each other, I try to
Help an Asian family
Obviously lost but they
Skitter away fearfully—
Me—old generic "white"
Man still scary?

Is it just the "war" news
Bringing almost everyone
Down except those
Causing it?—Or more?

The eyes of so many
"Black" women—so dark
And beautifully deep
Sometimes despite themselves—

A woman who could be
Sharon Stone without make-up—
With three kids, one still
Nursing—the woman's
Wearing a billed cap, her
Children as blonde and
Modestly beautiful as
She is—though their
Eyes aren't as tired
Looking, but still
Bright, as the woman's

[. . .]

Spring Street and Broadway—
My old neighborhood—
Unrecognizable from what
It was thirty years

Ago—at West Broadway
Even more unfamiliar
Except for Golden Pizza
One block over—

[. . .]

The rain and wind
Are whipping people—
Umbrellas almost beside
The point as I make it
Down into Prince Street
Station and onto the R train
Where four very large
And imposing African-
American men, and an
Equally large African-
American woman—all five
Distinctly different
Shades of skin color—
Push in before the doors
Close and the freckle
Faced reddish haired
One, what my Southern
Black friends used to
Call "redbone" makes
An announcement
That he and his "brothers
And sister" would like
To sing a song for us
And they break into
An accapela version
Of "The Lion Sleeps
Tonight" that rocks
The subway car
More than the tired

Old tracks and tunnels
We're pummeling
Through and puts a
Smile on my face—
And some coins
And greenbacks in
The brown paper
Collection bag—

[. . .]

Walking up Eighth Avenue
I spot the short gray
Haired man who played
A waiter in "Everyday
People" handing out
Flyers for some business—
I stop to tell him how
Much I liked his work
In the film—he seems
Very pleased, as I always
Am when someone
Stops me to tell of
Their appreciation
Of my work—his name
Is Victor—he goes back
To handing out flyers—

There's a taste of Fall
In the air today—
Even a leaf or two
Turning yellow or red
In the park cutting
Through Union Square—

[. . .]

The pear shaped woman
With purple hair ahead
Of me on lower Broadway—
The two young blondes
Obviously models—one
Giving off an almost
Tactile sense of petulance—

The Starbuck's on Astor
Place—the mix of semi-
Bohemian and generic
Normalcy in styles of
Dress and ornamentation—
Like the young almost
Attractive blonde woman
With the tee shirt ad-
Vertising the "original
Bada Bing Club" in
New Jersey, talking on
Her cell phone "Oh my God"—

The overweight black
Woman yelling at
Someone "I got a kid
At home yo size'll
Kick yo motherfuckin'
Ass" as she enters a
Parking lot booth past
A little girl, maybe eight
Or nine with her hair
In plaits like little black
Girls had even when I
Was a boy—is she talking
To her?—if so the child
Seems unfazed—but how
Could she be?—

[. . .]

The stunning red
Head walking up the
Slight incline of
Madison Avenue South
Of Forty-Second Street
Wearing a rust colored
Dress—she must be six
One at least—not model
Stunning—everyday
Woman stunning—
Refreshing in fact, like
A 1940s movie star
Without the studio hype
Or fabricated glamour—

Men in what remind
Me of 1950s "pedal pushers"
My sisters used to wear—
That leave the lower
Calf exposed—how un-
Expected—some things
Do seem new sometimes—

The mouse—large—or
Maybe baby rat—
Running across Broadway
At Madison Square
Park with me and
Others crossing in the
Crosswalk as if it
Too had been waiting
For the light to change—
People startled by it,
Exclaiming "Shit!"—

"Oh my God"—"Goddamn!"—
Or "What the fuck?!"—

It beats us all to the
Sidewalk where more
People notice—stop—swear—
Then changes course and
Runs back to the street
Only this time heading
South on Broadway
Hugging the curb—all
This in the middle of
A sunny Autumn day—

An older black bike messenger
Refuses to stop for a red light—
Going through it to
Veer around a bus in the
Cross street without
Knowing what's on the
Other side of it but
Obviously sensing the
Time he has to make it
As he just barcly does—

The variety! The various
Shades of skin and com-
Bination of features—
Some people could be
From places yet to be
Discovered—or the
Children of couples
So unexpected no
Film or novel or
TV show or current
History book has yet

To reveal them—

That beautiful woman—
Part African, part
Asian, part European,
Part island, part nomad,
Part city, part star,
Part future, part statue,
Part schedule, part job,
Part sport, part ambition,
Part dream, part answer—

The Gotham Book Mart
Gone from where it was—
My heart stops when
My eyes can't find
That familiar sign—
"Wise men fish here"—
I panic for a few moments
At the thought of all
That has passed away—

Then learn they only
Moved, as I knew they
Were planning to do—but
I also have seen that
"Move" turn into never—
Like the old Phoenix
Bookstore in the Village
Where I sold old signed
Books and reviewers copies
To feed my two oldest
Kids and me when we
Were barely surviving—

Walking through Washington

Square at night—the
Refurbished arch—the
Run down rest of it—
Rats scurry and squeak
On the cracked and
Bumpy paths that once
Were new or renewed—

[. . .]

After the reading
At Washington Square
Church, many teary
Eyed people asking:
"Has it ever been worse?"
Meaning our country's
Political situation—
In our lifetime—not
The country's obviously—
This is no civil war—yet—
[. . .]

Almost hit by another
Bike messenger—this
One a male Hispanic—
They just ignore signals
And foot traffic—which
Come to think of it most
Pedestrians, including me,
Do too—

I pass a white man
With a full head of
Gray hair in a perfect
Replica of what was
Common in 1954—and

He has on a white tee
Shirt with the hemline
Folds in the sleeves and
Denims, both also ala
1954—on a younger
Man it would be retro—
But this man is my
Age—is it possible he
Has kept this style
Intact through five
Decades?—why not?—

The black man with
Dreadlocks down to his
Waist on a bright green
Motorcycle with "Ninja"
Written in script on its side—

In Penn station, a few
Days before the convention—
I walk maybe twenty
Yards to the stairs
Down the platform
For my train and pass
At least fifty uniformed
Policemen—half of
Them yawning—working
Overtime obviously—

Back on the street—
The brightness of the day
And my heart that
All this beauty brings—

I love the women who enjoy
The pleasure their beauty
Gives the rest of us—

An overweight white
Woman in a pleated
Skirt passes me—
The way the skirt moves
As she walks by is
So feminine, so sensual—

Would any man feel
That way?—or only
Those my age who
Grew up in a time
Of pleated skirts and
The rhythmic allure
Of women's clothes that
Moved when they did,
But to their own secret
Beat beyond any man's
Capacity for counterpoint—

Today in Penn Station
Even more cops, and
Military in camouflage
Fatigues, which of course
Blend into nothing here
And only make their presence
Stand out more—the
Idea I assume—and
Canine cops too—
German Shepards who
Act like professionals—
More than the beat cops do—
Some of whom are
Very young and female
And beautiful in their
Ethnic variety—

The convention starts

Today—it's difficult
To get to Penn Station
Now—most trains to
Jersey stop running for
The entire week—

The mood on the street
Is festive if practical—
No minds are going to
Be changed here—too
Bad—life goes on as it
Has lately—seemingly
Normal except for the
Stress which the "be-
In" atmosphere of
The demonstrations—
To use Bill Lanigan's
Description—only
Temporarily relieves—

All types of people on
The street—all ages—
All sizes—all shades
Of skin color—all varieties
Of ethnicity—is it
Me or is our side
Just naturally more
Diverse?—To save my
Heart from the stress
I'm avoiding the con-
Vention coverage—just
Digging the anti-convention
Festive atmosphere of a
City that mostly doesn't
Seem to give a damn
Except for the inconvenience—

The police presence on
34th Street at Herald Square
Where barricades keep me
From jaywalking—mostly
Young officers or maybe
Still only cadets, quick
To anger, frustrated with
The normal New York
Pedestrian flow—then
On 35th St. a car runs
A red light almost hitting
Me, and there, a crowd of
Eight cops leans against
A black and white
Chatting, oblivious to
What might have
Been a terrorist bearing
Down on them through
The intersection but
More likely a commuter
From New Jersey—

The demonstrators
Are getting arrested
In the hundreds—
More than a thousand
With little or no media
Coverage beyond the
Local, unlike the '60s—

[. . .]

The convention is long
Gone—more arrests
Than in the so-called
Riots in Chicago in '68—

[. . .]

In the hospital—
More cleaning of the
Arteries, of the stent
That shouldn't need it—
How did Cheney and I
End up in the same boat—

The most beautiful
Day of the year!—
And tomorrow
The third anniversary
Of another beautiful day
When everyone realized how
Vulnerable we all are—

Though as always, some
More than others—

Last week the third
Anniversary of my cancer
Being removed, and of
My finally accepting the
Inevitable—or not so much
Acceptance as surrender—
[. . .]
My heart problems—though still
So difficult for me to
Comprehend—the cancer
Was so much more
Straightforward and clear—

And still that young light
Haired longhaired woman
In the beige jeans gives
Me a look of interest—

I wonder—but no—
She's doing it again—
Maybe it's the distance—
She can't see the fear
And disappointment in
My eyes—the age in
My neck and hands—
The shortness in my
Breath and discomfort
In my chest—I'm not
Ready for this—too bad—

[. . .]

In a cab going up
8th Avenue—Fall in
The air—I'd rather be
Walking, but just out
Of the hospital—not
Supposed to yet—though
Walking is the answer
[. . .]

At the Northeast corner
Of 42nd Street and Sixth
Avenue, eight motorcycle
Cops, parked, reading papers,
Lounging, in short sleeve
Summer uniforms—the rest
Of us a little more clothed
In the 8:30 AM Autumn chill—

[. . .]

Five mounted police riding
Their steeds down Seventh
Avenue—the incongruity

Of what, when my father
Was a boy a hundred years
Ago, would have been in-
Congruous in the other direction—

The way some black women
Use their long nails to
Scratch their heads between
The cornrows or extensions—

A summer day in Fall—
80 degrees at lunchtime
In Bryant Park—full of
People glowing in the sun
Light—three women—
In theirs 20s and 30s,
I would guess, stand
Out as I pass through—
One looks vaguely middle
Eastern—but in long
Fitted gray skirt and a
Top that suggests a woman's
Business suit and long
Thick curly black hair—
Olive skin—dark eyes—
Bright smile as she tries
To locate her friends on
Her cell phone, them waving
At her as I approach their
Table, her somewhere
Behind me now—another—
Tall, slim, light-skinned
African American with
Obvious European ancestry,
Mid length hair, glasses
Over green eyes, lovely

Smile as she passes
With a young white
Man as tall as her—
And me—her in jeans
And pastel shirt, shining
With health and heart—

The third I passed earlier,
An Asian woman also with
Some European "blood"
As they used to say, short
Hair, Buster Brown style
Only with blonde touches—
Glasses too, a fifties kind
Of summer dress, tight at
The waist, flared below,
Sitting at a table talking
To a more ordinary looking
Young Asian woman but
She catches my eye as I
Walk by and I feel flattered
By the sense I have of
Her being flattered by my
Attention—am I imagining
That, or is my ego? Or is
She truly pleased to be
Noticed for all her stylistically
Original flare—

Three black guys in
Herald Square, one with
Baseball hat backwards,
One side ways—Rootie
Kazootie or Flava Flav
Style, one hatless with
Shaved head—each

Seeming to fit that
Detail—the backwards
Hat guy all regular Joe,
Or Tyrone, the sideways
Guy the goof but with
An edge of danger, and
The shaven headed one
The authority, talking
Forcefully, making his point—

[. . .]

The funkiness of Eighth
Avenue as I cut from
34th to 49th—even the
Sidewalks seem dirtier—
A throwback to Manhattan
Of the 1970s—just
One block over, on Seventh
Avenue the young women
Are thinner, with more
Perfect features, except for
The pair of transsexuals I
Pass at 39th—black and white
And perfect in their "faux"
Femininity—

[. . .]

The handsome black man
In Penn Station, decked
Out in slim overcoat with
Suit and tie underneath,
All GQ upscale "clean"
As we used to say,
And on his arm an equally
Attractive Asian woman—

Both in their twenties or
Thirties I'd guess—young
To me—the glee I feel
In their impressive
Display of dapper
Fashion maturity—

[. . .]

Next day in Chelsea
Market, no Green Table
Anymore—that solicitous
Waitress gone with it—
And later
Try Victoria's in
The fashion district
But it too, after decades,
Closed—so much has
Passed, as I pass another
Woman, gray haired,
My age maybe, but
Beautiful in ways that
Seem new—like those
Gray haired models in
The TV commercials
Or magazine ads—my
Contemporaries finding
Life, after the so-called
"Change," more
Liberating than we knew—

[. . .]

God bless us all, as snow
Falls in Central Park and
My heart harks back to
Simpler times, no, not the

Times but us—or me—
Now comforted by
A glimpse of the dimple
On the back of a knee
Spied between the
High top boot and hem
Of skirt, winking at me,
As if to say, today's
Another day to be grateful
For being alive—again—
And when is just—eternity.

Jan-Dec 2004

TO MY SON FLYNN

Before you were born
I knew how to be happy.

The secret isn't a secret.
Just feel grateful enough

and the heart opens up
and becomes love going

out, which is the secret.
Ah, but what to be grateful

for, when they've robbed
the store, and are making

off with our money and
our country? That's easy:

you.

MOST MEMORABLE MOVIE MOTHERS

Bambi's
Dumbo's
Juno

Jane Darwell as Ma Joad in *GRAPES OF WRATH*

SHAFT

TWO POST-BRAIN-OPERATION OBSERVATIONS

1
Just took a pretty brisk walk, several blocks,
in the cool, crisp, air.

A bright and shiny day, at times almost chilly,
but felt so good to be out and feeling stronger.

The caw of a lone crow was so sharp and clarion,
it felt like the definition of what it means to be alive.

The last leaves still falling, the endless (we hope)
natural cycles.

How wonderful and fine life is when the possibility
of losing it becomes so current and realistic.

To be alive, what can disturb the awe of that
realization? Today, nothing.

2
It's been difficult for me to listen to music
since the brain surgery. The sounds that
normally blend into a cohesive whole in

most recordings, my brain was somehow
atomizing into discrete units that made
each musical moment sound overwhelm-
ingly complicated—jarringly, gratingly so.

Difficult to explain or articulate. I tried
one day on my first outing in my little
town where I was being helped by my
friend Sue Brennan and ran into another
friend, the great jazz pianist, Bill Charlap.
I was excited to communicate what I
was experiencing with music, but I'm
afraid I came off as a little out of my
mind, which is of course partly what
this whole experience has been about.

But yesterday, I tried listening to some
music again and it sounded close to
normal. I hit the shuffle key on my lap
top and the first tune was an old Billie
Holiday recording from the early '30s,
THESE'N'THAT'N'THOSE (beautiful tone
to her voice) followed, as it happened,
by Bill Charlap's trio's version of SOME
OTHER TIME, as close to Bill Evans as is
humanly possible, while still being Char-
lap. A haunting tune, one of my favorites.

BLIZZARD OF '16

So, I had the same sensation
when I went out this morning
after more than two feet of
snow had fallen that I always
have after an intense snow-

storm: awe and joy. You
might say easy for me since
neighbors charitably snow
blew the sidewalk in front of
the old house my apartment
is in, and others shoveled the
walk to the sidewalk before
I could (though I shoveled
the porch and steps late last
night and some more this AM).

But in previous years, before
my kids and loved ones kept
warning me not to shovel (well
actually they were doing it then
too but I ignored them) I loved
shoveling snow the morning after
a snow storm. I would do it in
short spurts with lots of resting
on the shovel handle digging
that unique post-snow silence—
none of the usual world's sounds
(aided by no cars driving by).
The brightness of the almost
cloudless sky, the blue of it
seemingly the only color
along with the pure white of
unsullied snow blown into
sensuous curves covering
everything—in some spots as
high as four foot drifts—and
the dark of tree trunks and limbs
where the snow had blown off.

I wish I could take a photo on
my phone and transfer it to this
poem, but I'm a little techno-

dyslexic. And the limitations of
any photograph would stop me
anyway. There's no way to
capture being surrounded by
a few feet of new fallen snow
under a bright blue sky with
the few nearby sounds coming
across as distant, or so muffled
they seem distant. In my almost
twenty years in L.A. I missed
just this, so I'm grateful for it,
at least today, before it begins to
melt and the slush in the street
gets sprayed onto the snowbanks
turning them into something less
pleasant. But for now, I can even
shrug off the old grammar school
friend turned rightwing troll who
can't stop his rightwing parroting,
this morning asking how I like
my two feet of global warming.

The guy actually thinks because
we had a blizzard after the most
snow-free winter ever, that some-
how that negates the reality that
2015 was the warmest year on
record and 2014 the warmest
before that. It would be pathetic
if it wasn't emblematic of the
brainwashing fossil-fuel coin
has bought in recent decades.

TAKE IT EASY

I.

Take it easy?
How many fuckin times
did I hear that when
I was a kid. And a
young man. And a
middle-aged man.

Take it easy Michael,
take it easy son, take
it easy brother, take it
easy man, take it easy
mister. Lot easier to
say than do.

How the fuck do you
take it easy when
you're born into a
world that's more
violent than it's ever
been.

I'm not talkin about
now I'm talkin about
when I was born into
World War Two the
bloodiest period in
history.

How you supposed to
take it easy when you
look around and people
are talkin about shit

you know isn't true as
though it is true.

I'm not talkin about
Trump I'm talkin about
people makin general-
izations when I was
young about black
people and white
people and I didn't
see anybody who was
white or black, I saw
people that were
gradations from fair
to dark, and everything
in between.

They even had fuckin
laws that didn't make
no sense. You could have
a man or woman who
looked as pale as a bone
who they said was legally
black and someone who
had darker skin than them
passing for so-called white
and how was a kid or a
young person or a middle-
-aged human or even an
old one supposed to take
it easy with so much fuckin
hypocrisy all around them . . . .

But I eventually learned,
how to at least sometimes
take it easy, because

not takin it easy cost me
so much, not just jobs and
friends and lovers and
careers and prizes and
money and security and
serenity and health but it
became clear that not
takin it easy often made
things worse than what
had made me not take it
easy at first . . .

2.

On the other hand, when
I was a kid and someone
said take it easy when they
were leaving, it was just
a hipper way of saying
goodbye, but it implied a
kind of admonition to be
cool, what I always longed
to be but couldn't quite
achieve because my
unforgiving temper was
so hot and got me into
all my troubles . . . it's not
that way as much anymore
since I learned and earned
the right to take it easy
more and more . . . though
if you get me at the right
or wrong moment, depending
on your view, I can seem
to take it easy now when
I'm secretly saying fuck you

TOO MANY CREEPS

Back when that Bush Tetras song
became the anthem of the down
town scene, in the 1970s I knew,
we'd add our own list of what
there were too many of, like
yuppies, lawyers and real
estate speculators buying up
the lofts we lived in illegally,
forseeing the powers that be
changing the laws in time
for the yuppies and lawyers
and real estate speculators to
buy up our neighborhoods
we never called "Soho" or
"Tribeca" but instead "So What"
and "Washington Market"
as it had always been known . . .

Now the list would go on
forever, like too many lies,
and too many people believing
them, and too many filthy
rich greedheads rigging the
game and then blaming
the rest of us for problems
they cause, and too many
people in poverty and
deprivation, too many of
them homeless, and too many
evictions of poor people, and
too many bullies, and too
many cars, and too many
TVs, and too many eyes on
too many screens, and too

many scams, and too many
overworked underpaid
people, and too many tax
exempt churches and
football stadiums, and too
many fundamentalist Christians
and Jews and Muslims and
Ayn Randians, and too many
hypocritical politicians and
pundits, and, What about too
many poems, you might ask,
and I'd respond There can
never be too many poems . . .

FIRST TWO REACTIONS:

1. THE NIGHT OF

You want someone to blame?
Blame the racists, cause maybe
not everyone who voted for him
was a racist, but every racist
who voted, voted for him. Blame
white women, more of whom
voted for him than for her.
Blame the Latinos who voted
for him at a higher percentage
than voted for Romney. Blame
the African-Americans who
didn't vote, or vote for her, but
voted for Obama. Blame the lefties
who spent the election campaign
bashing her, or the election
voting in protest for anybody

but her, which was in effect a
vote for him. Blame Julian
Assange and Wikileaks for
targeting her and not him.
Blame her for one of the
lamest slogans ever—I mean,
I'm with her?—what does
that promise?—and a logo
that looked like an Amtrak
sign from 1980. Blame the
Democratic Party which used
to know in its bones that "all
politics is local" but forgot,
letting the Republicans co-opt
that strategy, starting with
school boards that control what
our kids are taught. Blame the
media, or its audience, for not
being able to make money on
facts or anything else that isn't
sensational or divisive. Blame
old people for being afraid of
the future, and young people
for thinking the future was
theirs without a price to be
paid. Blame Russia, and China,
and Mexico, and Japan (wait,
scratch Japan, that was the
1980 election). Blame the
stars, blame the gods, blame
Ayn Rand and Fox News and
Irish-American traitors to their
ancestors: Hannity and O'Reilly
and their ilk. Blame fucking any-
one and anything, but yourself.

2. THE DAY AFTER

The day after I was born,
German U boat 106 sank
a US tanker in the Gulf of
Mexico. Twenty-two were
killed. Hitler and his allies
had been winning World
War Two and it looked like
they were about to take
over the world. Including
the USA. Three years later
Germany surrendered and
the war in Europe was over,
followed pretty soon after
by the end of the war in the
Pacific. In my brief three
year old life the world had
witnessed the greatest
death and destruction in
the history of humanity. It
was tragic and deeply sad
but even so, great acts of
courage and kindness,
sacrifice and love were
committed, great art and
music and movies and
more were made. Nothing
anywhere near as massively
brutal and deadly has occurred
since. Despite continuing wars
and oppression, the world has
not in my now seventy-four
years ever been as violent
or destructive as it was then.
That's not to slight the severity

of anyone's experience of
repression or cruelty, but
only to say as my old friend
Hubert Selby used to, that "You
can't have up without down,
success without failure,
pleasure without pain," and I
would add, dark days without
ones filled with light. Let us
be that light for those who will
need it now.

THE TIMES THEY'RE ALWAYS CHANGING

I was born into a war and world where
Most thought they'd be speaking German
Or Japanese soon. Then the times changed.

My paternal grandfather lived down the
Street. He'd been born into a thatch roofed
dirt floor cottage in Ireland at a time when

Native Irish were depicted In the English
Press as an inferior race, often equated with
Native Africans. Then the times changed.

My father was born into the end of the 19th
Century, dropped out of grammar school to
Go to work in a hardware store to help his

Family and ended up owning the store by
The time he was twenty and many more by
The time he was thirty at the height of The

Jazz Age. Then the times changed and The
Great Depression began, and, as he liked to
say: "The big boys bought back everything

I owned for a dime on the dollar, and some-
Times a nickel." My maternal grandmother
Burned all the I.O.U's to her husband after

He died and she moved in with us, saying
He would have wanted it that way. I helped
Care for her all through my boyhood and

Teenage years before I left home. The best
Lesson she taught me was: "If you're born
To be hung, you'll never be shot." My mother

Was a high school graduate making her the
Intellectual authority in our household. She
Was born in Newark in a neighborhood where

Her mother remembered what they called
Then "race wars" between the earlier German
Settlers and the newly arrived Irish. Then the

Times changed. Her mother couldn't vote
When she was twenty-one but my mother
Could, thanks to the new law letting women.

When I was stationed in the then legally
So-called racially segregated South Carolina
In 1962, African-Americans weren't allowed

To go to the drive-in movie in their own cars,
That's how bad it was. And when I went to a
Greenville bookstore looking for James Baldwin's

Latest book, they didn't have it, and wouldn't
Order it, and the library said the same, so I had
One of my sisters buy it in Newark and send it

To me. The only integrated place I found down
There was a home that hosted secret meetings
Of the Ba'Hai faith, one of many spiritual paths

I tried on in my youth. And then the times they
Changed. My oldest children were born into a
World where men didn't raise kids on their own

Even though I did. And then the times changed.
When my youngest was born at the end of the
Last century, Bill Clinton was called "The first

Black president." And then the times changed.
When our latest White House occupant won
Many citizens felt so despondent they found it

Hard to go about their daily lives and get any-
Thing done at all. But the day after he moved
In, The Resistance did begin, and once again:

"THE TIMES / THEY ARE / A-CHANGIN'."

LOVE IS THE ULTIMATE RESISTANCE

We are here. This is what is happening. And
the first step to changing any of it is acceptance
of what already is. It's bad enough politicians

use the phrase "The American People" followed
by "demand" or "want" or "believe" or "support"

or whatever. As if they aren't aware of the divi-

sions in our populace, that is so stridently po-
larized a cheap con artist can get appointed
president. Enough with the wishful-thinking or

deliberately-misleading or just-plain-ignorant
appellation "The American People" as subject
or object of any sentence from now on. I know:

If Only. Though the good going on—and going
to, and coming out of—recent hurricanes, earth-
quakes, fires, and even massacres, elevates us all

with the truth that there's a lot of love in a lot
of humans, manifested in caring about others in
trouble, including, most importantly, strangers.

The bad going on, and going to, and coming
out of, recent hurricanes, earthquakes, fires,
and massacres, is the direct result of personal

and corporate greed, and the actions of those
who serve it. Like the deliberate ignoring or
deregulation of safety standards for guns or

construction or overdevelopment, or our air
and water, screens and ear buds, planning
and lives. Human Need vs. Corporate Greed.

But, do not despair. The lies and hate and
fear, the mass hysteria and mass hypnosis,
smothering the so-called social media(s),

have always existed side by side with the
sweetness and romance and struggle to find
—to get as close as possible to—the truth,

no matter what it may be, or turn into. We
are all losers and winners, veterans of life
and naïve beginners. And one day will all

be the Finishers. For now, let the focus be
on the survival of the victims, innocent or
not. Love is always the ultimate resistance . . .

A former jazz musician, Hollywood actor, and radical organizer, the New Jersey–born **MICHAEL LALLY** has worn many hats over the course of his life. But throughout it all, he has written book after book of outspoken, soulful poems that have inspired countless other poets. Themes of identity, love, success, and failure pervade his body of work, but always with wry humor and the simple grace that is the mark of deep thought and conviction. Lally is the author of over thirty books of poetry and prose, including *White Lies* (1969), *It's Not Nostalgia* (1999), and *Swing Theory* (2015). He is the recipient of the PEN Oakland/Josephine Miles Award for Excellence in Literature and grants from the National Endowment for the Arts, among others. He lives in Maplewood, New Jersey.

EILEEN MYLES is a groundbreaking novelist, poet, and performance artist, whose books include *I Must Be Living Twice: New and Selected Poems* and *Chelsea Girls*.

ABOUT SEVEN STORIES PRESS

Seven Stories Press is an independent book publisher based in New York City. We publish works of the imagination by such writers as Nelson Algren, Russell Banks, Octavia E. Butler, Ani DiFranco, Assia Djebar, Ariel Dorfman, Coco Fusco, Barry Gifford, Martha Long, Luis Negrón, Peter Plate, Hwang Sok-yong, Lee Stringer, and Kurt Vonnegut, to name a few, together with political titles by voices of conscience, including Subhankar Banerjee, the Boston Women's Health Collective, Noam Chomsky, Angela Y. Davis, Human Rights Watch, Derrick Jensen, Ralph Nader, Loretta Napoleoni, Gary Null, Greg Palast, Project Censored, Barbara Seaman, Alice Walker, Gary Webb, and Howard Zinn, among many others. Seven Stories Press believes publishers have a special responsibility to defend free speech and human rights, and to celebrate the gifts of the human imagination, wherever we can. In 2012 we launched Triangle Square books for young readers with strong social justice and narrative components, telling personal stories of courage and commitment. For additional information, visit www.sevenstories.com.